Manager's Portfolio

of

Model Performance Evaluations

Ready-to-Use
Performance Appraisals
Covering All Employee Functions

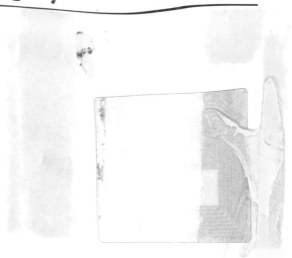

Contents

1

Getting Started

1

2

Assuring a Nondiscriminatory Review Process
15

3

Putting It in Writing
19

4

Model Evaluations for Secretarial and Clerical Workers
33

5

Model Evaluations for Trainers and Human Resource Professionals
93

6

Model Evaluations for Customer Service and Related Support Workers
155

7

Model Evaluations for Salespeople
209

8

Model Evaluations for Engineers, Programmers, and Other Technical Specialists
269

9

Model Evaluations for Administrative and Support Workers
313

10

Model Evaluations for Managers
367

11

Handling Salary Reviews Successfully
419

12

Preparing a Paper Trail for a Worker You Wish to Terminate
427

How This Book Will Help You

Short of firing or laying off an employee, the performance-review process is, for most managers, the single most unpopular part of their professional life.

Reviews are time-consuming, fraught with potential legal perils, and, all too often, the source of unpleasant face-to-face conflicts with disgruntled employees. The salary review is, in all likelihood, the setting for the vast majority of openly antagonistic exchanges between employees and their managers. It's no wonder most managers don't look forward to review time.

Manager's Portfolio of Model Performance Evaluations offers more than 100 model evaluations for employees, as well as strategies for conducting successful face-to-face meetings with employees at all levels and performance categories. It also features important advice on such matters as nondiscriminatory evaluation techniques, disabled employees, and termination. Thanks to its easy-to-find, easy-to-use reference format, this book allows managers to go right to the model that reflects the evaluation they must complete, select the appropriate performance category, and adapt text and rating materials to their own specific situation. They can also review key strategy points before the face-to-face meeting with the employee. The result? Less wasted time, less aggravation, and, perhaps most important, less potential for "static" from the employee during the evaluation process.

This book will *let managers handle evaluation and performance-review questions quickly, efficiently, and properly,* so they can focus their time and energy on the other pressing projects their organization needs them to complete.

1

Getting Started

First and foremost, all performance evaluations should be conducted using established guidelines that will effectively eliminate any subjectivity or appearance of subjectivity. Such guidelines must cover job standards that are both quantitative and qualitative. Therefore, preparation for any review should include a good, accurate job description and allowance for the setting, reviewing, and adjusting of goals.

Setting Standards for Honest and Consistent Reviews

Goals are probably the most important feature of any standards that are set for any job. What, specifically, is to be accomplished, and within what time frame? Both the employer and the employee should have long- and mid-range goals representing the steps that need to be taken to achieve particular results. For the employer, the worker's success in achieving those goals means enhanced corporate productivity, stability, and (it's hoped) prosperity. For the employee, successful achievement of goals can and should lead to job satisfaction and continued growth in his or her working life.

Short-term goals are equally important in the review process. They serve to address an employee's most immediate needs and issues and help to

1

move him or her toward long-term happiness in the job. As the saying goes, "A journey of a thousand miles begins with a single step." The key is in being able to identify and take that first step. Short-term goals are the means of defining what initial steps are needed at what stages in the employee's development in order to continue the journey toward the desired long-term goal.

Using a Rating System

In most corporate settings, the review includes a scale for rating certain qualities and abilities. The danger in this is that it often does not provide an accurate enough assessment of the employee's performance, relying as it does almost exclusively on a grading system. In addition, the large majority of the company's workforce will invariably end up in the top strata, because anything less than the top rating can be used to signal unacceptable performance. Therefore, careful thought and sound judgment have to be applied in the evaluation when using any sort of rating scale.

The ideal performance review would rate individuals on a two-tier system ("meets standards" and "needs improvement") or a three-tier system (add "unsatisfactory performance"), or some variation thereof. Space for brief statements should be provided for expanding on certain points. It is vital that these statements include substantive facts about the employee's performance; glowing generalities do not add any new information, nor do they provide accurate assessments of how the employee is or is not meeting established goals.

Using Job Descriptions

The cornerstone of any good employer–employee relationship is a clearly defined job description. In fact, one of your most important roles as a manager is to keep your workers fully informed of their job specifications and what is expected of them. Job descriptions serve to communicate your company's needs to your employees and to provide the structure that enables them to meet their job goals. Thus, if there are problems within your office or department and things are not working so well as they should be, it is most likely that you need to review job descriptions and revise them, as necessary.

You should ensure that the overall goals and needs of the company are adequately covered and defined by all job descriptions at all levels. Gaps in employee-performance requirements will inevitably lead to gaps in overall company performance. Therefore, it is helpful—if not imperative—to review all job descriptions on an annual basis to make certain that all your bases are being covered.

You should also ensure that each employee has a copy of his or her job description as well as a thorough understanding of what it entails. At review time, the job description should be close at hand in order to provide a tangible reference when discussing work performance. In unionized situations, job descriptions are legal documents that may provide cause for legal action if insufficient care is taken in preparing them. In cases where termination of an employee is necessary, the job description may be one of your most important tools in justifying the need for termination. Thus, it is of utmost importance that employee job descriptions be complete, accurate, and detailed, in terms of both quantitative and qualitative goals and expectations.

Establishing Performance Criteria

For an effective performance review, both the employee and the supervisor must be prepared to discuss what the position is about, the standards that are to be met, and past, present, and future goals. Some (but not all) of the questions that may be considered during the course of the evaluation are:

- What were the employee's major accomplishments during the time frame of the evaluation?
- How well did the employee meet both professional and personal goals established in the previous review?
- What goals were not met?
- What problems were encountered in meeting any of these goals?
- How can these problems be avoided in the future?
- What are the employee's strengths and weaknesses?
- Is any revision needed of the job description to more accurately represent job responsibilities?
- What goals or objectives should be set for the coming appraisal period?

Getting the Point Across

Here are some words and phrases you can use:

- Set up a new recordkeeping system.
- Initiated training sessions for the entire team.

- Learned a new spreadsheet program.
- Exceeded last year's goals of developing and implementing a new accounting program.
- Met last year's goal to enroll in an MBA program.
- Will need more time to meet last year's goal of hiring three new staff members.
- Goals were not met because of problems with vendors.
- Unexpected loss of personnel caused a slump in production; as a result, goals were not met.
- A new job description will be drafted and another performance evaluation will be held in six months.
- New goals for the coming quarter include gathering information on the proposed internal security system and making a full staff presentation.
- Has strong time-management skills.
- Handling interpersonal issues is one of the employee's strengths.
- Needs to improve speed and accuracy in generating reports.
- Is weak in making oral presentations.
- Will be expected to create ten sales presentations during the next six months.

Quantifying Performance

Some aspects of job performance are easy enough to quantify: attendance, amount of work done, meeting deadlines, meeting preset goals, and so forth. These details are measurable and can be addressed through what are sometimes called **"SMART"** goals: **S**pecific, **M**easurable, **A**chievable, **R**ealistic, and **T**imed. Obviously, specific quantifiable goals must be established with an understanding of each employee's unique circumstances, abilities, and aspirations.

Evaluation of all areas that can be quantified should be done in a fashion that illustrates clearly both current performance levels and future goals. Worker effort toward improvement in these areas is always stronger when goals are clearly stated and the worker is confident that increased effort will result in measurable improvement.

Following is a list of basic quantifiable criteria that may be used in a review.

- Quantity of work/productivity
- Job knowledge

- Work habits
- Accuracy/thoroughness
- Neatness
- Attention to detail
- Timeliness/time effectiveness
- Punctuality
- Use/management of resources
- Cost effectiveness
- Computer skills
- Business/industry knowledge
- Care of equipment
- Resourcefulness
- Organizational skills
- Accomplishment of goals/sales goals/quotas/etc.

Getting the Point Across

Here are some words and phrases you can use:

- Managed two major team projects.
- Handled an average of 50 customer complaints per day; received 20 notes of appreciation from customers.
- Submits clear, concise, detailed weekly reports.
- Has saved the company five million dollars by changing suppliers to keep up with new developments in the field.
- Has full knowledge of the job; is an important resource for the team.
- Uses time efficiently; gets timely results.
- Plans and organizes meetings well; chaired ten all-division meetings.
- Met last year's quota of developing three new products.
- Showed exceptional resourcefulness in handling conflict among several division groups.
- Despite last month's equipment breakdown, was able to increase units manufactured by efficient use of time and personnel.
- Is always careful in using equipment properly.
- Instructs others to avoid waste and use equipment carefully.
- Demonstrated superior computer skills.

- Was willing to train all team members to use the new computers.
- Trimmed the budget by fifty thousand dollars while not diminishing results.

Qualifying Performance

Other aspects of job performance are not so easy to quantify. For instance, the evaluation of attitudes and interpersonal relationships can be quite subjective. These are qualitative standards. In evaluating these points, it is helpful to give specific anecdotal illustrations of both desirable and unsatisfactory behavior. In many ways, the value of a worker is often dependent on these hard-to-quantify items. The ability to explain undesirable behavior in ways that are nonthreatening and not overly personal is important. Likewise, the ability to describe the desired behaviors in a way that is clear and seems achievable will more than likely result in a positive response from the employee and therefore a positive performance review.

Following is a list of qualifiable criteria that may be used in a performance evaluation.

- Quality of work
- Creativity
- Hospitality/courtesy
- Customer relations
- Customer responsiveness
- Communication skills
- Interpersonal skills
- Teamwork/cooperation
- Initiative/motivation
- Supervisory skills
- Decision-making skills
- Problem-solving skills
- Analytical skills
- Adaptability
- Dependability
- Flexibility
- Conscientiousness/perseverance
- Accountability

- Receptiveness to criticism
- Resilience
- Ability to set priorities
- Leadership abilities/influence on others
- Support and development of subordinates
- Professionalism
- Professional growth/self-development

Getting the Point Across

Here are some words and phrases you can use:

- Produces excellent work.
- Is strong team player; cooperates and shares ideas.
- Hands in well-written and informative reports.
- Speaks well and communicates ideas effectively.
- Is receptive to suggestions and constructive criticism.
- Shows eagerness to assume new responsibilities.
- Able to motivate subordinates to perform at highest levels.
- Can be depended on to make good decisions.
- Accepts full responsibility for consequences of decisions/actions.
- Has excellent people skills; well-liked by all.
- Is flexible in handling a variety of unfamiliar operations.
- Readily adapts to organizational change—new management, policies, and the like.
- Perseveres in solving knotty problems; doesn't give up.
- Treats clients with unfailing courtesy and professionalism.
- Has strong ability to analyze projections and make effective recommendations.

How Often Should Reviews Be Given?

The goal of an evaluation is—or should be—to provide the necessary feedback that will enable the employee to function at his or her highest level of performance. Thus, the timing of evaluations and reviews should be such that both employer and employee feel comfortable with and knowledgeable about how the employee is doing. In many cases, the evaluation process is built into the training and orientation of a new employee, providing a lot of feedback at the start and gradually reducing the frequency of that feedback until the employee is phased out of the training-and-orientation stage and into the regular-review stage.

Depending on the job, some orientation-review schedules include the initial shadowing of an employee by her or his supervisor; then working with a mentor; then independent work with daily reviews for a week or two. The employee may then graduate to weekly reviews for the first month and/or monthly reviews for the first quarter. After another quarterly review at midyear, the new employee is usually secure and ready to be evaluated through the regular annual or semi-annual review process.

Obviously, the more complex and responsible the position, the more extensive the training and orientation will be. Employees with routine jobs having little individual responsibility may require only a few days of close monitoring before they are essentially on their own. For all new employees, monthly evaluation for the first quarter and a mid-year review are a good idea. For many if not all of these reviews, the informal review process discussed below is a useful one that will help both parties avoid the "out-of-the-blue" syndrome, in which an employee has "no idea" about the existence of a particular problem area. Holding these informal meetings every three months seems to work best for most managers. The goal, after all, is to maximize performance through attention and support, not to harass employees or have them driven by fear.

An effective solution to handling a problem employee is to return to a "training-and-orientation" level of supervision. Supportive, sensitive, and well-timed supervisory attention can often reverse a downward trend or budding negativism. The employees you already have are almost always more cost effective than the employees you have to hire and train. Therefore, those are the employees you want to put some time and effort into bringing up to their highest level of performance, especially if they still show the ability and promise that won them the job in the first place.

Many employees don't find out how well (or how poorly) the boss thinks things are going until their annual performance appraisal. Implementing long-term constructive change is often difficult in this common scenario.

When performance assessments come but once a year, employees may see the review process as something quite distinct from their everyday routine. However sound or constructive the suggestions contained in the review may be, they are likely to be forgotten, or at least not acted on, when they are part of an isolated annual event that usually intimidates supervisors and subordinates alike.

Implementing the Informal Interim Review

Informal interim reviews, scheduled quarterly or every six months, or at least well in advance of the official review, can make the experience easier for everyone. These minireviews provide employees with much-needed feedback that *does not go into their files* and build in enough time for the team member to make needed changes. Some organizations make the *supervisor's* performance appraisal contingent on his or her holding informal meetings with all subordinates on a regular (usually quarterly) basis. Others make the results of a quarterly-review process a formal part of the employee's personnel record.

Informal reviews, like their formal counterparts, should be conducted using established guidelines, to avoid any possibility of subjectivity. For the informal interim review, it is best to work from an abbreviated outline sheet that covers basic work skills and attributes—organization, ability to cooperate with others, overall quality of work, and so on—and to grade each on a relative scale that preferably has no numerical values on it. Numbers have a way of intimidating employees in a way that circled dots, for instance, do not.

A brief section outlining past performance and current goals is also a good idea. In this section of the form, you can offer the specifics of what you feel the employee should be working toward in the future.

To take advantage of this system, consider the following steps.

- Sit down in private with the employee every three months and fill out a brief summary sheet in the employee's presence. (Ideally, you should tell the employee at the outset of the meeting that the sheet and the comments on it will not be part of the employee's permanent record.) The marks and comments you make on the summary sheet should reflect your assessment of the employee's performance in predetermined critical areas.
- During this meeting, discuss upcoming goals related to particular skill areas. Make appropriate brief notes.

- At the end of the short conference, *hand over the only copy of the completed sheet to the employee.*

Getting the Point Across

Here are examples of phrases to use:

- You have shown improvement in organizing your work schedule.
- Written work is much improved.
- Your reports are more detailed and better organized.
- You have made good progress in sharing information and ideas.
- There is a strong positive change in your attitude.
- You still need to improve your attitude.
- During the next three months, you should be able to complete the Special Report.
- The next six-month goal is to implement the new training program for three groups.
- Your appearance and professional manner have improved since the last review. Keep up the good work.
- Computer skills still need improvement.
- There has been a marked improvement in handling the new computer program.
- You seem to be better able to manage your time.
- Schedules have been met; there have been no delays.
- There has been a dramatic improvement in interpersonal relations; especially in handling multicultural issues.
- We will meet again, after you review my notes. I want to remind you that this informal review is not on record. I have not kept a copy of my notes.

Using this approach, you can lay the groundwork for issues that will be discussed at later formal evaluations, usually without incurring the defensiveness employees may show when they know that the results of the meeting are "on the record." From the supervisor's point of view, too, the informal review carries a distinct advantage: It's easier to be honest with someone when you know that doing so will not result in a permanent black mark in his or her files.

What to Cover in a Formal Review

All formal reviews should use the employee's job description as a guide. As a result of the review, the job description may need to be adjusted. Copies of the adjusted job description should be filed and made available to the employee in a timely manner.

- Review the quantity of work done since the last review.
- Review the quality of work done since the last review.
- Discover and discuss trends that may be found in these areas of quantity and quality.
- Discuss how specific tools or training have affected job performance.
- Identify specific tools or training that can be used to continue to improve job performance.
- Give the employee feedback on matters of job performance, attitude, and interpersonal relationships.
- Solicit feedback from the employee on matters of job performance, attitude, and interpersonal relationships.
- Review and evaluate progress made toward goals set in the prior review period (quarter-year, half-year, year).
- Set goals for the next review period, based on the overall development plan for the employee.
- If this is also a salary review, discuss the review process and give and receive feedback on that issue.

Getting the Point Across

Here are examples of phrases to use:

Quantity of work done:
- Prepared ten presentations.
- Brought in 75 new customers.
- Held 12 training sessions.
- Increased group productivity during the last three months.
- Saved three thousand dollars by handling the purchasing program efficiently.

Quality of work done:

- Maintained high standards of accuracy.
- Met or exceeded every schedule.
- Submitted excellent reports.
- Showed dramatic improvement in making oral presentations.
- Stayed within budget.

Trends in areas of quantity and quality:

- Showed reliability.
- Excelled as a leader.
- Demonstrated professionalism at the highest level.
- Has become a strong role model for the entire group.
- Continues to develop money-saving programs for the division.

Specific tools or training to improve performance:

- Should take advantage of the in-house seminars to enhance management skills.
- Needs to learn the new corporate accounting system to work more efficiently.
- Will be required to take sensitivity training to improve interpersonal relations.
- Plans to attend professional time-management workshops to improve efficiency.
- Is enrolling in an advanced computer programming course to enhance skills.

Review, evaluate, and set new goals:

- Last year's goal to bring in 80 new customers was not met; 60 new customers were brought in.
- In retrospect, last year's goal was unrealistic.
- This year's goal will be to bring in 65 new customers.
- The goal for the last quarter was to establish a new color-coding system. This was accomplished well within the quarter.
- The goal for the next quarter will be to train all departments to use the new system.

Solicit feedback from the employee:

- Avoid asking questions that can be answered "yes" or "no."
- Ask "How would you evaluate your handling of the Jones contract?"
- Ask "What system would you recommend we implement to keep track of the equipment?"
- Ask "Which seminar did you find most valuable?"
- Encourage the employee to comment on each aspect of the evaluation.

Salary:

- This year, annual raises will range from six to ten percent.
- In recognition of your overall good performance, you will receive an eight-percent raise.
- At this time, you will receive a two-percent raise. You will have another salary review in six months.
- You are not eligible for a salary increase this year.
- Your performance last year was outstanding; I am pleased to offer you a 12-percent raise.

What to Cover in a Special Review

All formal reviews should use the employee's job description as a guide. As a result of the review, the job description may need to be adjusted. Copies of the adjusted job description should be filed and made available to the employee in a timely manner.

- Be clear about the goal of the review. If it is an extraordinary review, then the real, and usually extraordinary, reason for the review should be clear to all.
- Review the quantitative matters that relate to the topic of the review.
- Review the qualitative matters that relate to the topic of the review.
- Always include opportunities for employee feedback and questions.
- Limit the review to the matter at hand and don't wander off into other, nonrelevant topics.
- Provide a process for giving the employee a summary of the review results, even if it is just a "for-your-eyes-only" informal interim review session.

Postponing a Review

Remember that all reviews are threatening to a certain extent. Most employees, while hoping for the best, always fear the worst, and this can become exaggerated in their minds when a review is postponed. Thus, try to convey in a sentence or two that "all is well" and that the reason for the postponement is a matter of schedule and workload, not a matter of gravity in terms of the review's content. If you can't make such a statement, don't postpone the review.

When postponing a review, be sure to set a new time right away. Both you and the employee need to complete the evaluation in a timely manner and get on with your jobs, rather than "waiting for the other shoe to drop."

Handling Performance Problems

If you have an employee who is not performing well, you should have a procedure for postevaluation follow-up. Here are some suggestions to make the process successful and turn a poor performer into a better performer—an organizational liability into an organizational asset.

- Make it clear, without unduly threatening, that continued poor performance will lead to disciplinary action and possibly termination.
- Communicate goals for individual performance.
- Jointly develop a work plan that addresses goals.
- Establish a tight review and a follow-up schedule.
- Set up a separate time for going over techniques for successfully accomplishing work plan (daily, weekly, monthly planning, how to avoid distractions and procrastination, etc.).
- Make sure the work plan includes a set of attainable, short-term goals, and reward their successful accomplishment (i.e., try to teach a new habit pattern of achievement).

2

Assuring a Nondiscriminatory Review Process

It is a powerful legal fact that no citizen may be denied access to the benefits of living in this country due to reasons such as race, religion, age, or sex. Those benefits include rightful employment, free from any harassment and discrimination that may result because one is, for instance, of a certain sex. In general, it is evident what this means for all corporate cultures: A person's age, race, or sex should have no bearing on the status of her or his position within the company and her or his chances for advancement. In theory, this should be easy enough to handle. National attitudes have developed well enough that it has become easier to accept such previously unusual phenomena as the male kindergarten teacher and the female fighter pilot.

Avoiding Sexism

It is still an unfortunate fact of life, however, that many companies, either consciously or unconsciously, will discriminate against an employee because he or she fails to meet certain unwritten, undiscussed standards and that such factors as sex can play a role in this discrimination. Where sexism is concerned, it is particularly true that women have a harder time competing in corporate cultures, which are often dominated by men who operate on frequently mysterious and inaccessible levels. If a woman cannot play the game according to the unwritten rules established by male managers and executives, she is more than likely going to be shut out of the loop or prevented from promotion. Additionally, women are much more likely to be harassed by their male coworkers (although cases of men being harassed on the job have also been documented).

These circumstances have frequently led to tricky legal territory in many companies. While most cases of discrimination or harassment are clear-cut, others are not so easy to resolve and are pinned on minutiae or misunderstandings. Harassment can often be in the eye of the harassed.

Your best resource in avoiding any charge of sexual discrimination or harassment is to simply separate sex from the equation as best you can. In other words, you must apply the rule that whatever sex you or your coworkers may be, it has no role in the way you or they do your jobs or interact with each other. This is a difficult task. Each state has its own set of extensive laws governing discrimination in the workplace, and it's impossible to be familiar with every single situation that might present you with legal trouble. Therefore, you can't allow yourself to become preoccupied by trying to live within the letter of the law. You can only take an open and honest stance that does not allow for sexism in the workplace—period.

Avoiding Racism

As it is with sex, discrimination based on race should have no place in any work environment. All employees should be judged and treated according to their skills and abilities, and not according to the color of their skin or the religion they happen to follow. Additionally, special care must be taken to avoid giving unintentional offense by way of jokes or jibes. No matter how benign or friendly such comments are originally meant, any remark made at the expense of another is inappropriate.

Particularly difficult are the sort of "in-the-family" racial slurs that populate the informal conversation of many people. Such verbal slights are inappropriate, however "innocent" they may be, and should not be tolerated. As a manager, it is up to you to monitor any open conversations where inappropriate talk can lead to wounded feelings or, worse, charges of sexual harassment. In essence, you need to be a bit of a "fuddy-duddy" about racial references in everyday office conversation, and especially in business-related matters. You must also monitor yourself to ensure that an employee's race does not enter into any decision that you make about admonishing or correcting a problem employee, especially if such actions are leading to termination.

Avoiding Age Discrimination

At times, the issue of age can be the most vexing of all. Aging cannot be avoided. People get older, and it does sometimes happen that with age comes a lessening in certain abilities, especially physical prowess. The question then becomes whether these diminished capacities play any sort of role in an employee's ability to effectively accomplish his or her job. If, for example, the employee is doing the job more slowly but is still producing the desired results, then speed should not be an issue at all. It is also important to note that many aspects of physical agility and strength are more than offset by hard-won experience and knowledge. If your goal is to have workers who do a spectacularly good job because they work "smart," then some of your older employees will often be your best.

However, if there is demonstrable proof that a worker's effectiveness and ability to make viable contributions to the company's goals have been seriously compromised as a result of age, then it is time to consider the prospect of either asking that employee to retire or easing her or him into another position. But such a decision has to be made with careful respect for the employee's skills and years of experience.

In all cases, there is no excuse for allowing anything beyond the basic facts of job performance to play a role in any evaluation. Sexism, racism, and ageism work at cross purposes to effective management and should be avoided at all costs.

Accommodating Employees with Disabilities

The purpose of the Americans with Disabilities Act of 1990 (signed into law on July 26 of that year) is "to provide a clear and comprehensive national mandate for the elimination of discrimination against individuals with disabilities." The primary intention of the ADA is to bring disabled people into the social and economic mainstream of American life by providing them with the same opportunities given to able-bodied people. Since the Act's passage, great strides have been made in accomplishing that goal.

Any employer today must be prepared to deal with issues of discrimination in the workplace. The ADA is the law, and cannot be ignored. Full understanding of what the law entails and how it affects your company is essential. Following are some salient points to assist you.

Making Reasonable Accommodations

The law mandates that reasonable accommodation for physical limitations must be made if the worker is otherwise qualified to do a job. Thus, the limitations of the handicap must be mediated through mechanical or other adaptations. Furthermore, this must be done in such a way that it is not demeaning and does not hold the worker up to public scrutiny or embarrassment.

Handling Complaints About the Workplace

More often than not, special help is needed to handle complaints and possible legal action against a company that is perceived to be discriminating against people with disabilities. There are boards and special advocates who understand the needs and the various means that exist for addressing these issues. The best plan is to check out your local American with Disabilities Act compliance center and make use of the resources you will find there.

Focusing on Performance and Predetermined Job Requirements

When you interview a person with disabilities for a position, be sure that you both understand the job description and that you both have agreed upon the performance level that will be expected and the accommodations that can be reasonably instituted for the disabled employee. In follow-up evaluations, you need to ensure that the employee is performing within the established parameters for job performance, without regard to her or his disability. On the other hand, special care has to be taken to refrain from pandering or condescending to the worker. Handicapped workers expect to do an excellent job and often have very high personal standards for their own performance which you should respect. In the long run, it is how well the individual accomplishes the job and meets established goals that count the most—just as it should be with any able-bodied employee.

3

Putting It in Writing

It is important to set the appropriate tone in written reviews. You want to make sure that there is nothing in the review that could provoke legal action. Remember that the purpose of the review is to reward excellence and to help employees improve their performance. Consider each work or phrase carefully before writing it down.

Words and Phrases to Avoid

Be extremely careful in setting the appropriate tone for your written salary review. Here is a list of words and phrases you should *not* use.

Imprecise and unmeasurable units of time:

always
never
a lot
soon
all the time

Imprecise and unmeasurable units of effort:

    a great deal
    very little
    zilch
    a weak try
    makes a big deal out of

Interpreting behavior negatively, rather than positively:

    Negative: Nit-picks every little thing. *Positive:* Has keen powers of observation.

    Negative: Gets hung up on details. *Positive:* Has a strong commitment to accuracy.

    Negative: Clams up whenever discussion is going on. *Positive:* Is able to stay objective in workplace discussions.

Emotionally charged or threatening vocabulary:

    doesn't deserve
    is lucky she isn't being . . .
    had better get it right . . .
    had better get his act together
    . . . or else!
    . . . and do it quick!

Personal slights:

    lazy
    slow
    mouthy
    nosey
    sloppy

You may never refer to a worker's:

    weight
    sex

age
marital status
race
sexual preference
political choices
family
religion
driving record
legal record

Unless it violates legal company policy, you may never refer to a worker's:

dress
leisure activities
grooming

Just the Right Words!

Here are examples you can use in evaluating 22 performance categories.

Excellent Employees

Accountability

Accepts responsibility for all actions and decisions.
Can be depended on to handle any situation in a mature and responsible manner.
Admits mistakes readily and corrects them quickly.

Adaptability and flexibility

Adapts readily to any management style/reorganization.
Willing to try new procedures, explore new methods of hand"
work/problems.
Can step into any position whenever the need arises.

Attendance

> Is punctual.
>
> Makes every effort to come to work, even under adverse weather conditions.
>
> Rarely uses sick days; has excellent attendance.

Attitude

> Has a professional attitude toward work and colleagues.
>
> Projects a positive outlook; a pleasure to work with.
>
> Is helpful to coworkers, supervisors, and clients.

Communication

> Has excellent verbal skills; communicates ideas well.
>
> Handles all speaking assignments extremely well.
>
> Runs very productive meetings; elicits high-level participation from those in attendance.

Dealing with stress

> Is able to handle stress productively; shares tight deadlines/unexpected problems with coworkers who work together to get results.
>
> Turns stress into a personal challenge to take charge and solve problems.
>
> Has a good perspective on job requirements; can deal with stress very well.

Decision making

> Can make timely, well-considered decisions.
>
> Is a careful, methodical decision-maker.
>
> Reviews major decisions with supervisors before implementing them.

Goals and objectives

> Consistently meets company goals and objectives.
>
> Establishes appropriate goals for those supervised, and implements successful plans to enable them to fulfill these goals.

Exceeds personal/professional goals and objectives.

Initiative and resourcefulness

Takes the initiative and shows resourcefulness in handling any problem.

Is eagerly sought after by coworkers and managers for resourceful solutions/ideas.

Will show initiative in taking on new responsibilities/tasks as needed, prior to being asked.

Intercultural sensitivity

Shows great sensitivity in dealing with people of different backgrounds and cultures. Is respectful of special accommodations necessary at certain times of year.

Treats all company personnel with respect and consideration.

Demonstrates special understanding of differences among people to manage the group effectively.

Interpersonal skills

Projects an open, friendly manner; is well-liked by all—coworkers and managerial staff alike.

Works well with others; is always ready to share information and ideas.

An excellent manager; has earned the trust and cooperation of the entire group.

Job knowledge

Is an expert in the field; continues to attend seminars and take in-service courses to keep up with the latest developments.

Knows every aspect of the job and performs with excellence.

Has an in-depth knowledge of the job; is an invaluable resource for the entire division.

Leadership

Demonstrates the ability to encourage others to cooperate and work together.

Shows natural leadership abilities.

Is looked up to by others in every respect—job knowledge, interpersonal relations.

Measurable performance qualities

Consistently exceeds goals.

Work is consistently accurate and on schedule.

Demonstrates positive attitude in handling the unexpected.

Planning/organization

Has excellent organizational skills.

Shows superior ability in developing and implementing successful plans.

Uses outstanding planning and organizational skills to get consistent high-level performance from subordinates.

Problem solving

Demonstrates originality and sensitivity in handling problems.

Has a direct objective approach to tackling all problems.

Regards any problem as a challenge to be met with eagerness and enthusiasm.

Professionalism

Is professional in appearance and behavior.

Treats coworkers and supervisors with courtesy and consideration.

Handles all aspects of the workplace in a professional manner.

Punctuality and dependability

Can be relied upon to be on time for every meeting.

Consistently dependable.

Is a strong role model for the group—dependable in any situation.

Receiving criticism and guidance

Handles criticism in a professional manner.

Is open to suggestions/guidance.

Shows a balanced view toward criticism; has a healthy perspective.

Reliability

Is reliable in carrying out any assignment.

Has a reputation for reliability within the entire division.

Can be relied on to work independently with superior results.

Use of resources

Uses equipment efficiently; has saved the company thousands of dollars.

Maintains a cost-efficient budget.

Encourages others to use resources carefully and avoid waste.

Summary comments

Is a valuable asset to the company.

A steady, reliable employee.

Continues to perform at the highest level.

Employees Who Need Improvement

Accountability

Must accept more responsibility for actions and decisions.

Should show a willingness to take responsibility for new projects.

Needs to admit mistakes readily.

Adaptability and flexibility

Has to be more accepting of change.

Needs to be more open to trying new ways of handling work/problems.

Should be more flexible in accepting new assignments.

Attendance

Must improve attendance.

Should make necessary arrangements to come to work every day.

Needs to adopt a more professional attitude toward attendance.

Attitude

Will need to improve attitude toward work and colleagues.

Needs to demonstrate a more positive outlook.

Should be more helpful to coworkers, supervisors, and clients.

Communication

Must improve ability to communicate with coworkers and supervisors.

Should practice clarifying written work.

Needs to work on handling speaking assignments.

Dealing with stress

Will need to learn how to deal with stress better.

Needs to improve ability to handle tight deadlines and other stress-producing projects.

Has to adopt a better perspective to cope with stress.

Decision making

Needs to work on improving decision-making skills.

Should ask for help in making decisions.

Must review major decisions with supervisors before implementing them.

Goals and objectives

Has to work on meeting company goals and objectives.

Should learn how to establish appropriate goals for subordinates.

Needs to improve fulfilling personal/professional goals and objectives.

Initiative and resourcefulness

Should show more resourcefulness in solving problems.

Needs to take the initiative in sharing ideas with coworkers and managers.

Must show initiative in undertaking new projects without being asked.

Intercultural sensitivity

Needs to be more sensitive in dealing with people of different backgrounds and cultures.

Must show more respect and consideration for cultural differences.

Should handle special circumstances with more diplomacy and sensitivity.

Interpersonal skills

Will have to project a more friendly manner.

Needs to improve ability to work with others—to share information and ideas.

Must focus on earning the trust of the entire group.

Job knowledge

Should attend seminars and take in-service courses to keep up with the latest developments in the field.

Needs to review job details to improve performance.

Will have to acquire more in-depth knowledge of the job.

Leadership

Has to develop the ability to encourage others to cooperate and work together.

Should act as a role model and set a good example for the team.

Needs to attend the corporate leadership training program.

Measurable performance qualities

Must work harder to meet goals.

Needs to improve accuracy and timeliness.

Will have to demonstrate a positive attitude in handling the unexpected.

Planning/organization

Needs to improve organizational skills.

Should follow company guidelines for development and planning.

Must sharpen planning and organizational skills to improve performance of subordinates.

Problem solving

Has to show more sensitivity in handling problems.

Needs to improve problem-solving skills.

Should work on viewing problems as challenges to be met with a positive outlook.

Professionalism

Must become more professional in appearance and behavior.

Needs to show more courtesy and consideration.

Should use more professional language.

Punctuality and dependability

Must be on time for every meeting.

Needs to show more dependability.

Should improve punctuality.

Receiving criticism and guidance

Needs to be more professional in handling criticism.

Should be open to suggestions/guidance.

Must develop a better attitude toward criticism.

Reliability

Will need to become more reliable in carrying out assignments efficiently.

Must show reliability as a team member.

Should be able to work independently.

Use of resources

Needs to use equipment more efficiently.

Must stay within budget.

Should encourage subordinates to use resources carefully and avoid waste.

Summary comments

If improvements are made, the employee will become a valuable asset to the company.

A good employee who fulfills job requirements.

Has the potential to grow and perform at a higher level.

Employees Who Face Termination

Accountability

Continues to behave irresponsibly despite many attempts to offer guidance and assistance.

Continues to make costly mistakes and makes no attempt to correct them.

Adaptability and flexibility

Is unable to adjust to the reorganization program.

Continues to be unwilling to implement the mandated new procedures.

Attendance

Has shown no improvement in punctuality.

Still has a poor attendance record. Hasn't worked a full week during the last three months.

Attitude

Demonstrates a hostile attitude toward work and colleagues.

Remains negative; is difficult to work with.

Communication

Has failed to improve the quality of written communication; reports are still submitted late, are poorly organized, and do not offer enough information.

Continues to have difficulty expressing ideas.

Dealing with stress

Is unable to function when under stress.

Becomes abusive toward subordinates when in stressful situations.

Decision making

Has shown no improvement in making independent decisions.

Continues to make inappropriate decisions.

Goals and objectives

Is still not able to establish appropriate goals for subordinates; as a result, their productivity is poor.

Has not shown any improvement in meeting company goals and objectives.

Initiative and resourcefulness

Continues to show a lack of initiative and resourcefulness in handling problems.

Has shown no improvement in taking on new responsibilities/tasks as needed, prior to being asked.

Intercultural sensitivity

Has not shown any improvement in respecting people of different backgrounds and cultures.

Continues to demonstrate a lack of sensitivity and understanding.

Interpersonal skills

Continues to display an arrogance that causes discomfort among coworkers and managers alike.

Has not improved in working with others; is still unwilling to share information and ideas.

Job knowledge

Has failed to attend seminars and take the required in-service courses to keep up with the latest developments.

Is still lacking in basic knowledge of the job; continues to need help from coworkers in handling even minimal projects.

Leadership

Has not demonstrated any growth in leadership skills; continues to be unable to manage the team.

Lacks the ability to be an effective role model—either by demonstrating strong professional skills or by demonstrating good interpersonal skills.

Measurable performance qualities

Work continues to be inaccurate and late.

Continues to demonstrate a negative attitude in handling the unexpected.

Planning/organization

Has shown no improvement in planning and organizational skills.

Is unable to develop or implement successful plans.

Problem solving

Continues to display a lack of originality and sensitivity in handling problems.

Has been unable to improve problem-solving skills.

Professionalism

Appearance has not improved; does not have a professional manner.

Does not treat coworkers and supervisors with courtesy and consideration.

Punctuality and dependability

Continues to be late for every meeting.

Has not shown any improvement in dependability.

Receiving criticism and guidance

Is still unable to handle criticism in a professional manner.

Has shown no improvement in accepting suggestions/guidance.

Reliability

Continues to be unreliable in carrying out assignments.
Cannot be relied on to work independently.

Use of resources

Continues to abuse equipment; has caused breakdowns and waste.
Has not improved in maintaining the approved budget.

Summary comments

As there has been no improvement since the last three-month review,
this review will serve as a two-week notice of termination.

4

Model Evaluations for Secretarial and Clerical Workers

This group consists of skilled and semiskilled detail-oriented workers. They are likely to work alone or in small, same-task groups. Their job titles include:

- Secretary
- Executive Secretary
- Managing Secretary
- Stenographer
- Pool Stenographer
- Typist
- Clerk
- Payroll Clerk
- Data-Entry Clerk
- Benefits Clerk

Gauging Performance

The work these employees perform is characterized by responsiveness and attention to detail. Individuals in these positions must be able to carry out tasks outlined by or begun by others. Their communication skills are important.

Quick, accurate, cheerful, and responsive individuals are highly sought in these positions. While innovation from these team members may be helpful, in most cases they are called upon to fulfill rather than initiate or design work projects.

The key issues in these positions usually revolve around the ability to adapt and respond to varying, frequently detailed tasks. The ability to be part of a task group and to cooperate on achieving group goals is important.

Performance Indicators

The top-level performer

- Has highly developed job skills
- Has a high degree of accuracy
- Is able to produce at a high level of accomplishment
- Is highly dependable
- Demonstrates a consistently cooperative manner
- Shows appropriate initiative without overstepping bounds
- Is punctual and regular in attendance
- Adapts well to changing situations and demands
- Is well organized
- Is comfortable and receptive to appropriate criticism

The good performer

- Has competent job skills
- Has a reasonable degree of accuracy
- Is able to produce at an acceptable level of accomplishment
- Is generally dependable and cooperative
- Sometimes shows initiative but sometimes oversteps bounds
- Has adequate attendance

- Can usually handle changing situations and demands
- Is generally organized but sometimes loses control of the details
- Is usually comfortable and receptive to appropriate criticism

The poor performer

- Has less than competent job skills
- Is lacking in job accuracy
- Produces at a less than acceptable level of accomplishment
- Is inconsistent in dependability
- Sometimes shows an uncooperative manner
- Show no initiative or has little skill at determining what areas of initiative are appropriate
- Has less than adequate attendance
- Is weak in adjusting to changing situations and demands
- Lacks organizational skills
- Is defensive and does not handle criticism well

Sample Reviews for Top-level Performers

PERFORMANCE EVALUATION
Secretarial/Clerical

Employee's Name: Lisa Livermore   Review Period: From 6/XX to 5/XX

Job Title: Receptionist/Clerk   Interim ___   Annual X

Name and Title of Evaluator: Anne Dutton, Registrar

Performance Guide

A — Consistently exceeds job requirements
Performance is exceptional, above and beyond what is expected

B — Meets job requirements
Does a good job; meets and sometimes exceeds requirements capably and competently

C — Improvement needed to meet job requirements
Is not performing at satisfactory level; extra supervision is required

O — Other
Not applicable to this area of evaluation

1. Job Knowledge   Grade: A

   Understands and effectively utilizes job-related information, procedures, and skills.

   Comments:

   Lisa is completely cognizant of all that she needs to do and how she should be functioning in her job. She keeps herself updated on all developments within the company so that she is able to field questions and direct people to the right location. Additionally, she ensures that she is kept informed at all times on the schedules of key employees so that she is able to provide relevant information regarding availability. Directories and brochures are always close at hand for her to refer to when taking calls or attending to visitors.

2. Quality of Work   Grade: A

   Completes assignments accurately and efficiently in accordance with department standards.

Comments:

As is made clear by other comments in this evaluation, Lisa's work is of the highest quality.

3. Timeliness   Grade: A

Finishes assignments within a reasonable or better time frame.
Comments:

In addition to her receptionist duties, Lisa is frequently given basic and sometimes complicated clerical tasks to do by many different people. She is always timely in the completion of these tasks and has impressed many due to the speed with which she works and the accuracy and pre-sentability of everything she does.

4. Work Habits   Grade: A

Plans and organizes work well, follows procedures, and makes efficient use of work time.
Comments:

Her work habits are superb. She has outstanding time management and organizational skills and is well able to juggle multiple tasks without becoming overwhelmed. Numerous people rely on her services and always get quality results from her.

5. Initiative and Resourcefulness   Grade: A

Demonstrates ability to work without direction and offer suggestions; can come up with creative solutions.
Comments:

She is rarely without something to do, but when she is, Lisa has always been able to find work to keep herself busy and involved. She was solely responsible for the reorganization of the reception area, changing the layout so that the receptionist's desk is more accessible to visitors, and has offered and implemented numerous suggestions that have contributed to the overall productivity of the office.

6. Decision Making   Grade: A

Evaluates situations, draws conclusions, and makes sound decisions.
Comments:

This would not normally be a criterion for somebody in Lisa's position, but in her case it applies. She applies thought and consideration to every task she is given and has sometimes found herself in the position of having to

37

make decisions regarding formatting of materials, correction of errors, ways to improve a project, and so on. She is entrusted with many important assignments because of her ability to make sound, rational judgments. She brings this ability into her receptionist work, as well, when she is able to screen phone calls and visitors and determine whether they will or will not reach the person they are seeking.

7. Adaptability and Flexibility   Grade: A

Adjusts to new ideas and situations and is receptive to new or additional work assignments.

Comments:

Lisa seems to love change and appreciates it when new challenges are presented to her. She is highly flexible and willing to do whatever is asked of her.

8. Accountability   Grade: A

Is willing to accept responsibility for job-related decisions and actions.

Comments:

Her errors are rare, but she always takes full responsibility for them. She is quick to apologize when the situation calls for it, and takes criticism well.

9. Punctuality and Dependability   Grade: A

Can be relied upon to be punctual and to do what is required without follow-up.

Comments:

Clearly we consider Lisa to be a highly dependable employee. She gives plenty of advance notice when taking time off, and the rare punctuality problem is always due to circumstances beyond her control. She knows that numerous people rely on her heavily, and she never fails to live up to that confidence and trust in her abilities and talents.

10. Use of Resources   Grade: A

Cares for and maintains equipment; conserves and economizes office resources.

Comments:

Lisa has effectively been an assistant office manager with her care and attention to office supplies and equipment. She looks after all machinery (fax, copier, printers, etc.) and ensures immediate attention whenever something breaks down. Additionally, she is economical and organized when it comes to ordering office supplies.

11. Communication Skills   Grade: A

Communicates with others clearly and effectively.

Comments:

Her responsibilities require her to be an effective communicator, and she lives up to the task admirably. Callers have frequently commented on her excellent telephone manner and her ability to provide clear, concise information. She is able to interpret messages and instructions so that there is no question about what is being said and how things are to be done. Her language skills are superb, and she has often rewritten letters for others to make them more comprehensible.

12. Interpersonal Skills   Grade: A

Interacts well with others; demonstrates courtesy, patience, diplomacy, discretion, and self-control; works well with a team.

Comments:

Once again, Lisa is superb in all ways. There is no question about her ability to get along with all with whom she comes into contact. She is dedicated and loyal and a team player to the core.

SUMMARY

Summarize employee's performance level since last review; indicate any improvement or decline.

It should be evident from my comments above that I think very highly of Lisa. She continues to excel in all areas, and has shown no evidence of any decline. She enjoys being busy and welcomes challenges, and in fact chafes at the bit when the work is slow. She is appreciated for her friendly, outgoing manner, her enthusiasm, her courtesy, tact, discretion, and diplomacy, and for her superb working skills. She took the receptionist's job to get a foot in the door, and now that she is all the way in, she should be encouraged to stay. It is clear that she is rapidly outgrowing the job. Having restructured her current position and made it more accessible and organized for another person to take over, it is now time for her to move on to a more responsible position. To that end, she has been going on interviews within the company and has her pick of potential jobs.

GOALS/OBJECTIVES FOR THE NEXT 12 MONTHS

Primary objective: Move on! Lisa's next review will undoubtedly be conducted by a different supervisor who will be establishing goals and criteria for her next position. I have no doubt that she will excel in whatever job she takes and wish her well as she moves onward and upward in her career.

EMPLOYEE'S COMMENTS

Employee's signature: _____ Date: _____

Evaluator's signature: _____ Date: _____

PERFORMANCE EVALUATION
Clerical

Name: Ronald McDougal   Title: File Clerk

Date: June 4, 20XX

Job Knowledge

Ron is an excellent file clerk who frequently works beyond the limits of his position to create a job that is more interesting and rewarding than one might ordinarily expect. Job knowledge is not an overriding factor in his evaluation, but he does ensure that he is on top of his work at all times and that he understands the nature of what he is filing, where it needs to go, who will need to draw on him for assistance, and how soon. He is alert and attentive at all times.

Quality of Work

As noted above, Ron goes beyond what some might consider to be a severely limiting job and manages to make it fulfilling for himself and for others. This is largely due to his attitude. He takes a positive approach to his work, works with a smile on his face at all times, and remains cheerful and unbowed by frequent periods of monotony. In fact, he frequently finds ways to break up the monotony and sparks the entire department with his wit and wisdom. He rarely falls behind in his work, and when he does he will work extra hours to get caught up. He has not been known to misfile materials and has earned high praise from numerous sources for his ability to find a file at a moment's notice. Overall, the quality of his work is superb.

Productivity/Timeliness

Ron is our most productive employee, getting both standard tasks and special assignments completed quickly and efficiently.

Work Habits/Organizational Skills

Ron is a superbly organized individual, who keeps the entire filing operation running smoothly with efficient shortcuts and an ability to reduce huge

41

stacks of files to nothing in no time. His skills in organizing his work and managing his time have resulted in his being the person to train new clerks in the File Room.

Resourcefulness

Ron's reorganization of the File Room has resulted in a more efficient operation that has enabled us to service employees with speed and efficiency. He is unquestionably resourceful and has made numerous suggestions that have improved overall efficiency.

Communication Skills

Ron's only possible drawback is that he sometimes tells off-color jokes that do not go over well with other employees. He should monitor his jokes so that he doesn't potentially offend somebody with an inappropriate comment. He is otherwise someone who expresses himself well, and is clear and easy to understand in all his business-related communications.

Interpersonal Skills/Teamwork

Ron is a leader within the department, well liked and respected by his peers and by employees throughout the company. He is a loyal and dedicated worker with extremely good interpersonal skills and a true dedication to team efforts.

Adaptability/Dependability

Ron is extremely dependable. He can be entrusted with important tasks without supervision, and many people rely heavily on him, to the point where, if he is out of the office, they will wait until his return before asking for assistance with something. He is a role model for dependable work habits and ethics.

Attendance/Punctuality

There have been no attendance or punctuality problems reported.

Goals for Next Review

Because of his talents, work ethic, and leadership abilities, it is my belief that Ron can and should move into a more administrative or managerial role. He is currently exploring other opportunities within the company, but has confessed himself quite happy working in the File Room. Given the upcoming expansion of the company, should he choose to stay in our department, then I will talk to Human Resources about creating the position of Assistant Manager for Ron, with the appropriate salary increase, and the understanding that he will succeed me as Manager at the appropriate time.

Employee's Comments

Employee's signature: _____ Date: _____

Evaluator's signature: _____ Date: _____

PERFORMANCE EVALUATION
Clerical (Interim Review)

Name: Barbara Byrne

Title: Office Assistant

Date of hire: September 12, 20XX

Department: Operations

Supervisor: Hillary Gogolin

Review Period: From 1/XX to 6/XX

Ratings: Employee is to be rated on a scale of 1 to 3, as described below.

1: Below expectations: Performance is substandard and requires improvement.

2: Meets expectations: Performance fully meets and occasionally exceeds standards.

3: Exceeds expectations: Performance consistently exceeds set standards.

N/A: Not applicable. Lack of sufficient knowledge to evaluate the performance factor.

Section I: Basic Job Skills

	Below	Meets	Exceeds	N/A
Job knowledge	1	2	<u>3</u>	N/A
Quality of work	1	2	<u>3</u>	N/A
Productivity/Timeliness	1	2	<u>3</u>	N/A
Dependability	1	2	<u>3</u>	N/A
Work habits	1	2	<u>3</u>	N/A
Organizational skills	1	2	<u>3</u>	N/A
Resourcefulness	1	<u>2</u>	3	N/A
Problem solving	1	<u>2</u>	3	N/A
Care of office equipment	1	<u>2</u>	3	N/A

Comments:

Barbara is an excellent worker. She is willing to do whatever is asked of her and does it quickly, efficiently, and cheerfully. She brightens the office with her sunny attitude and a cooperative nature that makes it possible to trust her with work assignments and not have to follow-up or double-check to make sure she's doing it right.

Section II: Personal Attributes

	Below	Meets	Exceeds	N/A
Attendance/Punctuality	1	2	3	N/A
Ability to take direction	1	2	3	N/A
Initiative	1	2	3	N/A
Cooperativeness	1	2	3	N/A
Adaptability	1	2	3	N/A
Receptiveness to criticism	1	2	3	N/A
Communication skills	1	2	3	N/A
Interaction with coworkers	1	2	3	N/A
Courtesy/Hospitality	1	2	3	N/A

Comments:

Barbara has a tendency to arrive anywhere from 5 to 15 minutes late 2-3 days a week. She always makes up the time, but it would be better if she could be more consistent in her arrival and departure times. Otherwise, she has amply demonstrated her ability to meet all the criteria of her job.

Section III: Strengths and Weaknesses

Describe employee strengths:

Cooperative attitude; dedication to her job; determination to see a job through to its finish; tremendous flexibility; cheerful disposition.

Describe areas for improvement:

Punctuality; initiative (see below).

Describe goals for next performance review, and means by which goals will be achieved:

- Improve punctuality by arriving earlier in the morning to ensure 9:00 start.

- Develop job description by proposing ideas to change or enhance current work routine.

- Make more of an effort to solve problems on own initiative, rather than asking for help.

45

Section IV: Comments

Evaluator:

Barbara has the potential to advance. She has proven herself to be a capable, hard worker, but perhaps lacks sufficient confidence in herself to completely take charge of her job and turn it into something more. She should take more initiative in developing her job description and polishing the skills that will win her recognition and job advancement.

Employee:

Employee's signature: _____ Date: _____

Evaluator's signature: _____ Date: _____

PERFORMANCE EVALUATION
Clerical

Name: Bill Johnson   Department: (Front office)

Title: Receptionist/Clerk   Supervisor: Jill Bowen

Date of hire: March 13, 20xx   Review period: From 3/xx to 2/xx

Ratings: Employee is to be rated on a scale of 1 to 3, as described below.

1: Below expectations: Performance is substandard and requires improvement.

2: Meets expectations: Performance fully meets and occasionally exceeds standards.

3: Exceeds expectations: Performance consistently exceeds set standards.

N/A: Not applicable. Lack of sufficient knowledge to evaluate the performance factor.

Section I: Basic Job Skills

	Below	Meets	Exceeds	N/A
Job knowledge	1	<u>2</u>	3	N/A
Quality of work	1	2	<u>3</u>	N/A
Productivity/Timeliness	1	2	<u>3</u>	N/A
Dependability	1	2	<u>3</u>	N/A
Work habits	1	2	<u>3</u>	N/A
Organizational skills	1	2	<u>3</u>	N/A
Resourcefulness	1	2	<u>3</u>	N/A
Problem solving	1	<u>2</u>	3	N/A
Care of office equipment	1	2	<u>3</u>	N/A

Comments:

Bill has consistently met the requirements of his job and sometimes has exceeded them. He faced some difficulties at the beginning of his employment because many perceived his to be a "woman's job." However, he has persevered and has made the job his own. His greatest strengths are his dependability and his resourcefulness. He is always punctual and never too far from his desk at any time. When he needs to leave his desk for any period of time, he ensures that somebody will cover the phones for him. He keeps the main reception area looking clean and welcoming, frequently adding flowers or decorations to liven things up. He also takes excellent care of all the equipment for which he is responsible. He is willing to do special projects that are requested of him. In short, he is a dependable, dedicated worker.

Section II: Personal Attributes

	Below	Meets	Exceeds	N/A
Attendance/Punctuality	1	2	<u>3</u>	N/A
Ability to take direction	1	<u>2</u>	3	N/A
Initiative	1	2	<u>3</u>	N/A
Cooperativeness	1	2	<u>3</u>	N/A
Adaptability	1	2	<u>3</u>	N/A
Receptiveness to criticism	1	2	<u>3</u>	N/A
Communication skills	1	2	<u>3</u>	N/A
Interaction with coworkers	1	2	<u>3</u>	N/A
Courtesy/Hospitality	1	2	<u>3</u>	N/A

Comments:

These job factors constitute Bill's strongest suits. He is perfectly suited to his area of responsibility thanks to his enthusiastic approach to his job. He never fails to be courteous and respectful of others, whether visitors, executives, or coworkers. He greets everybody with a smile and has a pleasant and appealing telephone manner. He is willing to help out wherever and whenever he is needed and has never complained about any task to which he has been assigned. He has the welcome ability to learn from his mistakes, which are almost never repeated. In short, Bill represents the company well!

Section III: Evaluator's Comments

Describe employee strengths:

Pleasing and enthusiastic attitude; willingness to do any task that is assigned to him; excellent interpersonal skills.

Describe areas for improvement:

Bill should be more ambitious in his career goals. Several department managers have spoken to him about advancing to a higher position, but Bill seems to be content to stay where he is. Of course, this is not a big flaw, but he is clearly an intelligent and talented individual who can make even more valuable contributions to the company should he choose to tackle some more complex assignments.

Describe goals for next performance review and means by which goals will be achieved:

I have suggested that Bill spend a little time each day familiarizing himself with the different departments and the job opportunities within each department. He is not required to move to a different position if he truly doesn't want to, but he should be encouraged to explore his options and to be open to other possibilities where he can learn new things and be more creative and better challenged by his work. His intelligence and enthusiasm are a valuable asset to the company, and he should be urged to pursue professional growth.

Section IV: Employee's Comments

Employee's signature: _____ Date: _____

Evaluator's signature: _____ Date: _____

PERFORMANCE EVALUATION
Secretarial/Clerical

Name: Joan Valentine   Title: Typist

Date: February 20, 20XX   Interim   Annual X

I. JOB FACTORS: *RATING:*

1. Job knowledge   (poor) 1 2 3 <u>4</u> 5 (excellent)
   Comments:

   Not a major factor in the performance of her duties.

2. Quality of work   (poor) 1 2 3 4 <u>5</u> (excellent)
   Comments:

   Joan has excellent typing skills, as well as a good eye for formatting every document she works on, making everything neat and presentable. Managers who send work to her have expressed their appreciation of her careful attention to spelling and grammar, as well as her ability to spot errors, which she then brings to their attention.

3. Productivity   (poor) 1 2 3 4 <u>5</u> (excellent)
   Comments:

   Joan is fast and efficient in her output; has excellent completion time. On many days she is able to complete two or three times the work of other typists in the pool.

4. Initiative   (poor) 1 2 3 4 <u>5</u> (excellent)
   Comments:

   She welcomes opportunities for new and creative assignments. When there is a lull in the flow of work, she asks around to see if there is other work she can do for people.

5. Dependability   (poor) 1 2 3 4 <u>5</u> (excellent)
   Comments:

   She is focused on her work and willing to do whatever is asked of her. A lot of trust is placed in her abilities, and managers will specifically ask for her to do their work.

6. Interpersonal skills/Teamwork   (poor) 1 2 3 4 <u>5</u> (excellent)
   Comments:

50

She has an excellent rapport with her fellow typists and frequently initiates challenges to see who can produce the most work in a set amount of time. She also brightens the office with decorations during the holidays. She maintains a cheerful attitude at all times and interacts well with employees at all levels.

7. Decision-making abilities   (poor) 1 2 3 4 <u>5</u> (excellent)
Comments:

Ordinarily this would not be a criteria for evaluation on Joan's level, but she has frequently demonstrated decision-making capabilities when she has caught errors or problems in a particular document. On one occasion, she spotted a contradiction in a report that would have caused the manager considerable embarrassment had it been sent out to clients without the appropriate correction. Thus, her attention to details such as these and her ability to follow through on them show that she is always thinking, which is a great asset. I believe she is capable of making even more important decisions.

8. Problem-solving abilities   (poor) 1 2 3 4 <u>5</u> (excellent)
Comments:

As already explained in other comments.

9. Organizational skills   (poor) 1 2 3 4 <u>5</u> (excellent)
Comments:

Joan's desk is always neat and presentable. When presented with multiple tasks, she is able to prioritize without any additional directions and to organize her work schedule for maximum, efficient output.

10. Communication skills   (poor) 1 2 3 4 <u>5</u> (excellent)
Comments:

Joan is well-spoken and communicates her thoughts and ideas easily. Her writing skills are nothing short of perfect.

11. Analytic skills   (poor) 1 2 3 4 <u>5</u> (excellent)
Comments:

As already explained in other comments.

12. Receptiveness to criticism   (poor) 1 2 3 4 <u>5</u> (excellent)
Comments:

It should be pointed out that Joan's work is rarely if ever criticized.

13. Management of resources   (poor) 1 2 3 <u>4</u> 5 (excellent)
Comments:

Not a major factor in her evaluation. She meets the criteria.

14. Professionalism   (poor) 1 2 3 4 <u>5</u> (excellent)
Comments:

She always maintains a very professional attitude toward her work and toward other employees.

15. Punctuality   (poor) 1 2 3 <u>4</u> 5 (excellent)
Comments:

She is almost always on time.

Overall Rating   (poor) 1 2 3 4 <u>5</u> (excellent)

II. SUMMARY/COMMENTS

Joan is clearly interested in moving on to a more responsible and creative position, and she is unquestionably capable of doing so. Unfortunately, recent downsizing in certain areas has prevented the opening of any suitable positions at the present time. However, she knows she is first in line for any job that opens up for which she would be qualified. Several of our managers have indicated their desire to have her join their departments, so in time she should have no lack of opportunity for advancement. In the meantime, I would very much like to keep her as part of our team rather than lose her to another company. To that end, I wish to offer her an incentive to stay by recommending a 3-percent merit increase on top of her approved 2-percent cost-of-living raise.

III. GOALS FOR NEXT REVIEW

Joan should just keep on doing the fine job she has been doing from the start.

IV. EMPLOYEE COMMENTS

Employee's signature: _____ Date: _____

Evaluator's signature: _____ Date: _____

Sample Reviews for Midlevel Performers

EVALUATION FORM

Employee Name: Sandra Rodriquez   Date: January 15, 20xx

Employee's Job Title: Department Secretary   Department: Research

Name of Evaluator: Andy Stillwell   Title: Supervisor

Period covered by this evaluation: From 1/xx to 1/xx

Reason for this evaluation: Interim   Annual X   Other _____

(Specify)

Rating levels and definitions

Level 5 = *Performance exceeds job requirements.*

Level 4 = *Performance meets job requirements.*

Level 3 = *Performance meets job requirements with room for further development.*

Level 2 = *Performance needs improvement.*

Level 1 = *Unacceptable performance.*

PERFORMANCE CRITERIA

A. Job Knowledge   Rating Assigned: 3

Evaluate the extent to which the employee understands the responsibilities of his or her position: is knowledgeable in the latest techniques, skills, and methods pertinent to his or her area of responsibility; and pursues further training or education to improve job know-how and professional capabilities.

Explanation:

Since her six-month review, Sandra has become proficient in her understanding of what is required of her. She has taken some computer courses and shows interest in learning to do her job more efficiently. However, she waits too often for instructions and has not yet learned to apply previous experience to new situations.

B. Quality of Work   Rating Assigned: 3

Evaluate the extent to which the employee's work conforms to established standards and procedures: demonstrates attention to specific directions; is accurate, thorough, and presentable; and is concise and timely.

Explanation:

Sandra is always neat and does her best to be organized. However, she needs to demonstrate more attention to the details of her work. In addition, she is often too slow in completing assignments. Improvement in speed is desirable.

C. Accomplishment of Goals and Objectives   Rating Assigned: 3

Evaluate the extent to which the employee sets appropriate goals and objectives: demonstrates commitment and enthusiasm in carrying out his or her plan of action; and achieves objectives in a timely and competent manner.

Explanation:

Sandra has the basics of her job down pat now and should be setting more goals for herself rather than waiting for directions from others. She is brighter than she realizes and has the capability of turning what may seem to her like a mundane job into something more creative and exciting. But she needs to apply herself more to specific goals to achieve this.

D. Initiative and Creativity   Rating Assigned: 2

Evaluate the extent to which the employee is aware of what needs to be done and demonstrates the energy and self-motivation to begin and complete work requirements without prompting from others: approaches his or her work in creative or imaginative ways.

Explanation:

See above. More initiative needs to be demonstrated.

E. Analytic Skills   Rating Assigned: 0

Evaluate the extent to which the employee can analyze a situation or problem and draw logical and valid conclusions: identifies all critical areas of the issue and can make sound recommendations; and is able to propose several viable alternatives based on recognition of multiple options.

Explanation:

N/A

F. Problem Solving   Rating Assigned: 3

Evaluate the extent to which the employee identifies different problems requiring attention: can isolate causes and propose solutions; and is able to foresee the impact decisions made may have on other people or departments and therefore will consult with them.

Explanation:

Currently little comes up that requires Sandra to be a problem solver. She turns to others for solutions if any difficulty arises during the course of her duties.

G. Interpersonal and Communication Skills   Rating Assigned: 4

Evaluate the extent to which the employee demonstrates conciseness, clarity, tact, and cordiality in both written and verbal communications: listens carefully and understands directions; provides accurate and timely information when required; and is considerate and respectful of different levels of personnel as well as people of different types and cultures.

Explanation:

This is Sandra's strength. She expresses herself well and is both forthright in her opinions and respectful of others. She is unfailingly courteous and interacts effectively with her coworkers.

H. Teamwork and Cooperation   Rating Assigned: 3

Evaluate the extent to which the employee works effectively and efficiently with others: is willing to offer or accept assistance when necessary; and is flexible and willing to compromise or make concessions in the best interests of the organization.

Explanation:

Sandra interacts well with others and is cooperative and friendly. She is willing to help out when asked, but rarely offers her services outside her normal routine.

I. Consumer Relations/Hospitality   Rating Assigned: 4

Evaluate the extent to which the employee achieves positive relationships with customers, visitors, and all levels of company staff: contributes to a favorable public image of the company; is accessible to users of department services; and has merited the trust and respect of others within and outside the department.

Explanation:

A good portion of Sandra's job entails her fielding phone calls and receiving visitors to the department who desire to use our resources. She directs them to the right person or location and is always gracious and helpful. She also needs to be accessible and willing to work on special projects that can be generated from several different sources. This means that she interacts on a daily basis with dozens of visitors and personnel and needs strong people skills. In this regard, she more than meets the criteria for the position.

J. Cost Effectiveness   Rating Assigned: 3

Evaluate the extent to which the employee budgets time and remains organized and focused on work assignments: effectively preserves and economizes on expendable supplies and resources; cares for and maintains office equipment; and adheres to departmental cost-containment policies.

Explanation:

Sandra is weak when it comes to prioritizing her work and in finishing tasks on a timely basis—improvement is definitely needed. She has also been overly enthusiastic in ordering supplies for the office when she should be practicing a better sense of economy. This has been discussed with her previously, and she is desirous of improving herself in these areas.

OVERALL PERFORMANCE RATING: 3

DEVELOPMENTAL GOALS

Describe goals for the next 12-month period, along with agreed-upon plan for obtaining goals, the time frame for achieving goals, and the method to be used for measuring achievement.

Sandra must do a better job of staying on top of the jobs that should be a part of her daily routine—for example, posting the schedule for use of the library, checking the fax machine on a regular basis, checking the status of supplies, etc. I have suggested that she create a daily checklist to ensure that routine jobs are not overlooked.

She also needs to work on prioritizing her work better. To that end, I have asked her to write a daily diary of her activities over the next two weeks in order to get a better idea of how she is utilizing her time and make suggestions for improvement. Thereafter, she is to write a weekly summary of her job, detailing what she is doing and for whom and the time being spent on various projects. I would also like her to summarize problems she encounters and how she has dealt with them. We will review these periodically.

Sandra is also to think about her job—what it entails and how she would like it to be different. She will be meeting with me again to go over her goals and to see how the scope of her job might be expanded and made more interesting for her. When a plan has been developed, we will review it on a regular basis to see how well she is meeting her goals and what might be done to help her meet them.

EMPLOYEE'S COMMENTS AND SIGNATURE

Employee's signature: _____ Date: _____

EVALUATOR'S COMMENTS AND SIGNATURE

Sandra has occasionally expressed frustration at the limited scope of her job. She was informed when she was hired that it was a position with the potential for growth, and she feels that that opportunity has not been presented to her. I have reiterated the need for her to show more initiative and to make things happen for herself by making suggestions, volunteering for extra assignments, and implementing any ideas she has to improve her current routine. Although she has shown improvement since her interim review, she has not yet demonstrated the self-motivation that will earn her increased recognition and responsibilities.

Evaluator's signature: _____ Date: _____

57

PERFORMANCE EVALUATION
Clerical

Name: William Merriman   Title: Legal Stenographer

Date: 12/14/20XX

Job Knowledge

Bill's overall basic job knowledge is good. He has strong typing skills and is aware of all the legal terminology and fundamental legal procedures that he needs to know in his position. This makes it possible for him to understand and correctly transcribe tapes, depositions, and court proceedings with an adequate amount of accuracy. He knows when to ask questions and is able to apply previous learning to new situations as they arise.

Quality of Work

For the most part, Bill's work quality is good. Transcribed documents are neat and presentable, and he is careful and attentive to details. However, he sometimes does not take enough care to proofread, and his spelling skills are weak, so that there are often spelling errors in his documents and court reports, as well as occasional grammatical errors.

Quantity of Work

Turnaround time is fine, and he does a pretty good job of staying on top of his workload. However, he doesn't seem to work so well as he should under pressure. His speed and accuracy tend to deteriorate when a crunch is on and he is required to produce something in more of a hurry, which makes him push himself hard and leads him to get nervous about what he is doing.

Work Habits/Organizational Skills

As already noted, Bill does a fairly good job of staying on top of his workload. His organizational skills are fine; he keeps himself well supplied with all the materials he needs and shows up in court and at depositions fully prepared with the necessary supplies and equipment. His desk is always neat and clean, his files are in order, and he manages his time well.

Initiative

Bill can be depended upon to do what is expected of him—to be where he is told to go and to produce the expected output. He has not demonstrated too much in the way of initiative, but this is largely because the nature of the job does not require that particular skill.

Interpersonal Skills

Bill is a quiet worker, very respectful of those around him. He feels he should be part of the background in any proceeding, rather than intrude in any way, and he succeeds in this admirably. Because he is so quiet, it is difficult to judge his interpersonal skills. He certainly gets along well with others and has never had any problems in either personal or business interactions.

Adaptability/Dependability

The nature of Bill's work requires him to be adaptable to any situation, and he meets all the criteria in this regard. He is steady and hard-working and is regarded as very dependable by all with whom he works.

Attendance/Punctuality

There have been rare punctuality problems. Bill is a dependable employee who rarely takes a day off and has never failed to show up where he has been expected to be.

Comments/Goals for Next Review

By and large, the best word for Bill would be "steadfast." For what is expected of him, he meets all the established criteria and is a dedicated and reliable employee. He understands the work he must do as well as the reasons behind it. The only reason I cannot rate him as superior is his difficulty in working under stressful conditions, as well as his subpar spelling and grammatical skills. His work is clean, neat, and presentable, but he needs to pay closer attention to these particular areas, as they are crucial in what he does. On my recommendation, he recently purchased a dictionary and a style manual, which he keeps close by at his desk. In addition, he is to make better use of the spell checker in the computer; he has tended to overlook this resource in the past in the interest of speed. Even if it slows him down for the time being, I want him to concentrate on spelling and composition skills. We will also work together on techniques to improve his ability to handle more pressurized conditions.

Employee's Comments

Employee's signature: _____ Date: _____

Evaluator's signature: _____ Date: _____

PERFORMANCE EVALUATION

Name: Wendy Williamson   Title: Office Assistant
Date: November 1, 20XX   Interim   Annual X

I. JOB FACTORS: *RATING:*

1. Job knowledge   (poor) 1 2 <u>3</u> 4 5 (excellent)
2. Quality of work   (poor) 1 2 <u>3</u> 4 5 (excellent)
3. Productivity   (poor) 1 2 3 <u>4</u> 5 (excellent)
4. Dependability   (poor) 1 2 3 <u>4</u> 5 (excellent)
5. Work habits   (poor) 1 2 <u>3</u> 4 5 (excellent)
6. Care of equipment   (poor) 1 2 <u>3</u> 4 5 (excellent)
7. Interpersonal skills/Teamwork   (poor) 1 <u>2</u> 3 4 5 (excellent)
8. Adaptability   (poor) 1 <u>2</u> 3 4 5 (excellent)
9. Organizational skills   (poor) 1 2 <u>3</u> 4 5 (excellent)
10. Communication skills   (poor) 1 2 <u>3</u> 4 5 (excellent)
11. Initiative/Resourcefulness   (poor) 1 2 3 <u>4</u> 5 (excellent)
12. Ability to take direction/Cooperation (poor) 1 2 <u>3</u> 4 5 (excellent)
13. Receptiveness to criticism   (poor) 1 2 <u>3</u> 4 5 (excellent)
14. Attendance/Punctuality   (poor) 1 2 <u>3</u> 4 5 (excellent)

Overall Rating   (poor) 1 2 <u>3</u> 4 5 (excellent)

II. SUMMARY/COMMENTS

Wendy is a good, capable employee whose performance rating has improved considerably since her last review. She still displays some areas of inconsistency, but by and large I am very pleased with the progress she has made in the last six months. Her strongest areas are in productivity, dependability, and resourcefulness. She has improved her turnaround speed on work assignments almost trifold and has proven herself to be very dependable and conscientious when it comes to completing any task given to her. The biggest pleasure has been in regard to her ability to take more initiative in her job. This was a goal established at her last review, and she has met the challenge admirably, coming up with suggestions for improving the filing system for patient records and implementing a number of changes on her own to improve her job efficiency. She has improved her overall job knowledge considerably and applied herself well to the tasks of improving her organizational skills (there are still some problems there, but she is working on them) and bettering her communication skills and her attitude. The temper that she displayed in the past whenever a criticism was made of her has largely disappeared, and she has become more amenable to suggestions.

All in all, I am extremely proud of the progress Wendy has made. I feel certain that at the rate she is progressing, she will undoubtedly be earning a superior performance evaluation in the future. Two areas still need a bit of work: adaptability and interpersonal skills. Wendy still struggles with change and tends to resist whenever new policies or procedures are introduced into the office. In addition, she still tends to be a bit grating or sarcastic with her coworkers. She prefers to work alone and does not do exceptionally well on projects that require her to work in tandem with others. Teamwork is a large point of concern.

III. GOALS FOR NEXT REVIEW

Wendy is to continue making headway in all areas, and I have no doubt that she will do well in the months ahead, with continued self-application and encouragement from me and others in management. Interim evaluations are no longer necessary, although she and I will have biweekly informal meetings to review her progress and any points of concern as they come up. Meanwhile, she will work on her ability to adapt to change, and on her interpersonal skills. To deal with this last matter, I will be assigning her to work on a number of projects with others in the office, and I will be on hand to mediate any disputes or problems that result, with the goal of helping her to monitor her behavior and to learn the skills she needs to work as part of a team.

IV. EMPLOYEE COMMENTS

Employee's signature: _____ Date: _____

Evaluator's signature: _____ Date: _____

PERFORMANCE EVALUATION

Name: George Kawinski   Department: Data Entry
Title: Data Entry Operator   Supervisor: Nancy Perkins
Date of hire: 10/20/XX   Review period: From 10/XX to 9/XX

Ratings: Employee is to be rated on a scale of 1 to 3, as described below.

1: Below expectations: Performance is substandard and requires improvement.

2: Meets expectations: Performance fully meets and occasionally exceeds standards.

3: Exceeds expectations: Performance consistently exceeds set standards.

N/A: Not applicable. Lack of sufficient knowledge to evaluate the performance factor.

Section I: Basic Job Skills

	Below	Meets	Exceeds	N/A
Job knowledge	1	2	3	N/A
Quality of work	1	2	3	N/A
Productivity/Timeliness	1	2	3	N/A
Dependability	1	2	3	N/A
Work habits	1	2	3	N/A
Organizational skills	1	2	3	N/A
Resourcefulness	1	2	3	N/A
Problem solving	1	2	3	N/A
Care of office equipment	1	2	3	N/A

Comments:

George consistently meets expectations. He is well organized, works well within established procedures, and never fails to meet his daily goals. He is one of our most dependable workers.

Section II: Personal Attributes

	Below	Meets	Exceeds	N/A
Attendance/Punctuality	1	2	3	N/A
Ability to take direction	1	2	3	N/A
Initiative	1	2	3	N/A
Cooperativeness	1	2	3	N/A
Adaptability	1	2	3	N/A
Receptiveness to criticism	1	2	3	N/A

Communication skills	1	<u>2</u>	3	N/A
Interaction with coworkers	1	2	<u>3</u>	N/A
Courtesy/Hospitality	1	2	3	<u>N/A</u>

Comments:

George is part of a large team of operators and works well with all of them. He is often a resource for answering questions when the supervisor is not present. He expresses himself well and maintains a good attitude towards his work.

Section III: Comments

Describe employee strengths:

George does everything that is expected of him, willingly and efficiently. He gets along well with his coworkers and is cooperative with his supervisor. He is one of our most dependable operators.

Describe areas for improvement:

He does no more than what is expected of him. He has the ability to move on to a supervisory position but has not yet demonstrated any initiative in this direction, such as making suggestions for improving data-entry efficiency.

Describe goals for next performance review and means by which goals will be achieved:

I have asked George to consider the possibility of advancement and he has agreed to act as a trainer for new employees, as well as to offer ideas for changes in current procedures.

Section IV: Employee Comments

Employee's signature: _____ Date: _____

Evaluator's signature: _____ Date: _____

PERFORMANCE EVALUATION
Secretarial/Clerical

Name: Nanette Nickerson   Title: Receptionist

Date: January 2, 20XX

Job Knowledge

Nanette is aware of all the basics regarding the company, its various departments, and its employees, so that she is able to process routine phone calls and requests for information, as well as to direct visitors to their destinations. She is sometimes perplexed by more complicated calls and has demonstrated no desire to learn any more than what she absolutely needs to know to get her job done.

Quality of Work

General work quality is good, but cannot be considered outstanding, although I believe Nan has the capability of achieving more than she is currently achieving. She is fine with the basic details of her job, but does not seem to be motivated to go beyond the limits of her position. For instance, when she is asked to type a report, she will do so without putting enough thought into how it looks and how she might improve the visual appearance of what is given to her. Details of formatting and style do not seem to interest her all that much. In other words, she does what is expected of her, but no more than that, and does not demonstrate much initiative to improve on her own work.

Productivity

Nan produces a good turnaround rate on all projects given to her. She rarely turns something in late and is conscientious about producing the desired results in a timely fashion.

Organizational Skills

Nan has inconsistent organizational skills. She goes through periods where she is on top of everything and keeps everything neat and well organized. Then she gets into other periods where her desk becomes piled high with paper and she has difficulty finding anything. She has a pronounced distaste for filing, and has to push herself to get it done. When she falls behind on her filing, this adversely affects other areas of her job responsibilities, especially when she has to stop and search for important documents or necessary materials that have become lost in the maze of paper on her desk.

Initiative

As previously noted, Nan largely does only what is expected of her. She had a burst of creativity last year, when she determined that the layout of the reception area was rather uninviting to visitors. She suggested changes and improvements that made the area much more friendly and open to our guests. For the most part, she is willing to do a good job according to the dictates of her job description, but little more than that, unless it satisfies a creative urge inside her.

Interpersonal Skills/Teamwork

Nan's interpersonal skills are excellent. She gets along well with other employees and provides a bright and cheerful introduction to outsiders by way of her friendly, outgoing manner. She is well liked by all who come into contact with her.

Adaptability/Dependability

Nan has demonstrated herself to be very adaptable to any new situation and—except for occasional lapses—is a good, dependable employee. These lapses center around the amount of time she spends on the telephone and chatting with other employees, which frequently takes her attention away from her job for excessively long periods of time.

Attendance/Punctuality

No attendance or punctuality problems have been noted (but see above).

Comments/Goals for Next Review

Nan needs to be more conscientious about sticking closer to her desk and not disappearing for great lengths of time to socialize with other employees. She has been warned that too much time spent away from her post will be noted in her employee file if it continues. She must also demonstrate improved consistency in her organizational abilities, specifically as it applies to staying on top of her filing chores. It is possible that Nan doesn't have enough to do in her position, therefore I am requesting that other staff give her projects to do, as they see fit. Nan will be monitored for her willingness and ability to take on extra work assignments as well as for the degree of care and creativity with which she completes them.

Employee's Comments

Employee's signature: _____ Date: _____

Evaluator's signature: _____ Date: _____

PERFORMANCE EVALUATION

Name: Ralph Mazzeo   Title: File Clerk
Date: March 22, 20XX   Interim   Annual X

I. JOB FACTORS: *RATING:*

   1. Job knowledge   (poor) 1 2 <u>3</u> 4 5 (excellent)
   2. Quality of work   (poor) 1 2 <u>3</u> 4 5 (excellent)
   3. Productivity   (poor) 1 <u>2</u> 3 4 5 (excellent)
   4. Dependability   (poor) 1 2 <u>3</u> 4 5 (excellent)
   5. Work habits   (poor) 1 2 <u>3</u> 4 5 (excellent)
   6. Care of equipment   (poor) 1 2 <u>3</u> 4 5 (excellent)
   7. Interpersonal skills/Teamwork (poor) 1 2 3 <u>4</u> 5 (excellent)
   8. Adaptability   (poor) 1 2 <u>3</u> 4 5 (excellent)
   9. Organizational skills   (poor) 1 <u>2</u> 3 4 5 (excellent)
  10. Communication skills   (poor) 1 2 <u>3</u> 4 5 (excellent)
  11. Initiative/Resourcefulness   (poor) 1 2 <u>3</u> 4 5 (excellent)
  12. Ability to take direction/Cooperation (poor) 1 2 <u>3</u> 4 5 (excellent)
  13. Receptiveness to criticism   (poor) 1 2 <u>3</u> 4 5 (excellent)
  14. Attendance/Punctuality   (poor) 1 2 <u>3</u> 4 5 (excellent)

Overall Rating   (poor) 1 2 <u>3</u> 4 5 (excellent)

II. SUMMARY/COMMENTS

In the year that he has been with our company, Ralph has proven himself
to be a steady and reliable employee whose best asset is his ability to get
along with others and to be part of a team. In fact, he works best in group
situations, when he can work in tandem with others on various projects and
have his efforts integrated with team goals and achievements. Left to
his own devices, the quality of his work dips a bit, especially in the areas
of productivity and organization. The latter is probably his weakest point.
He has not yet been able to attain a real sense of control over his work
area or his schedule unless he has somebody directing him. He lags behind
other clerks in turnaround time on projects and in fact has one of the low-
est productivity rates in the department. However, it invariably improves
when he is assigned to team projects. Working with others seems to spark
him into increasing his speed, as well as his accuracy.

In all other areas, Ralph has maintained an even level of quality and reliability. He has a good work ethic and is both dependable and adaptable to change. Although he does not excel and takes little to no initiative to improve his position or his career goals, he does meet all the criteria for his position, and there has never been a serious problem with or complaint about his work. He generally gets his work done with a fair amount of accuracy and attention to detail, and he maintains a good attitude about what he is doing, even when it gets to be very rote. My main concern is with his ability to work on his own, as well as the speed of his turnaround time.

III. GOALS FOR NEXT REVIEW

Ralph has proven himself to be a good team player, but still needs to focus on his ability to work independently, with a minimum of direction. To that end, he will be given primarily solo assignments over the next few months so far as basic filing projects are concerned. However, because of his strong people skills, I am also going to move him into a frontline position. For two days a week, he will work at the service counter, responding to requests, delivering files to the requesting offices, and assisting with problems. I believe Ralph will thrive working in a more service-oriented situation, and if it works out, we will move him into the position on a permanent basis. In the meantime, he is to work on improving his productivity rate and organizational skills and to become more independent in his work, so that he can be given more important assignments without the need for heavy supervision or additional support.

IV. EMPLOYEE COMMENTS

Employee's signature: _____ Date: _____

Evaluator's signature: _____ Date: _____

69

PERFORMANCE EVALUATION
Clerical

Name: Bill Woodhouse   Title: Payroll Clerk

Date: November 30, 20XX   Interim   Annual X

I. JOB FACTORS   *RATING:*

1. Job knowledge   (poor) 1 2 <u>3</u> 4 5 (excellent)
    Comments:
    Bill understands what is expected of him and meets those expectations.

2. Quality of work   (poor) 1 2 3 <u>4</u> 5 (excellent)
    Comments:
    He usually takes extra care to double-check his work and reconfirm final figures before sending his assignments on to check processing.

3. Productivity   (poor) 1 2 <u>3</u> 4 5 (excellent)
    Comments:
    He meets expectations, although some improvement in speed would be desirable.

4. Initiative   (poor) 1 2 <u>3</u> 4 5 (excellent)
    Comments:
    Although he is willing to go the extra mile when it's asked of him, he does not generally take any extra measures to go beyond what is expected.

5. Dependability   (poor) 1 2 <u>3</u> 4 5 (excellent)
    Comments:
    Meets expectations.

6. Interpersonal skills/Teamwork (poor) 1 2 3 <u>4</u> 5 (excellent)
    Comments:
    He works well with the rest of the staff and is willing to take on extra assignments to help out his coworkers at crunch time. He remains calm at times of stress and exerts a calming influence on others.

7. Decision-making abilities   (poor) 1 2 <u>3</u> 4 5 (excellent)
    Comments:
    Bill is not usually called upon to make major decisions. Those that he has to make in the normal pursuance of his duties are handled fine.

8. Problem-solving abilities   (poor) 1 2 <u>3</u> 4 5 (excellent)
   Comments:
   Same as 7.

9. Organizational skills   (poor) 1 2 <u>3</u> 4 5 (excellent)
   Comments:
   He meets standards for neatness and organization. He files all his paper-work immediately so is usually able to retrieve documents easily.

10. Communication skills   (poor) 1 2 <u>3</u> 4 5 (excellent)
    Comments:
    None.

11. Analytic skills   (poor) 1 2 <u>3</u> 4 5 (excellent)
    Comments:
    Within the scope of his duties, Bill's analytical abilities are fine.

12. Receptiveness to criticism   (poor) 1 2 <u>3</u> 4 5 (excellent)
    Comments:
    None.

13. Management of resources   (poor) 1 2 <u>3</u> 4 5 (excellent)
    Comments:
    None.

14. Professionalism   (poor) 1 <u>2</u> 3 4 5 (excellent)
    Comments:
    Bill occasionally dresses a little too casually and sometimes inappropriately for the office. His equally casual attitude sometimes comes off as indif-ference. He needs to raise his degree of professionalism in his personal appearance and attitude.

15. Punctuality   (poor) 1 2 3 <u>4</u> 5 (excellent)
    Comments:
    None. Punctuality has never been an issue.

Overall Rating   (poor) 1 2 <u>3</u> 4 5 (excellent)

II. SUMMARY/COMMENTS

Bill is a classic competent worker. He strives to do no more than what is expected of him, although he will take on extra assignments when asked. He is not a career-oriented individual in terms of the position he holds with our company. His real interests lie in music and the creative arts, in which respect he engages in numerous activities outside working hours. I have the impression that he gets very little sleep at times because of all his outside interests, and on some days he is clearly fatigued. However, he manages to complete his work assignments with minimum errors and maintains a neat enough paper trail that others are easily able to follow up on routine problem solving when he is not in the office.

All in all, Bill is not one of our most outstanding workers, but he gets the job done.

III. GOALS FOR NEXT REVIEW

Bill needs to improve his professional appearance, particularly on days when there are departmental or interdepartmental meetings. This does not mean he must wear a jacket and tie every day, but he should get away from the jeans and overly casual shirts he has been prone to wearing.

I would also like to see him make more of an effort to share any ideas he may have and take a more active role in creating systems for streamlining and/or improving current operations.

IV. EMPLOYEE COMMENTS

Employee's signature: _____ Date: _____

Evaluator's signature: _____ Date: _____

Sample Reviews for Poor Performers

PERFORMANCE REVIEW
Secretarial/Clerical Employees

Name: June Tupper

Job Title: Secretary

Date: March 16, 20XX

Type of Evaluation:

Interim   Annual X

Evaluation Guide

1 = Excellent (exceptional; exceeds expectations)

2 = Good (consistently meets, and frequently exceeds, usual expectations)

3 = Satisfactory (conforms to standards; meets expectations)

4 = Fair (marginal; meeting only minimum requirements)

5 = Poor (below standard and unacceptable; improvement required or termination will result)

Factors for Review

Job Knowledge   Rating: 3

Degree to which the employee knows and understands his/her job and its functions

June understands what is expected of her and performs her job strictly within that understanding. She does not attempt to push herself beyond the boundaries of her job expectations.

Quality of Work   Rating: 4

Accuracy, presentability, neatness, etc.

Although she has been reprimanded several times for sloppy work, she continues to make errors and overlook important details. Her letters frequently require proofreading and it is necessary to follow up on tasks that have been assigned to her to make sure she is doing things correctly.

Quantity of Work   Rating: 4

Amount of work consistently produced within requirements of the position

June is slow and frequently falls behind on her work assignments. Because of her difficulty in meeting deadlines, most managers prefer to use other secretaries rather than June.

Work Interest   Rating: 5

Employee's attitude toward his/her work, specialized knowledge of the job, receptivity to new work assignments, efforts to acquire new or broader job knowledge

June has been warned that her continued apathy towards her job will bring about its termination if she doesn't make some effort to improve.

Resourcefulness   Rating: 5

Adaptability, versatility, dependability, self-reliance, initiative, ease of learning

Unfortunately, June cannot be trusted to work on her own. She requires frequent monitoring and must have her work checked and double-checked. She is clearly unmotivated.

Judgment   Rating: 5

Ability to evaluate situations, draw conclusions, and make sound decisions

She is not able to exercise individual judgment in her work; constant supervision is necessary.

Interpersonal Skills   Rating: 4

Tact, courtesy, self-control, patience, loyalty, and discretion

She is friendly with other secretaries and is fine with fielding phone calls. But she seems to regard anybody from management as the enemy and often behaves in a sullen, defensive manner.

Dependability   Rating: 3

Punctuality, regular attendance at meetings, overall reliability

June manages to be punctual.

Work Habits   Rating: 5

Ability to plan and organize work, make efficient use of work time, adhere to established rules and procedures, follow through on work assignments

As is made clear in other comments, she does not meet the criteria for this job factor.

Use of Resources   Rating: 4

Conservation and economization of expendable resources; care of equipment

There is an excessive waste of paper due to her repeated errors causing numerous retyping of letters and reports. She eats over her computer key-

74

board, despite being told not to. She was recently observed striking the photocopying machine in a moment of frustration.

Growth Potential   Rating: 5
Ability to progress to higher level work and assume more responsible duties
This is not an option for June.

OVERALL RATING

Since employee's last appraisal, his/her performance has: ____ Improved
                                                            ____ Maintained same level
                                                            _X_ Declined

COMMENTS

Noteworthy performance strengths:
None.

Areas needing improvement:
June's disinterest in her job and in making improvements is clear. Despite repeated meetings and attempts to help her, both verbal and written warnings had to be issued regarding her sullen attitude, her overall sloppiness, and her complete lack of initiative. After discussing it with her thoroughly, she has agreed that secretarial work is not her strength and she should begin looking for another job immediately.

Plan of action:
As above.

EMPLOYEE'S COMMENTS

Employee's signature: _____   Date: _____

Evaluator's signature: _____   Date: _____

PERFORMANCE EVALUATION
Secretarial/Clerical

Employee's Name: Judy Jonas   Review Period: From 9/xx to 3/xx

Job Title: Staff Assistant   Interim   Annual X

Department: Registrar's Office

Name and Title of Evaluator: Anne Dutton, Registrar

Performance Guide

A — Consistently exceeds job requirements

Performance is exceptional, above and beyond what is expected

B — Meets job requirements

Does a good job; meets and sometimes exceeds requirements capably and competently

C — Improvement needed to meet job requirements

Is not performing at satisfactory level; extra supervision required

O — Other

Not applicable to this area of evaluation

1. Job knowledge   Grade: C

Understands and effectively utilizes job-related information, procedures, and skills

Comments:

Despite strong commitment to contribute, Judy frequently needs to be reminded of established procedures.

2. Quality of work   Grade: C

Completes assignments accurately and efficiently in accordance with department standards

Comments:

Judy's completion of both routine tasks and special assignments is excessively tardy. She often needs assistance and guidance on projects.

3. Timeliness   Grade: C

Finishes assignments within a reasonable or better time frame

Comments:

See above.

4. Work habits   Grade: C

   Plans and organizes work well, follows procedures, and makes efficient use of work time

   Comments:

   Judy requires constant monitoring to ensure that tasks are in the process of completion. Her desk and files are not well organized, and she often misplaces important documents.

5. Initiative and resourcefulness   Grade: C

   Demonstrates ability to work without direction and offer suggestions; can come up with creative solutions

   Comments:

   This is not a strength for Judy, for reasons made clear by above comments.

6. Decision making   Grade: N/A

   Evaluates situations, draws conclusions, and makes sound decisions

   Comments:

7. Adaptability and flexibility   Grade: B

   Adjusts to new ideas and situations and is receptive to new or additional work assignments

   Comments:

   Despite her problems, Judy has attempted to improve and to learn in order to expand the scope of her job. She is flexible and willing to take on whatever is asked of her.

8. Accountability   Grade: N/A

   Is willing to accept responsibility for job-related decisions and actions

   Comments:

9. Punctuality and dependability   Grade: B

   Can be relied upon to be punctual and to do what is required without follow-up

   Comments:

   She is conscientious about showing up on time and seeing a task through to the end.

10. Use of resources   Grade: B

    Cares for and maintains equipment; conserves and economizes office resources

    Comments:

    This is Judy's strength. She takes good care of all office equipment, and her coworkers frequently turn to her for help when the photocopy machine breaks down or there are other mechanical failure. She is also careful not to waste supplies or other resources.

11. Communication skills   Grade: B-

    Communicates with others clearly and effectively

    Comments:

    This is marginal. Judy has problems dealing with abstract questions and is often unable to clearly explain details or summarize a situation. However, she has made efforts to improve in this area, and we recognize a certain amount of progress.

12. Interpersonal skills   Grade: B

    Interacts well with others; demonstrates courtesy, patience, diplomacy, discretion, and self-control; works well with a team

    Comments:

    She tries hard, and her friendly attitude brightens the office. Although she has difficulty herself in answering questions from students, she knows where to direct them.

13. Supervisory skills   Grade: N/A

    Supervises employees effectively; maintains sound working relationships

    Comments:

14. Skills development   Grade: C

    Works to develop new skills and takes advantage of opportunities for training and development

    Comments:

    She doesn't seem to be interested in moving beyond her current position, and commitment to on going improvement could be stronger.

SUMMARY

Summarize employee's performance level since last review; indicate any improvement or decline.

Judy provides a mixture of helpfulness and friendliness with a disorganized approach to her work that has seriously affected the quality of her output. She is trusted with only the simplest of tasks, which she does willingly, but she cannot be relied upon to be put into any situation requiring independent thought or judgment. She is aware of her deficiencies and makes stabs at improving herself, but eventually slides back into lazy, disorganized habits. She is popular and well-liked, but if her poor working habits continue on their present course, we will have to consider terminating her.

GOALS/OBJECTIVES FOR THE NEXT 12 MONTHS

Indicate whatever goals or criteria the employee must meet for the next review period.

Determined and consistent attempts to improve the organization of her work area and the timely and efficient completion of her tasks must take place within the next six months. Judy must be persistent in her efforts to improve and demonstrate real results in terms of accuracy, neatness, timeliness, and the confidence of others to trust her with work assignments with only a minimum of supervision.

EMPLOYEE'S COMMENTS

Employee's signature: _____ Date: _____

Evaluator's signature: _____ Date: _____

PERFORMANCE EVALUATION
Clerical

Name: Jeannette Olivier
Title: File Clerk
Date of hire: January 1, 20XX

Department: Technical Information
Supervisor: Gene Tilton
Review period: From 1/XX to 12/XX

Ratings: Employee is to be rated on a scale of 1 to 3, as described below.

    1: Below expectations: Performance is substandard and requires improvement.

    2: Meets expectations: Performance fully meets and occasionally exceeds standards.

    3: Exceeds expectations: Performance consistently exceeds set standards.

N/A: Not applicable. Lack of sufficient knowledge to evaluate the performance factor.

Section I: Basic Job Skills

	Below	Meets	Exceeds	N/A
Job knowledge	1	<u>2</u>	3	N/A
Quality of work	<u>1</u>	2	3	N/A
Productivity/Timeliness	<u>1</u>	2	3	N/A
Dependability	1	<u>2</u>	3	N/A
Work habits	<u>1</u>	2	3	N/A
Organizational skills	<u>1</u>	2	3	N/A
Resourcefulness	1	2	3	<u>N/A</u>
Problem solving	1	2	3	<u>N/A</u>
Care of office equipment	1	<u>2</u>	3	N/A

Comments:

    Jeannette tends to be too slow in completing work assignments and frequently does not file papers in the correct location. She is also easily distracted, and this has resulted in misfiled documents. Although she has made an effort at improvement in recent weeks, she needs to concentrate on her work more and pay attention to where she is putting things.

Section II: Personal Attributes

	Below	Meets	Exceeds	N/A
Attendance/Punctuality	1	<u>2</u>	3	N/A
Ability to take direction	1	<u>2</u>	3	N/A
Initiative	<u>1</u>	2	3	N/A

80

Cooperativeness	1	<u>2</u>	3	N/A
Adaptability	1	2	3	<u>N/A</u>
Receptiveness to criticism	<u>1</u>	2	3	N/A
Communication skills	<u>1</u>	2	3	N/A
Interaction with coworkers	1	<u>2</u>	3	N/A
Courtesy/Hospitality	1	2	3	<u>N/A</u>

Comments:

Jeannette arrives on time every day. However, it takes her a while to get started, frequently spending too much time in the bathroom and chatting with friends before starting her work. She has agreed to make more of an effort to start her work within ten minutes of her arrival at the office.

She generally takes direction well; however, she relies too much on direction and waits too often for somebody to tell her what to do. She needs to take some initiative and to seek out work or begin new assignments without waiting for the "go" signal. She should also try using what she has already learned and apply it to new situations as they arise rather than always relying on others to solve any problems that arise in the course of her work. She also needs to be more consistent in seeking out help when it's needed rather than putting work to one side and not dealing with it, as she is currently doing.

Finally, she tends to overreact when any criticism is made of her work and fails to take responsibility for her errors. She often conveys a negative attitude toward her job and frequently puts off work by socializing with other employees. She should display a more serious attitude and accept constructive criticism of her work as an attempt to help her improve rather than as a personal attack on her.

Section III: Strengths and Weaknesses

Describe employee strengths:

Jeannette seems willing enough to do what is asked of her, including working overtime when it's necessary. She has a neat and presentable appearance and she gets along well with her coworkers.

Describe areas for improvement:

Jeannette has a problem with authority. She does not respond well to criticism, which she frequently regards as a personal attack on her; therefore

81

she gets very defensive and is perceived by many as having an attitude problem. She should try to display a more serious attitude and accept constructive criticism of her work as an attempt to help her improve rather than as a personal attack on her. She also needs to complete assignments at a faster pace and demonstrate some initiative and willingness to solve problems on her own rather than wait for others to solve them for her.

Describe goals for next performance review:

(1) Improve attitude.

(2) Improve speed and accuracy in completion of assignments.

(3) Begin work within 10 minutes of arrival at office.

Section IV: Comments

Evaluator:

Although there have been a number of complaints about Jeannette's attitude problem, and the quality of her work is not at the level it could or should be, it is my belief that Jeannette has the ability to really apply herself to her work and make significant improvements in how she is currently approaching her job. If we see improvement within the next six months, we will discuss with her any opportunities that may exist for advancement.

Employee:

I have read the above review and discussed it with my supervisor. I will try to meet the goals that have been set for me in the next review.

Employee's signature: _____ Date: _____

Evaluator's signature: _____ Date: _____

INTERIM PERFORMANCE EVALUATION
Clerical Employee

Performance evaluation for: Daphne Jones

Date: June 30, 20XX

Job Factors:

1. Quality of Results (accuracy, neatness, thoroughness)
   (weak) 1 2 3 <u>4</u> 5 (superior)
   Comments:

   You certainly try very hard to be accurate and neat, but you often slow yourself down because you are perhaps trying too hard. Try to find ways to be thorough without falling behind in the completion of your assignments.

2. Productivity (amount of satisfactory work completed)
   (weak) 1 2 <u>3</u> 4 5 (superior)
   Comments:

   See above. Try to improve your speed.

3. Job Knowledge (skills and knowledge necessary for the job)
   (weak) 1 2 <u>3</u> 4 5 (superior)
   Comments:

   Try asking more questions of others to improve your job knowledge. Your skills are adequate, but there is some room for improvement, especially to get your speed up.

4. Dependability (perseverance and conscientiousness)
   (weak) 1 <u>2</u> 3 4 5 (superior)
   Comments:

   Don't give up so easily. You need to push yourself a little harder and put more effort into solving problems yourself.

5. Initiative (motivation and determination)
   (weak) 1 <u>2</u> 3 4 5 (superior)
   Comments:

   Have more faith in yourself and your abilities!

6. Cooperation (ability to work with others)

(weak) 1 2 3 <u>4</u> 5 (superior)

Comments:

Definitely one of your strongest areas!

7. Attendance and Punctuality

(weak) 1 <u>2</u> 3 4 5 (superior)

Comments:

As we have discussed, you are tardy 3-4 days every week. This must be improved.

8. Adaptability (resourcefulness, problem solving, learning)

(weak) 1 <u>2</u> 3 4 5 (superior)

Comments:

You get along well with people. Use that ability to learn from others, and then find inventive ways to solve problems on your own.

9. Organization

(weak) 1 2 <u>3</u> 4 5 (superior)

Comments:

You are sticking closely to established procedures to keep your work organized, and this is fine. However, don't be afraid to be creative and try out new methods of doing things.

10. Receptiveness to Criticism

(weak) 1 <u>2</u> 3 4 5 (superior)

Comments:

Try not to be so defensive when criticism is offered.

OVERALL RATING:

<u>X</u> Needs improvement in job performance

___ Meets job requirements

___ Exceeds job requirements

1. *Work over the past three months:*

You have adequately learned the minimum requirements of your job. You have tried very hard to do exactly what was asked of you and always within the prescribed boundaries of your job, but without putting in any effort to "go the extra mile." You have been neat and accurate in your work, but have frequently caused missed deadlines on report submissions because you have been too slow in completing typing assignments. Overall, you have been neat and organized, but there is much room for improvement.

2. *Goals for the coming three months:*

   • Improve punctuality. Arrive at the office by 9:00 A.M. or before.

   • Work on speed in completion of assignments. Find better ways to prioritize your work.

   • Take the initiative in problem solving. Try to find a possible solution before you go to somebody else for help. If you are extremely uncertain about your solution, consider identifying three possible courses of action for discussion.

3. *Additional comments:*

   You have demonstrated a willingness to learn and an ability to work well with others; these are strong attributes that should enable you to make improvements in your job performance. You know the basics—now it's up to you to take charge of your job!

EMPLOYEE'S COMMENTS:

Employee's signature: _____ Date: _____

Evaluator's signature: _____ Date: _____

PERFORMANCE EVALUATION
Clerical

Name: Fiona MacIntosh   Title: Payroll Clerk

Date: August 1, 20XX

Job Knowledge

Unfortunately, Fiona does not yet seem to have grasped all the essentials of her job and what is required of her, nor is she able to take previously acquired job knowledge and apply it to new situations as they arise. She has made a number of costly errors in processing the payroll for her section that should not have happened at all, given the length of time she has now served in the job and the amount of job knowledge she should have accumulated and retained. Recently she failed to enter vacation time taken by several employees, and on many occasions she has overlooked and therefore failed to report employee sick days, with the result being that we have an inaccurate record of vacation and sick time and need to go back to re-create and update all records for her section, a time-consuming task. These and other errors on Fiona's part have frequently brought about duplication of effort and unnecessary extra time spent on extraneous tasks.

Quality of Work

Due to the number of errors she has made, the overall quality of Fiona's work has been very poor. Timesheets and workcharts often lack the proper signatures, and computer reports must be double-checked for possible inaccurate or incorrect entries. She has sometimes misplaced reports and records, and there have been complaints about the illegibility of her writing.

Quantity of Work

Technically, Fiona's production rate is fine, and she stays up to quota. However, she rushes her work and doesn't pay close enough attention to the details of what she is doing, so the fact that she is able to produce at the appropriate rate is irrelevant, given the quality of the work produced.

86

Work Habits/Organizational Skills

As indicated, Fiona tends to rush her work and is not very attentive to the details of what she is doing. She has also misplaced numerous files and reports, creating problems when certain records are needed and they are lost in a maze of paper on her desk. Her work area is sloppy and poorly organized, which adds to the overall problem.

Initiative

Fiona seems to lack the initiative necessary to improving her job performance. She responds well to direction, but her follow-through is lacking and she has little to no ability to work independently, without supervision.

Problem-Solving Skills

As should be evident from the above remarks, Fiona needs to work on effectively identifying problems and offering sound resolutions.

Interpersonal Skills/Teamwork

Fiona has a couple of good friends with whom she spends a great deal of time—perhaps too much so. She tends to be a bit standoffish with other clerks in the department, and does not function very effectively as part of a team effort. She often conveys an attitude of disinterest in what she is doing and in her role as part of the department.

Adaptability/Dependability

Because of the many errors she has made and continues to make in the execution of her work, as well as her poor attitude, Fiona is not regarded as a very dependable employee, nor is she considered to be very adaptable. She frequently balks when given a new assignment and has openly expressed her resentment at the close supervision she has received, especially lately.

Attendance/Punctuality

She is frequently late arriving at work and on occasion has taken time off without proper advance notice.

Comments/Goals for Next Review

This is Fiona's third formal review since she began working with XYZ Company a year ago. She has also had two informal interim evaluations. Every effort has been made to work with Fiona on the problems she has been experiencing and to find solutions that will work for both her and for the company. Nevertheless, she has continued to make unwarranted and sometimes costly mistakes in the daily execution of her job, and we find that we are no longer able to support her errors, in addition to which she has maintained a poor attitude that has clearly conveyed a lack of interest in or enthusiasm for what she is doing. Therefore she will be given two weeks' notice and assurances of help in finding a more suitable position.

Employee's Comments:

Employee's signature: _____ Date: _____

Evaluator's signature: _____ Date: _____

PERFORMANCE EVALUATION
Secretarial

Name: Buster Keeley   Title: Typist

Date: December 22, 20XX

Job Knowledge

Job knowledge is not a major factor in Buster's position. He needs to be able to type quickly and accurately and to be familiar with scientific and medical terminology. Except for accuracy, he generally meets these criteria.

Quality of Work

The overall quality of Buster's work has been poor. He is often inattentive to details and fails to run spell checks on his documents. Several projects have been submitted poorly formatted, with no eye to the overall form and style of the document. In addition to numerous misspellings, grammar is often poor. Buster seems to lack the language skills necessary to correcting the errors of those who give him work to do.

Quantity of Work

His production rate is poor. In the six months since he began with the company, he has failed to get his typing speed up, and if anything it seems to have dropped in recent weeks. Several managers have complained of his inability to return their projects in a timely manner. All in all, Buster needs to improve his turnaround time.

Work Habits/Organizational Skills

His poor turnaround record seems to have a lot to do with his lack of organizational skills and generally poor work habits. His desk is often sloppy and disheveled looking, and he has misplaced important documents more than once. He takes numerous breaks to go outside for a smoke and sometimes disappears for extended periods. He has been spoken to about this tendency, and for a short period of time he improves, but then quickly returns to old habits. Overall, his working skills leave a lot to be desired.

Initiative

Largely undependable, Buster prefers to do no more than what is expected of him. He tends to gripe when he is given extra assignments and has shown no interest in taking any initiative whatsoever.

Problem-Solving Skills

On occasion, Buster has shown that he has the ability to spot problems in the making and to offer solutions, or at the very least to point them out to those from whom he received his assignments. However, he is inconsistent in this, and when he is feeling down or discontented about his job, which seems to be often, he takes a laissez-faire attitude and will make no effort to either identify or propose solutions to problems as they arise.

Interpersonal Skills/Teamwork

Buster is very gregarious with his coworkers and often spends more time socializing with others than he should. He certainly works better as part of a team than he does as an individual worker responsible only for himself and his own job. When he has been called upon to work with others on a major project, he has met the challenge and in fact has seemed to thrive.

Adaptability/Dependability

Buster's adaptability often depends on the situation. He is conducive to changes in policy and procedure and works well in any new situation that requires him to work in tandem with others. However, on independent projects, his ability to adapt drops dramatically, and he frequently needs intense supervision to ensure that he is handling it all right. He has inconsistent rates of dependability, once again depending on the situation. He cannot always be relied upon in circumstances where he must work solo and exercise independent judgment.

Attendance/Punctuality

As noted, he often disappears from his desk for long periods. In addition, he is usually late anywhere from two to four days out of the week.

Comments/Goals for Next Review

Buster has never seemed to be put off by the fact that he is a man doing what is generally considered to be a woman's job, nor has he encountered any prejudice because of this. This is all to the good. However, he has demonstrated a very inconsistent job performance, on some occasions showing what he is capable of doing, and on other occasions taking little to no interest in his job or in putting out quality work. The most common complaint about his work has been with regard to his inattention to details and general sloppiness. Buster's primary goal is to improve his attendance and punctuality and to be more consistent in his work. There must be a noticeable improvement in attitude and a reduction in errors and inattentiveness. An interim review will be conducted in three months' time.

Employee's Comments:

Employee's signature: _____ Date: _____

Evaluator's signature: _____ Date: _____

5

Model Evaluations
for Trainers and
Human Resource Professionals

This group consists of people-oriented workers who often have professional training. They work closely with other employees and have a great impact on the overall morale of the entire workforce. Their job titles include:

- Trainer
- Mediator
- Program Developer
- Training Assistant
- Training Specialist
- Personnel Benefits Assistant
- Affirmative Action Officer
- Human Resources Generalist
- Placement Officer

Gauging Performance

The work these employees perform is characterized by flexibility and responsiveness to the people with whom they work. Because individuals in these positions must interact with other people, they have to be adaptable and creative in their interpersonal skills. Communication skills are very important.

Cheerful, attentive, and detail-oriented individuals are highly sought in these positions. Innovation in the overall design of their work is seldom expected from these workers, but they must be unceasingly innovative in their handling of the people with whom they work and interact.

The key issues in these positions usually revolve around the ability to deliver the product needed (healthy, happy, and well-trained and supported employees) within specific time frames and the financial restraints of the organization. The ability to be part of a task group and to cooperate on achieving group goals is important. It is often also important that these workers have the ability to be self-starters and to work independently.

Performance Indicators

The top-level performer

- Has a high degree of appropriate knowledge (often as the result of a varied set of experiences)
- Has a track record of delivering a high-quality product within the limits of the situation
- Is able to consistently achieve a high level of accomplishment
- Is highly dependable
- Demonstrates a consistently cooperative manner and outstanding interpersonal abilities
- Demonstrates a high level of sensitivity to cultural diversity and individual special needs
- Shows appropriate initiative and works independently
- Is punctual and regular in attendance
- Adapts well to changing situations and demands
- Is well organized
- Is comfortable and receptive to appropriate criticism

The good performer

- Has an acceptable degree of appropriate knowledge, perhaps with some limitations
- Usually delivers a quality product within the limits of the situation
- Is able to consistently achieve an acceptable level of accomplishment
- Is usually dependable
- Demonstrates a generally cooperative manner and acceptable interpersonal abilities
- Demonstrates an acceptable level of sensitivity to cultural diversity and individual special needs
- Shows adequate initiative and independence
- Has acceptable attendance
- Usually adapts to changing situations and demands
- Is adequately organized
- Is usually comfortable and receptive to criticism

The poor performer

- Has a less than acceptable degree of appropriate knowledge
- Is uneven in the ability to deliver a quality product within the limits of the situation
- Is inconsistent in reaching an acceptable level of accomplishment
- Is less than dependable
- Demonstrates at times an uncooperative manner and unacceptable interpersonal abilities
- Demonstrates an unacceptable level of sensitivity to cultural diversity and individual special needs
- Shows inadequate initiative and independence
- Has unacceptable attendance
- Usually does not adapt to changing situations and demands
- Is poorly organized
- Is not consistently comfortable and receptive to criticism

Sample Reviews for Top-level Performers

PERSONNEL BENEFITS GENERALIST—TOP LEVEL
Interim Review

Name: Lois Schwartz   Date: 10/4/XX

Performance Rating

On a scale of 1–10, your overall performance rating is a 9. You have demonstrated excellent consistency and are fully knowledgeable in staff benefits and insurance coverage. You have a good ability to work independently. You take responsibility for your assignments, and your work is almost always of the highest quality. You interact well with employees and never seem to be stymied by their requests for information, but are able to find the answers with great efficiency and care taken to fully answering their questions. Your efforts have had a direct bearing on positive employee morale. All in all, you have been doing an outstanding job!

Strengths

Your strongest elements are your interpersonal and communication skills. You seem to get along well with all people, regardless of their social or cultural background. You have a reputation for cordiality and cooperation that is unmatched by any other employee.

Weaknesses

Your weakest elements are scheduling and status reports. You seem to overbook yourself quite often and have difficulty bringing a meeting to a conclusion in order to make it to the next meeting in a timely manner. Thus, you often keep other people waiting, which affects worker efficiency. Some complaints have also been received about the incompleteness of your status reports, with the general feeling being that you would prefer to talk to people.

Goals and Directions

Continue to hone your people skills, as they are your strongest asset. People feel comfortable coming to you for help, and that is a good part of what makes you such a valued employee. However, you must try to find ways to manage your time more effectively, particularly as it relates to how you schedule meetings and keep appointments. Establish a starting and ending time as well as goals for each meeting. Work to stay on the relevant topic(s), rather than venturing off into subjects that are not pertinent to the immediate discussion. Manage your schedule—don't let it manage you.

In addition, it is clear that you don't have a fondness for paperwork. Unfortunately, it's a fact of life in any corporation, so you need to apply yourself a little harder to thoroughly completing all status reports in a timely manner. I strongly recommend that you attend a workshop to learn how to better organize your schedule and your work so that you are able to carve out the time you need for doing the necessary paperwork.

Forecast

Overall, you have done an excellent job, and with continued improvement you are in line for a possible promotion to supervisor and/or trainer. Work on your organizational and scheduling problems, and we will review your performance in three months.

Employee's Comments

Employee's signature: _____ Date: _____

Evaluator's signature: _____ Date: _____

PERFORMANCE APPRAISAL

Employee Name: Jane Dalwich   Interim   Annual X
Job Title: Benefits Coordinator
Supervisor: Patrick Halper   Date: October 16, 20XX

I: Job Skills

	Sometimes	Usually	Always
Job Knowledge			X

Uses/demonstrates the skills and tools necessary to
perform job effectively. Can draw upon previous
experience to handle new problems or challenges.
Makes effort to stay current in field.

Comments:

Jane is thoroughly versed in all aspects of benefits administration. She
played a key role in the recent switch to a new HMO for all corporate
employees, as well as the formation of updated policies for insurance coverage. Her knowledge and understanding of our various benefits programs
has made her the go-to person whenever a question can't be answered by
anybody else. She stays current with all new developments and organizes
regular workshops for employees to help them stay abreast of any changes
in benefits coverage.

	Sometimes	Usually	Always
Organizational Skills			X

Can plan, organize, and prioritize work effectively.
Meets deadlines and completes assignments within
specified time frames. Uses time and resources effectively to meet goals.

Comments:

Jane is extremely well organized and able to juggle a complicated schedule and workload with ease.

98

	Sometimes	Usually	Always
			X

Teamwork

Works effectively with other employees. Gives assistance to others when needed. Shares credit and can balance personal and team goals.

Comments:

> She has excellent interpersonal skills. She has no trouble relating to employees who come to her for help, no matter what their position in the company may be. Jane is always ready and willing to answer questions and to be available for assistance when it's needed. She is always cheerful and cooperative and is well liked by all with whom she works.

	Sometimes	Usually	Always
			X

Communication Skills

Communicates thoughts and ideas clearly and demonstrates ability to listen and offer sound feedback. Is concise in both written and verbal communications. Keeps management and peers well informed.

Comments:

> Jane's communication skills are top-notch. She is able to interpret questions and requests for information with no difficulty and to provide answers that are concise and comprehensible, whether verbally or in writing. Her presentations in staff meetings are always easy to understand and provide a sound basis for working out solutions.

	Sometimes	Usually	Always
			X

Problem Solving

Can identify and analyze problems and present solutions, using available resources or creative ideas.

Comments:

> She has a remarkable ability for identifying problem areas and coming up with creative solutions. She is rarely stymied by a difficult problem.

	Sometimes	Usually	Always
			X

Professionalism

Accepts responsibility for all aspects of job and is willing to be held accountable for errors. Displays professional attitude and appearance in approach to job.

Comments:

> Jane maintains a professional attitude and full responsibility for her job at all times. When she makes the occasional error, she admits it and corrects it without fuss. She serves as an excellent role model for many of our younger employees.

	Sometimes	Usually	Always
			X

Initiative and Motivation

Can handle multiple tasks and responsibilities and is willing to take on new challenges. Displays interest in and enthusiasm for job and completes assignments quickly and efficiently.

Comments:

> She clearly loves what she is doing! On any given day, Jane has an overwhelming amount of paperwork to tackle, meetings to go to, and voice-mail messages with urgent questions to answer, yet she handles it all with aplomb and efficiency. She never turns down a project and is eager to accept new challenges.

	Sometimes	Usually	Always
			X

Flexibility

Adapts to new situations and changing work responsibilities. Is open to suggestions and criticism and able to utilize input from others. Looks for acceptable solutions in conflict situations.

Comments:

> As should be made clear by comments in other areas, Jane excels as a flexible and adaptable employee.

100

	Sometimes	Usually	Always
		X	

Punctuality

Adheres to work hours and is present for work every day. Provides adequate notice of vacation or personal time, and makes arrangements for coverage.

Comments:

Jane is often late in arriving at work, and sometimes takes days off without prior notice. She works to make up the time, but much of her job is contingent upon her being present and available during normal office working hours. She needs to be more punctual.

II: Achievements and Contributions

List the employee's major contributions to company goals, growth, and/or profitability during the appraisal period. Describe what actions the employee took to make these achievements.

As mentioned above, Jane was a major player in the recent overhaul of the company's employee-benefits packages and was the one to research and recommend the HMO that we are now using, which has saved the company over $100,000 in contributions to employee medical-insurance coverage. In addition, she made major contributions to the revamping of both the corporate life- and disability-insurance policies. All this was done while still carrying out her regular daily duties of answering questions and solving individual employee problems. She has truly done a remarkable job overall, managing a huge workload with ease and equanimity.

III: Plans and Goals

List and describe what the employee must achieve for the next performance appraisal period, including skills development, areas of improvement, projects, etc.

The only area Jane needs to improve in is her punctuality problem. Because so much relies on her presence in the office, it is important that she arrive at the start of regular working hours and to give adequate notice of when she is going to be taking time off. I have spoken to her about this problem, and she has agreed to work on it.

IV: Evaluator's Summary

Describe employee's overall performance rating.

On a scale of 1 to 10, I would definitely rate Jane as a 10!

V: Employee's Comments

Employee's signature: _____ Date: _____

Evaluator's signature: _____ Date: _____

PERFORMANCE EVALUATION

Employee's Name: Harold Andersen   Review Period: From 3/XX to 2/XX

Job Title: Training Specialist   Interim   Annual X

Department: Program Development

Name and Title of Evaluator: Betsy Grogan, Program Manager

Performance Guide:

A — Consistently exceeds job requirements

Performance is exceptional, above and beyond expectations

B — Meets job requirements

Does a good job; meets and sometimes exceeds requirements capably and competently

C — Improvement needed to meet job requirements

Is not performing at satisfactory level; extra supervision is required

O —Other

Not applicable to this area of evaluation

1. Job Knowledge   Grade: A

Understands and effectively utilizes job-related information, procedures, and skills

Comments:

Hal consistently displays thorough knowledge and understanding of all that his job entails. He keeps up with all the latest methodologies, attends workshops to sharpen his skills and expand his expertise in various areas, and makes suggestions for improvement in current procedures. He frequently comes up with ideas to improve on-the-job training techniques, which have proven to be extremely useful to other specialists.

2. Quality of Work   Grade: A

Completes assignments accurately and efficiently in accordance with department standards

Comments:

Hal meets all standards for high-quality work. He continues to excel in survey techniques and improving methods of training. He is often able to detect and correct problems before they occur, saving the company thousands of dollars in the process. He is always ready and willing to assist other staff members with questions or problems and is frequently called upon to help resolve disputes. His presence on the training staff has helped to stabilize and enhance overall program development.

3. Timeliness   Grade: A

Finishes assignments within a reasonable or better time frame

Comments:

Hal is fast and accurate in all that he does. He sets company records for accomplishing numerous tasks within tight time frames.

4. Work Habits   Grade: B

Plans and organizes work well, follows procedures, and makes efficient use of work time

Comments:

While Hal certainly uses his time efficiently, he is occasionally disorganized, resulting in lost files or time lost while he searches for important documentation. He also sometimes fails to follow established corporate procedure. This is due largely to the fact that he is an innovative person who likes to try out new methods and techniques. There is no problem with his innovations, except that he should seek my approval first before launching ahead with new ideas. In some cases, the established company procedure works best, and he needs to be able to recognize when that is the case.

5. Initiative and Resourcefulness   Grade: A

Demonstrates ability to work without direction and offer suggestions; can come up with creative solutions

Comments:

This is undoubtedly one of Hal's major strengths. He has shown exceptional creativity in adapting his training sessions and workshops to the individual employee or to the particular situation. He is a real self-starter whose contributions have resulted in noticeable improvements to our overall training programs development.

6. Decision Making   Grade: A

Evaluates situations, draws conclusions, and makes sound decisions

Comments:

Hal has excellent decision-making capabilities. He is sometimes a little too impulsive and proceeds to implement a decision without consulting me first, but this has yet to lead to any serious errors in judgment. I would ask only that he keep me better informed.

7. Adaptability and Flexibility   Grade: A

Adjusts to new ideas and situations and is receptive to new or additional work assignments

Comments:

Another strength for Hal. He is one of the most adaptable people I have ever worked with and in fact seems to love changing situations so that he can come up with new ideas and prove his worth all over again.

8. Accountability   Grade: B

Is willing to accept responsibility for job-related decisions and actions

Comments:

Hal's mistakes are rare, but when he does make them, he has a hard time admitting that they were his fault. I would like to see him make more of an effort to recognize when he is wrong and not attempt to place the blame on somebody else.

9. Punctuality and Dependability   Grade: A

Can be relied upon to be punctual and to do what is required without follow-up

Comments:

Hal's enthusiasm for his job leads him to arrive early and work late. He can always be counted on to do what is needed in any situation.

10. Use of Resources   Grade: A

Cares for and maintains equipment; conserves and economizes office resources

Comments:

No comments necessary. Hal does a fine job in this area.

11. Communication Skills   Grade: B

Communicates with others clearly and effectively

Comments:

Hal's verbal skills are terrific, although he occasionally gets so excited when he's talking that he goes too fast, making him hard to understand. This is something to watch out for when he is conducting a training session; it's important that his trainees can follow him without needing an interpreter. When he does slow down and think about what he is saying, he comes across more clearly and effectively. His writing skills could use some improvement. His reports are occasionally difficult to read due to poor syntax. I would like to see him work with somebody on grammar and sentence construction to improve his abilities in writing.

12. Interpersonal Skills   Grade: A

Interacts well with others; demonstrates courtesy, patience, diplomacy, discretion, and self-control; works well with a team

Comments:

This is absolutely Hal's strongest suit and what makes him our number-one Training Specialist. His people skills are superb in every way.

13. Supervisory Skills   Grade: O

Supervises employees effectively; maintains sound working relationships

Comments:

He is not currently supervising anybody.

14. Professional Growth   Grade: A

Works to develop new skills and takes advantage of opportunities for training and development

Comments:

Hal has expressed a keen interest in moving up, and I believe he is capable of taking on a more managerial role in time. He is self-motivated and a hard worker who has acted on just about every suggestion I have made to further his professional growth.

SUMMARY

Summarize employee's performance level since last review; indicate any improvement or decline.

Hal is an exceptional employee with numerous skills and talents, as well as with a great capacity to meet new challenges and take on additional responsibilities. He is resourceful and energetic and a credit to our company. He never balks at a challenge and has proven himself willing and able to take on whatever opportunities we can provide him. He operates at the highest possible level, with only minor areas requiring improvement.

GOALS/OBJECTIVES FOR THE NEXT 12 MONTHS

Indicate whatever goals or criteria the employee must meet for the next review period.

(1) Work on improving writing skills. The company is willing to pay for any supplemental courses that may help in this regard.

(2) Find a way to better organize personal work space and keep files in order.

(3) Work on improving attitude as regards accountability for mistakes.

(4) Look into other opportunities within the company to move up to a supervisory or managerial position. Talk to Human Resources about management training classes.

EMPLOYEE'S COMMENTS

Employee's signature: _____ Date: _____

Evaluator's signature: _____ Date: _____

PERFORMANCE EVALUATION

Name: William Kunkle   Department: Planning & Programming
Title: Training Assistant   Supervisor: Fred Unterholz
Date of hire: 9/22/XX   Review period: From 9/XX to 8/XX

Ratings: Employee is to be rated on a scale of 1 to 3, as described below.

- 1: Below expectations: Performance is substandard and requires improvement.
- 2: Meets expectations: Performance fully meets and occasionally exceeds standards.
- 3: Exceeds expectations: Performance consistently exceeds set standards.

N/A: Not applicable. Lack of sufficient knowledge to evaluate the performance factor.

Section I: Basic Job Skills

	Below	Meets	Exceeds	N/A
Job knowledge	1	2	3	N/A
Quality of work	1	2	3	N/A
Productivity/Timeliness	1	2	3	N/A
Dependability	1	2	3	N/A
Work habits	1	2	3	N/A
Organizational skills	1	2	3	N/A
Resourcefulness	1	2	3	N/A
Problem solving	1	2	3	N/A
Care of office equipment	1	2	3	N/A

Comments:

Bill has come along very well as a training assistant, and it won't be long before he will be promoted to full Specialist. His knowledge of all programs for which training is required is top-notch, and he has worked hard on the recent studies conducted of employee assessments and retention. The quality of his work is also excellent. On occasion he can be a little lax in his organizational skills and sometimes shows up at training sessions without all the materials he needs. However, he is capable of "winging it" very well. Some laxness has also been noted regarding his care of office equipment, with some complaints regarding his use of the photocopy machine noted in particular. He has been asked not to bang the machine's doors and cover if he gets frustrated when it breaks down. A little patience is clearly needed. This aside, Bill has been a great asset to the company, with an excellent production record. He particularly excels at employee retention, with a 90-percent success rate.

Section II: Personal Attributes

	Below	Meets	Exceeds	N/A
Attendance/Punctuality	1	2	<u>3</u>	N/A
Ability to take direction	1	<u>2</u>	3	N/A
Initiative	1	2	<u>3</u>	N/A
Cooperativeness	1	<u>2</u>	3	N/A
Adaptability	1	2	<u>3</u>	N/A
Receptiveness to criticism	1	<u>2</u>	3	N/A
Communication skills	1	2	<u>3</u>	N/A
Interaction with coworkers	1	2	<u>3</u>	N/A
Courtesy/Hospitality	1	2	<u>3</u>	N/A

Comments:

Bill is a dedicated worker who takes his job seriously. There have been no attendance problems reported, and he has been a strong presence at all planning meetings. He interacts well with his coworkers, but at the same time he occasionally has problems taking direction and sometimes reacts negatively to criticism. I believe this is because he is a perfectionist as well as a bit of a loner. He clearly likes taking the bull by the horns and often prefers to work out new ideas and alternative solutions on his own rather than as part of a team effort. His work is otherwise exemplary, and his efforts have had positive and valuable results overall.

Section III: Strengths and Weaknesses

Describe employee strengths:

Bill is dedicated and enthusiastic and maintains a strong and consistent work record. He applies his best efforts to every task assigned to him. He has natural leadership abilities and is eager to move ahead into a more supervisory position. He is self-reliant and presents a professional appearance and attitude.

Describe areas for improvement:

Before one can become a real leader, one has to learn to be part of the team. I would like to see Bill concentrate on his interactions with others, particularly when it comes to problem-solving issues and creative ideas. Additionally, some improvement is needed in his organizational skills and his attitude toward office machinery.

Describe goals for next performance review:

I am assigning Bill to a team project, working with Edna Murray and Sam Williams on ways to improve employee retention. He will be monitored for cooperativeness and sharing of ideas. Tangible proof of improvement in his organizational abilities should also be demonstrated.

The ultimate goal for Bill is to be promoted to Training Specialist, and I fully expect that such a promotion will take place within four to eight months.

Section IV: Comments

Evaluator:

Bill's only real weakness is his occasional lapse into impatience, which affects both his organizational skills and his ability to cope with the vagaries of office equipment. He also sometimes displays impatience with others, especially when he is trying to make a point and the other person is not "getting it." I would like to see him monitor this tendency and try to correct it before his rare burst of temper erupts. This aside, his track record with the company has been impressive, and he shows the makings of a strong future leader. He has made remarkable progress since he was first hired, and I am certain that he has a great future with this company.

Employee:

Employee's signature: _____ Date: _____

Evaluator's signature: _____ Date: _____

PROGRAM DEVELOPMENT COORDINATOR
—TOP LEVEL
Interim Performance Review

Employee name: Keiji Notokino
Date: October 5, 20XX

Performance Rating 1-10

> Your overall performance rating is a 10. You have done an exceptional job of creating and implementing programs that help employees prepare for promotion and expanded responsibilities. What is terrific about your programs is that they are often geared to the needs and talents of individual employees, as well as to the requirements of the company as a whole. By doing so, you have improved overall efficiency at many levels and have also helped contribute to employee morale, since they know that you are tuned in to what they need. Well done!

Strengths

> Your strongest abilities are in setting up individualized development plans to strengthen existing skills and to teach new skills to employees. You are well organized, and your skills enable you to tailor development programs according to the existing situation. You also maintain a consistent professional attitude. You get along well with both coworkers and supervisors, who like and appreciate your ability to be cheerful and outgoing, even in the face of enormous pressure at times. Your interpersonal skills are superb and play a large role in the success of your programs.

Weaknesses

> You have demonstrated some weakness in your ability to develop executive potential among current employees in lower level positions. Specifically, you concentrate largely on job skills and less on professional development that involves character and personality traits. The company's management feels we would do much better by promoting current, seasoned staff than to procure new prospects who are not familiar with our overall family-

style structure. Therefore, we would like to see you work on strengthening those programs that help established employees realize and develop their inner potential for professional growth.

Goals

Your primary goal for the next review period will be to implement a program that identifies and trains potential executives from our current pool of rank-and-file workers. Within the next three months you should research and study successful programs in other companies and make recommendations to management; then you will take charge of implementing the new program(s). The methods you choose will be up to you; you will be evaluated according to the success of whatever program you set up, and how employees respond to it.

Forecast

On the whole, it is clear that you have an excellent future with this company. Feel free to come to me for help as you plan and initiate your executive development program. The company feels this program has great possibilities. Your belief in it and the same dedicated effort you bring to all your other work will help it to succeed. You are well regarded as a great asset to this company, and your hard work is greatly appreciated. It is clear that among the potential executives within our ranks, you are a top candidate and can fully expect to be promoted into an upper managerial position within 1-2 years. Congratulations on a job well done!

Employee's Comments

Employee's signature: _____ Date: _____

Evaluator's signature: _____ Date: _____

PERFORMANCE EVALUATION
(Mediator —Top Level)

Performance evaluation for: Andre Ferrar

Date: October 1, 20XX

JOB FACTORS:

1. Job Knowledge

    (weak) 1 2 3 4 <u>5</u> (superior)

    Comments:

    Andre is on top of all the latest in mediation techniques. He regularly attends workshops and seminars to improve his job knowledge and is good about sharing what he has learned with other mediators. He also uses every mediation case he handles as an opportunity for self-examination and personal growth in refining and enhancing his techniques for dispute resolution.

2. Productivity

    (weak) 1 2 3 <u>4</u> 5 (superior)

    Comments:

    Andre's current production record is 87 percent resolved of all disputes he handles. He can and should be working at 90 percent or better, especially given the way he has been applying himself to learning and improving his mediation techniques.

3. Quality of Results

    (weak) 1 2 3 4 <u>5</u> (superior)

    Comments:

    His ability to get top-notch results from the cases he resolves successfully has meant fewer cases resurfacing after resolution. That is, once a problem is solved, it generally stays solved due to his admirable ability to find solutions that are agreeable to all parties involved.

4. Initiative

    (weak) 1 2 3 4 <u>5</u> (superior)

    Comments:

    Andre has great initiative and works hard to find creative solutions to problems.

113

5. Teamwork

   (weak) 1 2 3 4 <u>5</u> (superior)

   Comments:

   Andre is a team leader in the mediation department. He is quick to assist when called upon to do so and is equally quick to share with other mediators what he knows or has learned.

6. Decision Making

   (weak) 1 2 3 <u>4</u> 5 (superior)

   Comments:

   Andre sometimes hesitates when making an important decision and will come to me for advice before implementing any decisions that may have certain consequences—for instance, if he fails to reach an agreeable compromise in a dispute and must come down firmly on the side of one party or the other. This is fine in some cases, but not in others, and I think it's this hesitation that is keeping his resolution rate to under 90 percent. His decisions are almost always sound, and he should trust them and himself more.

7. Problem Solving

   (weak) 1 2 3 <u>4</u> 5 (superior)

   Comments:

   As above. Andre has a keen instinct for solving problems, and I would like to see him trust that instinct more.

8. Organization

   (weak) 1 2 3 4 <u>5</u> (superior)

   Comments:

   Andre is extraordinarily well organized and is a model to the rest of the department for keeping his office clean and neat and his files in order. He plans well for the times when he is going to be absent, and other mediators are always able to locate necessary materials when they're needed. He also manages his time very effectively.

9. Communication

   (weak) 1 2 3 4 <u>5</u> (superior)

   Comments:

   This is unquestionably a strength for Andre. He communicates his ideas to others very effectively and makes good use of his language and interpersonal skills to provide a comfortable and comprehensible forum in dispute-resolution meetings. He is well liked and appreciated for his ability to put others at ease and to express his thoughts and solutions in ways that are nonoffensive and easy to understand. His written reports are excellent.

10. Receptiveness to Criticism
(weak) 1 2 3 4 <u>5</u> (superior)
Comments:
Andre takes criticism very well and uses it as an opportunity to better understand both his job and himself.

OVERALL RATING:

__ Needs improvement in job performance
__ Meets job requirements
<u>X</u> Exceeds job requirements

1. *Work over the past twelve months:*
Andre is an exceptional mediator who has done exemplary work. He has maintained and lived up to the high standards he has set for himself. His production rate is excellent, but could be better.

2. *Goals for the coming twelve months:*
Andre is to work on his self-confidence, in terms of his decision-making and problem-solving skills, which I believe is key to raising his production status. By this time next year, he should be well over the 90-percent resolution rate, and he has indicated that he will shoot for 95 percent.

Employee's signature: _____ Date: _____

Evaluator's signature: _____ Date: _____

Sample Reviews for Mid-level Performers

PERFORMANCE EVALUATION
(Mediator—Mid-level)

Performance evaluation for: Randolph Harrison

Date: August 1, 20xx

JOB FACTORS:

1. Job Knowledge

   (weak) 1 2 <u>3</u> 4 5 (superior)

   Comments:

   Randy's success rate in resolving disputes averages out at 77 percent. While this is okay, it could be a bit better, especially if he puts a little effort into expanding his job knowledge to be able to anticipate questions and potential problems between any two parties involved in a dispute. We have discussed several self-training techniques to make him more keenly aware of what he needs to know, but it would also help if he could take a workshop to learn the latest in dispute-resolution techniques.

2. Productivity

   (weak) 1 2 3 <u>4</u> 5 (superior)

   Comments:

   On the whole, Randy's productivity rate is above the average and meets company standards with a little room to spare. He often handles numerous cases at one time, but does not allow this to overwhelm him too much.

3. Quality of Results

   (weak) 1 2 <u>3</u> 4 5 (superior)

   Comments:

   His success rate could be a little better, especially where it concerns disputes between new and seasoned employees. I have recommended that he work with a training specialist for assistance in this area.

4. Initiative

   (weak) 1 <u>2</u> 3 4 5 (superior)

   Comments:

   Initiative has declined since the last review. He seems to struggle with pro-

116

jects that require him to work independently. He does better in situations where he can draw on the resources of others for help.

5. Teamwork

(weak) 1 2 3 <u>4</u> 5 (superior)

Comments:

Randy works well in team situations. On those occasions when he has to work in tandem with another mediator, he frequently excels. I believe he works best in circumstances that allow him to have the support and feedback of another individual.

6. Decision Making

(weak) 1 2 <u>3</u> 4 5 (superior)

Comments:

For the most part, Randy relies on the "tried-and-true" formulas for making decisions. I would like to see him become more daring and try different approaches to decision making. He will do this with my guidance and the support of other mediators to whom he can go for assistance and feedback.

7. Problem Solving

(weak) 1 <u>2</u> 3 4 5 (superior)

Comments:

This is one of Randy's weakest areas. As with decision making, he often has problems in seeking out creative new approaches to problem solving.

8. Organization

(weak) 1 2 3 <u>4</u> 5 (superior)

Comments:

Randy meets company standards for organizing his desk and his work. He manages to stay on top of his workload, and there have been no complaints about his inability to produce the desired results. He manages his time and his tasks very well.

9. Communication

(weak) 1 2 <u>3</u> 4 5 (superior)

Comments:

Randy interacts with others on an average level. His communication skills serve him well.

10. Receptiveness to Criticism

(weak) 1 2 3 <u>4</u> 5 (superior)

Comments:

Randy is open to criticism —perhaps a little too open. He needs to know that not every critical word should be taken as gospel, and he is free to disagree when he feels the criticism is unjust.

OVERALL RATING:

__ Needs improvement in job performance

<u>x</u> Meets job requirements

__ Exceeds job requirements

1. *Work over the past 12 months:*

Randy has largely retained the same level of performance as he was demonstrating at his last review. He is competent and works hard and would like to improve his position with the company.

2. *Goals for the coming 12 months:*

I would like to see Randy become a little more independent and a little less reliant on the help of others in resolving disputes. The workshop he is going to next month will be a start toward achieving this goal. I will aim to give him more assignments that he should be capable of handling on his own, to prove his capabilities.

Additionally, I would like to see Randy improve his 77-percent dispute resolution rate to 80 percent or better within the next three months, with the ultimate goal of achieving a 100-percent retention rate in a year's time. He is free to come and discuss his goals and the methods he will use to achieve them at any time.

Employee's signature: _____ Date: _____

Evaluator's signature: _____ Date: _____

INTERIM PERFORMANCE EVALUATION
(Personnel-Benefits Manager—Mid-level)

Name: Grace Harlow
Supervisor: Mary McCall
Date: 4/6/XX

Performance Rating

On a scale of 1 to 10, you are working at about level 7. Your performance has generally been uneven, with moments of good productivity offset by moments when you appear to be apathetic about your job. You've proven in the past that you have the capability to stay on top of your work and get the training and education you need to succeed. You can work independently, but it has become necessary to monitor you to ensure that you are meeting all your goals and not lapsing into those occasional periods when you seem to have no interest in or drive to do your job. The quality of your work needs to improve in such a way that it is consistent on a daily basis, and not just with occasional splashes of productivity.

Strongest Elements of Your Work

You have strong organizational abilities. Your files are always in impeccable order, and your desk area is clean and neat. You are also very pleasant and have a good attitude about what you are doing, even when you're struggling with it. This positive approach serves you well.

Weakest Elements of Your Work

Time management appears to be an issue. You are frequently late to meetings and are always falling behind on your work because you haven't been able to schedule your day efficiently. In addition, communication skills are lacking when it comes to reporting to senior staff on problems and the status of certain projects. There are indications that you have failed to properly present relevant data in your status reports that would affect any decisions made by management. You need to prepare reports that are both thorough and concise, omitting no pertinent details, as you are currently doing. We've discussed the specific areas in which this

119

seems to be happening, and you have agreed to monitor yourself more closely and for the next month will pass all status reports by me for review.

Goals and Training

You have the organizational skills to be able to manage your schedule better than you are now doing. There should be evidence of timeliness and time effectiveness clearly demonstrated within the next three months. Additionally, as discussed above, there needs to be tangible improvement in your communication skills, particularly as regards written reports. The workshop we talked about would be a good place to start.

Forecast

Although there have been some problems, I strongly believe you have the ability to improve and become more consistent in your work. It would help to know what your personal goals are for career advancement and how this job factors into your goals. I would like to have follow-up meetings with you to discuss this and to map out a plan of action whereby both you and the company can benefit from improved job performance.

Employee's Comments

Employee's signature: _____ Date: _____

Evaluator's signature: _____ Date: _____

PERFORMANCE APPRAISAL

Employee Name: James Stuart   Interim   Annual X
Job Title: Trainer
Supervisor: Lewis Meyer   Date: December 1, 20XX

I: Job Skills

	Sometimes	Usually	Always
Job Knowledge		X	

Uses/demonstrates the skills and tools necessary to perform job effectively. Can draw upon previous experience to handle new problems or challenges. Makes effort to stay current in field.

Comments:

Jim generally approaches his work with consistency and good attention to detail. He sometimes doesn't keep up with the latest developments and techniques in the field, but quickly catches up when they are brought to his attention. In this regard, he needs to take more initiative in seeking out information and data pertinent to what he is doing. Overall, his job performance is consistently up to par.

	Sometimes	Usually	Always
Organizational Skills		X	

Can plan, organize, and prioritize work effectively. Meets deadlines and completes assignments within specified time frames. Uses time and resources effectively to meet goals.

Comments:

Jim occasionally has problems prioritizing his work. He has a heavy training schedule that requires him to be out in the field often, conducting sessions. When he returns to the office, he can be overwhelmed by messages and paperwork that need to be done. I have suggested that he draw on the services of the department secretary to help him get his files into manageable shape. Additionally, he needs to apply some time-management techniques that will help him prioritize his work better. On the plus side, he

121

never fails to meet a deadline, although it often means having to put in extra hours to do so.

	Sometimes	Usually	Always
			X

Teamwork

Works effectively with other employees. Gives assistance to others when needed. Shares credit and can balance personal and team goals.

Comments:

Jim is a good team player. He frequently coordinates special training sessions led by teams of trainers that allow them not only to handle large groups but also to speak on their individual areas of specialty. He shows real leadership potential.

	Sometimes	Usually	Always
		X	

Communication Skills

Communicates thoughts and ideas clearly and demonstrates ability to listen and offer sound feedback. Is concise in both written and verbal communications. Keeps management and peers well informed.

Comments:

While Jim is great as a public speaker, his writing skills leave a little something to be desired. His presentation materials need to be reviewed for grammar and spelling before they can be handed out at training sessions. He has not allowed this to bother him too much because he is so good at working "off the cuff," and he has no trouble expressing himself verbally. He does need to improve in this area, however, particularly as regards his monthly reports to management, which should be written better and made easier to understand.

	Sometimes	Usually	Always
		X	

Problem Solving

Can identify and analyze problems and present solutions, using available resources or creative ideas.

Comments:

Jim is a very good problem solver. He occasionally makes errors because he jumps to conclusions and fails to think out a situation fully and carefully before applying the solution. In other words, he can be impulsive. Most times, however, his instincts are correct.

	Sometimes	Usually	Always
Professionalism		X	

Accepts responsibility for all aspects of job and is willing to be held accountable for errors. Displays professional attitude and appearance in approach to job.

Comments:

Jim sometimes dresses a little too informally. While this is fine for the office, he should be presenting a more professional appearance when conducting sessions out in the field. He is also sometimes loath to admit when he has made a mistake, although once he does admit it, he takes full accountability for his actions.

	Sometimes	Usually	Always
Initiative and Motivation			X

Can handle multiple tasks and responsibilities and is willing to take on new challenges. Displays interest in and enthusiasm for job and completes assignments quickly and efficiently.

Comments:

Jim is super-motivated, creative, and highly innovated. He is always introducing new ideas into his training sessions and has a zeal that is infectious. He may sometimes take too much initiative and introduce new concepts before they have been approved, but his overall enthusiasm and creativity make up for his occasional impulsiveness.

	Sometimes	Usually	Always
		X	

Flexibility

Adapts to new situations and changing work responsibilities. Is open to suggestions and criticism and
able to utilize input from others. Looks for acceptable solutions in conflict situations.

Comments:

Jim introduces many innovative ideas, not all of which are accepted by
company management. He often becomes upset when something in which he
believes is rejected. He is also touchy about criticism. He knows he is good
and doesn't like to admit to flaws, although once he is able to accept
that he is not perfect, he is able to handle the criticism and use it to
improve his job performance. He does react well to ideas from others and
can often improve on those suggestions, to the betterment of the entire
department.

	Sometimes	Usually	Always
		X	

Punctuality

Adheres to work hours and is present for work
every day. Provides adequate notice of vacation or
personal time and makes arrangements for coverage.

Comments:

Jim can often be lax about arrival and departure times at the office,
particularly for staff meetings, although he is faithful about making it to
training sessions in a timely manner.

II: Achievements and Contributions

*List the employee's major contributions to company goals, growth, and/or profitabili-
ty during the appraisal period. Describe what actions the employee took to make
these achievements.*

Jim has made innumerable and invaluable suggestions that have improved
training methods department-wide. He is intelligent, innovative, and ambitious, and the success of the training sessions he has conducted has
resulted in a higher employee-retention rate. He has made tremendous

strides in both professional and corporate development since he was first hired a year ago.

III: Plans and Goals

List and describe what the employee must achieve for the next performance appraisal period, including skills development, areas of improvement, projects, etc.

Jim has great potential, and improvement in the areas indicated above will undoubtedly result in his promotion to Training Specialist. I expect him to take more of a leadership role and will continue to utilize his ideas and suggestions, as his innovations are of great benefit to us all.

Employee's Comments

Employee's signature: _____ Date: _____

Evaluator's signature: _____ Date: _____

PERFORMANCE EVALUATION
Training Specialist—Mid-level

Name: Mathilda Johanssen

Date: 4/9/XX

1. Job Knowledge

Matty has met the established standards for the job for the most part. She attends all staff meetings and does her best to stay on top of current training techniques and methodologies. At my suggestion, she has attended some workshops to learn better interactive skills. She seems to be interested in improving her job knowledge, but sometimes has difficulty applying what she has learned to new situations as they arise, preferring instead to ask for help or direction.

2. Quality of Work

The quality of her work is generally good, although she should be quicker in her responses to employees who need her assistance. In one instance, she took too long in correcting an error made by an associate, who subsequently came to me to get the problem resolved. This should not have happened, and Matty realizes that she made an error in delaying her return of the associate's calls. New recruits in particular need a sense of stability and the feeling that somebody will be there for them when they need help. Matty has agreed to work on being more accessible to all employees, but particularly to new people who need her services the most.

3. Quantity of Work

Matty maintains a good consistency in her work flow and volume. Her overall rating is high in this area, although she has demonstrated some weaknesses in the on-the-job training program, as detailed above.

4. Initiative and Motivation

Matty has occasional problems with initiative, particularly as it relates to working independently and problem solving. She relies too much on turning to others for help rather than working things out for herself. This also relates to the problem described above. In talking it over with Matty, it became clear that the reason for her delay in returning the associate's call was that she was unsure of the answer and wanted time to talk to others about it. Again, she should have worked out a possible solution based on her job knowledge and experience rather than wait for direction on how to handle it. This is clearly an area to work on. I would like to see Matty more motivated to take some risks and find ways to solve problems on her own.

5. Attendance and Adherence to Work Schedule

There have been some days of tardiness, but Matty is usually punctual and can be relied upon to adhere faithfully to her prescribed work schedule, as well as to make up any lost time.

6. Interpersonal Relations

People skills are a little on the weak side, in terms of responsiveness. Matty is unfailingly friendly and courteous, but seems to be afraid of damaging feelings or not providing a correct response to a question, which causes her to be too reticent. I would like to see her become more assertive and willing to take risks in order to speed up her response time to employee questions and concerns.

7. Cultural Diversity and Sensitivity

Matty has shown no evidence of prejudicial or insensitive behavior and seems to relate well with employees of all backgrounds.

8. Overall Rating and Goals

Matty currently rates a 6 on a scale of 1–10. She has many strengths, which include her sensitivity to others and her sincere willingness to improve her job performance. I have spoken to her about ways in which she can take firmer control of her job and become more of a risk taker. We have set a date for an interim review in six months' time, when we will review her progress in taking initiative and being more responsive to employees.

Employee's Comments

Employee's signature: _____ Date: _____

Evaluator's signature: _____ Date: _____

PERFORMANCE REVIEW

Name: Gloria Friday
Job Title: Placement Officer
Date: August 22, 20XX_

Type of Evaluation:
Interim   Annual X

Evaluation Guide

1 = Excellent (exceptional; exceeds expectations)
2 = Good (consistently meets, and frequently exceeds, usual expectations)
3 = Satisfactory (conforms to standards; meets expectations)
4 = Fair (marginal; meeting only minimum requirements)
5 = Poor (below standard and unacceptable; improvement required or termination will result)

Factors for Review

Job Knowledge   Rating: 3
Degree to which the employee knows and understands his/her job and its functions
Gloria has adequate working knowledge of her job and what it entails.

Quality of Work   Rating: 3
Accuracy, presentability, attention to detail, etc.
Gloria has maintained a consistent level in the quality of her work since her last review, with no discernible improvement or deterioration.

Quantity of Work   Rating: 4
Amount of work consistently produced within requirements of the position
She could still use some improvement in this area. She seems to be continuously backlogged, and the problem has gotten worse since the layoffs that occurred three months ago. I have authorized the hiring of a temp to help her catch up on all the paperwork and leave her more time to concentrate on helping employees with placements.

Work Interest   Rating: 3
Employee's attitude toward his/her work, specialized knowledge of the job, receptivity to new work assignments, efforts to acquire new or broader job knowledge

129

Gloria seems to be content to stick with what she knows and makes no strong effort to create something more out of her job and make it more interesting for herself. On occasion she has displayed sparks of interest, usually when she is required to be more creative and more interactive with others. But she seems to be apathetic about completing paperwork.

Initiative   Rating: 4
Ability to act independently without specific instructions

See above. Gloria does not seem to be interested enough in her job to take the initiative to make improvements or instill more variety and creativity into what she does.

Judgment   Rating: 4
Ability to evaluate situations, draw conclusions, and make sound decisions

This is Gloria's weakest area. Despite nearly two years in this position, she seems to lack the confidence in herself and her knowledge of the job to be able to make sound, rational judgments, especially when she is under stress. She frequently turns to others for help, but does so a little too often, without stopping to reason things out for herself first or to draw on her experience to help work out new situations as they arise. I have been working with her on ways to trust her own judgment more.

Interpersonal/Communication Skills   Rating: 3
Tact, courtesy, self-control, discretion, ability to communicate verbally and in writing

Gloria gets along well with her coworkers and clients, and in fact is working in this field because she most enjoys the interactions with other people. Her writing skills are weak, however, and I believe this ties in with her aversion to paperwork.

Dependability   Rating: 2
Punctuality, regular attendance at meetings, overall reliability

This is her strong suit. She is unfailingly punctual and can be depended on to be there when she is needed.

Organizational Skills   Rating: 3
Ability to plan and organize work, make efficient use of work time, adhere to established rules and procedures, and follow through

> She follows established policies and procedures to the letter and make good use of any advice offered her for improving her organizational abilities. I would like to see her take some more initiative and come up with new ways to organize and handle her workload.

Growth Potential   Rating: 3
Ability to progress to higher level work and assume more responsible duties

> She is currently not ready to move on to a higher work level.

OVERALL RATING

Since employee's last appraisal, his/her performance has: ____ Improved
                                                              _X_ Maintained same level
                                                              ____ Declined

COMMENTS

Noteworthy performance strengths:

> Gloria is a dedicated employee who is trying her best to improve her job performance, especially in recent months. She is self-aware and open to criticism, and she maintains a positive attitude, even when she is struggling. Her interpersonal skills are very good, and she is dependable, often willing to stay late or come in early when a crunch is on.

Areas needing improvement:

> I would like to see her take more initiative and make more of an effort to reason things out for herself, rather than always relying on others. For instance, when an employee who comes to her for placement presents challenging requirements, she needs to use more of her own skills and job knowledge to come up with an answer before talking it over with me or anybody else. She also needs to get on top of her paperwork and complete reports in a more timely fashion. I'm hoping the assistance of a temp for the next two months as well as improvement in her organizational skills will help her do this. She also needs to improve her writing skills.

Plan of action:

As noted above, Gloria needs to be making certain changes in how she approaches her work. She is going to check in with me on a weekly basis to let me know how she is doing with the paperwork and what she is doing. Additionally, she is to come only to me when she is having any trouble with a placement so that I can assist her in ways to work out solutions on her own more. Improving her writing skills is a more difficult proposition. I have suggested that she take a couple of courses at a local university, for which the company will pay, focusing on grammar and syntax.

Employee Comments

Employee's signature: _____ Date: _____

Evaluator's signature: _____ Date: _____

PERFORMANCE EVALUATION

Employee's Name: Jerry Fielding   Review Period: From 9/XX to 8/XX
Job Title: Human-Resources Generalist   Interim   Annual X
Department: Human Resources
Name and Title of Evaluator: Alice Moser, Department Manager

Performance Guide

A — Consistently exceeds job requirements

   Performance is exceptional, above and beyond what is expected

B — Meets job requirements

   Does a good job; meets and sometimes exceeds requirements capably and competently

C — Improvement needed to meet job requirements

   Is not performing at satisfactory level; extra supervision is required

O —Other

   Not applicable to this area of evaluation

1. Job Knowledge   Grade: B

   Understands and effectively utilizes job-related information, procedures, and skills

   Comments:

   Jerry displays and utilizes adequate job knowledge for effective performance. He does not take any real initiative to learn any more than he needs to know to get the job done. I would like to see him attend more seminars and job-related workshops to improve his job knowledge and, it's hoped, incite more interest in what he is doing.

2. Quality of Work   Grade: B

   Completes assignments accurately and efficiently in accordance with department standards

   Comments:

   Generally, Jerry's work is fine. He is especially good with in-house transfers, matching employees who are looking for a different venue for work with managers who need suitable experienced candidates for a particular job. Employees and managers are comfortable working with him, and he gets along well with his fellow generalists. I would like to see some improvement in certain areas, as described below.

3. Reliability   Grade: B

   Is timely, accurate, and dependable

   Comments:

   Jerry has sometimes been late for departmental meetings and occasionally misses appointments. Otherwise he can generally be counted on to do whatever is asked of him, although sometimes he is late in completing assignments or takes a little too long to handle an employee request or complaint.

4. Work Habits   Grade: C

   Plans and organizes work well, follows procedures, and makes efficient use of work time

   Comments:

   Given his habit of missing or being late to meetings, I feel that Jerry could use better time-management skills. He also has a hard time staying on top of paperwork. His office is usually quite messy, and when people come to see him, he has to shift piles of paper around. He has admitted that his organizational skills are his weakest area and has already begun working to make improvements. At my suggestion, he has been using a department secretary to help clean up and better organize his office and will be attending a time-management seminar within the next couple of weeks.

5. Initiative and Resourcefulness   Grade: B

   Demonstrates ability to work without direction and offer suggestions; can come up with creative solutions

   Comments:

   He shows the ability to be resourceful, often coming up with some top-grade ideas for handling certain standard situations. However, he frequently hesitates to take any initiative and is often shy about expressing his ideas. I suspect Jerry has latent talents that can and should be uncovered to our benefit, as well as his.

6. Decision Making   Grade: B

   Evaluates situations, draws conclusions, and makes sound decisions

   Comments:

   Jerry often needs assistance in handling sticky situations that require him to mediate a dispute or something similar. He is quite capable in other situations and has made no rash errors or unsound judgments.

7. Adaptability and Flexibility   Grade: B

Adjusts to new ideas and situations and is receptive to new or additional work assignments

Comments:

Jerry sometimes demonstrates a reluctance to adapt to any changes in current procedures, as he admits he likes the "tried-and-true" way best. However, he does not make an issue of it and applies himself to learning what he needs to know. He is willing to be flexible, even if not always able.

8. Accountability   Grade: B

Is willing to accept responsibility for job-related decisions and actions

Comments:

Jerry is willing to be accountable for any decision he makes and any action he takes. He rarely if ever points the finger of blame at anybody else when something goes wrong. I believe this to be one of his strengths.

9. Communication/Interpersonal Skills   Grade: B

Communicates with others clearly and effectively

Comments:

Jerry expresses himself very well in writing, but often becomes tongue-tied and hesitant when giving presentations at meetings. He needs to have more confidence in himself when speaking in a public forum. On a one-on-one basis, he is fine and gets along well with his coworkers, as well as with the employees who come to him for assistance. He is a good team player.

10. Professional Growth   Grade: B

Works to develop new skills and takes advantage of opportunities for training and development

Comments:

A lot depends on Jerry's ability to stir up his own interest in the job. He's not going to take advantage of other opportunities unless he recognizes the advantages he has now.

SUMMARY

Summarize employee's performance level since last review; indicate any improvement or decline.

In some ways, Jerry seems to have lost interest in his job and in recent months has not demonstrated the drive and enthusiasm with which he started working a year ago. I attribute this to the fact that he has a lot of outside interests that seem to interfere with his concentration on his job. He has also been overwhelmed due to additional work being assigned to him after the loss of two generalists earlier this year, only one of whom was replaced after some time. Jerry did not let me know that he was feeling so overwhelmed and also somewhat resentful of the burden being placed on him. We have since been able to redistribute some of the "wealth," and he is not so overwhelmed at this point and is showing signs of renewed interest in his job.

GOALS/OBJECTIVES FOR THE NEXT 12 MONTHS

Indicate whatever goals or criteria the employee must meet for the next review period.

Demonstrable improvement in his organizational skills is a must. Jerry also has to show that he's interested enough in the job and in making a go of it and must not allow outside distractions to keep him from focusing on his job when he is in the office. He is also to maintain a daily log of how he is managing his time, as well as to attend any recommended workshops.

He seems to be strongest in any part of his job that requires him to interact with others. I am increasing his duties with regard to in-house transfers, as I believe this suits him best.

EMPLOYEE'S COMMENTS

Employee's signature: _____ Date: _____

Evaluator's signature: _____ Date: _____

136

Sample Reviews for Poor Performers

PERFORMANCE EVALUATION
(Mediator—Poor Level)

Name: Grant Nicholsen

Date: July 8, 20xx

Job Knowledge

Grant has sufficient job knowledge to be able to turn in an effective performance. Unfortunately, he is not using what he knows to his own advantage and does not seem to be able to work beyond established protocols for mediating a dispute. Thus, if something doesn't work according to the formula, he tends to give up. This has resulted in a poor percentage of staff disputes resolved—that is, only about 60 percent. This demonstrates a general failure to utilize job knowledge effectively.

Quality of Work

Grant's problems have affected the overall quality of his work. In addition to a poor success rate in resolving disputes, he has demonstrated an apathetic attitude toward turning in reports in a manner that is both timely and presentable. Written reports in particular have demonstrated his poor attention to form, style, and grammar and have been both sloppy and consistently late. It is unfortunate, since he didn't start out this way, but has been heading in a downward spiral for some time.

Productivity

Grant concentrates on labor disputes between management and employees. He has a heavy workload and currently is a good month behind due to the backlog of cases he has yet to handle. He is not producing at a fast enough rate, and will fall further and further behind at the rate he is going. Some assistance will be needed to help him catch up.

Initiative

This is not one of Grant's strong points. He is generally apathetic about his work and shows no interest in taking charge of his job and making some-

137

thing more of it. He follows established policies and procedures to the letter, but doesn't provide input at staff meetings, nor show any inclination to improve his job knowledge or further his job opportunities.

Attendance and Adherence to Work Schedule

Grant has frequently been late getting into the office and has not made up the time for his periods of tardiness. Additionally, he is often late to meetings.

Interpersonal Relations

Although he seems to handle his mediating sessions fine, Grant is a bit of a loner who does not mix much with his coworkers, and he can in fact be a bit standoffish. There have been no complaints received of any instances of racial insensitivity, although I have caught him making an inappropriate remark or two and have cautioned him about being more circumspect in what he says around the office. As interpersonal skills are such an important element of mediating work, I am a bit concerned about this aspect of Grant's job performance and am talking to him now about ways he can become more actively involved with his coworkers and thus be more alert and sensitive to interpersonal relations throughout the company.

Overall Rating and Goals

On a scale of 10, I would rate Grant to be a 4. His production record is below average, and the success rate of staff dispute resolutions is entirely too low. Grant is going to work on his interpersonal skills, and will have as his primary goal the raising of his production rate to 75 percent within the next three months and to 90 percent or better within the next nine months.

Employee Comments

Employee's signature: _____ Date: _____

Evaluator's signature: _____ Date: _____

PERFORMANCE EVALUATION

Name: Frances Greenacre
Title: Benefits Specialist_
Date of hire: 6/1/XX

Department: Human Resources
Supervisor: Amy Chodoroff
Review period: From 6/XX to 12/XX

Ratings: Employee is to be rated on a scale of 1 to 3, as described below.

1: Below expectations: Performance is substandard and requires improvement.

2: Meets expectations: Performance fully meets and occasionally exceeds standards.

3: Exceeds expectations: Performance consistently exceeds set standards.

N/A: Not applicable. Lack of sufficient knowledge to evaluate the performance factor.

Section I: Basic Job Skills

	Below	Meets	Exceeds	N/A
Job knowledge	1	2	3	N/A
Quality of work	1	2	3	N/A
Productivity/Timeliness	1	2	3	N/A
Dependability	1	2	3	N/A
Work habits	1	2	3	N/A
Organizational skills	1	2	3	N/A
Resourcefulness	1	2	3	N/A
Problem solving	1	2	3	N/A

Comments:

Fran has unfortunately been experiencing difficulties from the start of her employment with our company. She came with good recommendations from the XYZ Company, where she performed a variety of duties in the Human Resources Department, all of them in the administrative support area. This is her first position of real responsibility, which she and I both felt she was up to. However, it has become clear that she is not yet ready to take on a position in which she is essentially autonomous and must work for prolonged periods without direction. She has struggled to learn all the aspects of our various benefits offerings, which differ in many ways from XYZ Company's, and is often confused and frazzled when talking to employees about their options. She is not yet fully cognizant of the terms of insurance policies and what employees on various levels are or are not entitled to. Her uncertainty about herself and what she is doing has manifested itself in all other aspects of her work. She has not been able to

139

keep herself organized, is frequently tardy in submitting reports, and has lacked the resourcefulness and initiative to take charge of her job. Several times I have found her in tears in her office and have had to counsel and encourage her to have more confidence in herself and her abilities. However, her difficulties have been getting the best of her, and it is clear that the job is too stressful for her.

Section II: Personal Attributes

	Below	Meets	Exceeds	N/A
Attendance/Punctuality	1	<u>2</u>	3	N/A
Ability to take direction	1	<u>2</u>	3	N/A
Initiative	<u>1</u>	2	3	N/A
Cooperativeness	1	<u>2</u>	3	N/A
Adaptability	<u>1</u>	2	3	N/A
Receptiveness to criticism	<u>1</u>	2	3	N/A
Communication skills	<u>1</u>	2	3	N/A
Interaction with coworkers	1	<u>2</u>	3	N/A

Comments:

Fran has been trying as hard as she can, and in some areas she has met the criteria for her job. However, she is very self-critical, and sensitive to criticism from others. Because of her self-doubts, her communication skills are poor, and she lacks the ability to take any initiative to improve her position or her interest in her job.

Section III: Strengths and Weaknesses

Describe employee strengths:

Fran does take direction well, and she can't be faulted for not trying to do her best. She is always punctual, and some days has come in early or stayed late in an effort to apply herself to learning the job better or catching up on paperwork. She is cooperative and gets along well with her coworkers. She is earnest and sincere and well liked by others, who have tried to help her through her difficulties.

Describe employee weaknesses:

Fran's lack of confidence in herself is probably her biggest weakness. She has good basic skills that have been done in by the distress she feels over the mistakes she has made and the enormity of her responsibilities, which require

140

her to do more independent thinking rather than always relying on direction from others. If she can get past this mental stumbling block, I believe she is capable of improving in all other aspects of her job responsibilities.

Describe goals for next performance review:

Despite her lack of managerial experience, Fran had enough gumption to try for a position of greater responsibility. I still believe it is possible for her to achieve more success in what she does and to gain better self-confidence in the process. Therefore, we are going to retool her job over the next three months and put her back into training mode. She will work in conjunction with me and other specialists on special assignments and will sit in on counseling sessions to observe how others handle questions and concerns from employees. At the end of three months, she will be allowed limited autonomous responsibilities, and her workload will be gradually increased as she understands more and experiences growing success in what she does. She and I will have periodic "spot-check" reviews to go over what and how she has been doing and to identify the problem areas that need to be worked on.

Section IV: Comments

Evaluator:

It is possible that part of Fran's problems stem from being left "in the lurch" when she first joined the company. At that time, a number of people had left the company and many jobs were still in transition. I found myself preoccupied with handling numerous crises and was always putting out fires in other areas of the department. As a result, I probably did not spend enough time with Fran to help her learn and understand the functions of her job better. Because of this, I am taking on some of the responsibility for Fran's poor job performance and will be spending more time with her in the next three months to help her improve and gain more confidence in herself.

Employee:

Employee's signature: _____   Date: _____

Evaluator's signature: _____   Date: _____

141

PERFORMANCE EVALUATION

Employee's Name: Lilian Hallwell   Review Period: From 9/XX to 8/XX

Job Title: Human-Resources Generalist   Interim   Annual X

Department: Human Resources

Name and Title of Evaluator: Daniel Benson, Department Supervisor

Performance Guide

A — Consistently exceeds job requirements

     Performance is exceptional, above and beyond what is expected

B — Meets job requirements

     Does a good job; meets and sometimes exceeds requirements capably and competently

C — Improvement needed to meet job requirements

     Is not performing at satisfactory level; extra supervision is required

O — Other

     Not applicable to this area of evaluation

1. Job Knowledge   Grade: C

    Understands and effectively utilizes job-related information, procedures, and skills

    Comments:

    Lillian has been given every opportunity to acquire the knowledge she needs to do an effective job. Unfortunately, she has resisted any efforts to assist her, preferring instead to rely on an instinctual approach to her work in which, as she puts it, she "operates from the gut" rather than from any organized, logical method based on company history and established methods and procedures. This attitude has seeped into all areas of her job performance.

2. Quality of Work   Grade: C

    Completes assignments accurately and efficiently in accordance with department standards

    Comments:

    Her work quality has generally been poor. There have been numerous complaints regarding her accessibility—that is, she frequently doesn't return calls, keeps people waiting for meetings, and has been unresponsive to ques-

142

tions asked of her. People looking for answers to a particular question or issue often have to follow up several times before they get a response from her. There is a general feeling from those who deal with her that she is indifferent to their concerns. Additionally, she has been consistently late in filing reports, and her paperwork has been sloppy on the whole.

3. Reliability   Grade: C

   Is timely, accurate, and dependable

   Comments:

   For some time now, Lillian has been operating under her own rules, rather than those of the company. Because of this, there is a feeling that she can't be trusted to do what is expected or needed of her.

4. Work Habits   Grade: C

   Plans and organizes work well, follows procedures, and makes efficient use of work time

   Comments:

   Lillian has never been very organized, and lately the problem seems to have become worse. She cannot handle multiple tasking and tends to be peevish when she's interrupted. As already indicated, she fails to follow established procedures in favor of following her own lights.

5. Initiative and Resourcefulness   Grade: C

   Demonstrates ability to work without direction and offer suggestions; can come up with creative solutions

   Comments:

   Lillian feels that her approach to her work is taking initiative. Unfortunately, I do not agree. She has displayed little respect for the way things are done in this company—for instance, her habit of doodling during meetings rather than paying attention or offering input—and her idea of resourcefulness is merely her way of thumbing her nose at company procedures.

6. Decision Making   Grade: C

   Evaluates situations, draws conclusions, and makes sound decisions

   Comments:

   Her decisions have often been hasty and uninformed by appropriate experience and reasoning.

7. Adaptability and Flexibility   Grade: C

Adjusts to new ideas and situations and is receptive to new or additional work assignments

Comments:

This is probably Lillian's weakest area, as should be made clear by the comments above. She is inflexible more often than not and refuses to adapt to established company policies and procedures.

8. Accountability   Grade: C

Is willing to accept responsibility for job-related decisions and actions

Comments:

When things go wrong, Lillian points the finger of blame at others a little too readily and becomes overly defensive when called to account for an error or a rash decision.

9. Communication/Interpersonal Skills   Grade: B

Communicates with others clearly and effectively

Comments:

This is Lillian's strength. However much she may be at odds with others, she manages nonetheless to express herself very articulately, both verbally and in writing.

10. Professional Growth   Grade: C

Works to develop new skills and takes advantage of opportunities for training and development

Comments:

She is not comfortable with suggestions meant to help her in her professional growth, nor does she desire to take any further opportunity offered to her for further training. Her resistance on this score is quite certain.

SUMMARY

Summarize employee's performance level since last review; indicate any improvement or decline.

Lillian and I have been at odds almost from the day I took over as supervisor of the department. It has partly been a clash of personalities, and recognizing this, I started working early on to overcome our differences and to help her find her voice within the company. She has definite ideas about the way things should be run, which I respect; however, she seems to be unable to work as part of a team. She is a strong-willed individual who prefers to do things her own way, rather than according to established protocol, and she goes on the defensive a little too easily whenever her way is questioned. She does not participate in meetings and has maintained an uncooperative attitude for too long. It is my feeling that the constant battles that erupt between her and any other person, including myself, have been seriously affecting department morale. Furthermore, the overall inferior quality of her work, especially as regards her responsiveness to employees (which is her primary responsibility), has become too blatant to ignore. All in all, the past year has seen a serious shift downward in Lillian's job performance.

GOALS/OBJECTIVES FOR THE NEXT 12 MONTHS

Indicate whatever goals or criteria the employee must meet for the next review period.

None. After considerable discussion, Lillian and I have come to an agreement that her goals and the goals of this company are not in accord. Therefore, she is being given a month's pay in lieu of notice, and will leave the company as of August 15 to pursue other career opportunities.

EMPLOYEE'S COMMENTS

Employee's signature: _____ Date: _____

Evaluator's signature: _____ Date: _____

145

PERFORMANCE REVIEW

Name: Bernice Detwiler
Job Title: Placement Officer
Date: 11/10/xx

Type of Evaluation:
Interim   Annual X

Evaluation Guide

1 = Excellent (exceptional; exceeds expectations)
2 = Good (consistently meets, and frequently exceeds, usual expectations)
3 = Satisfactory (conforms to standards; meets expectations)
4 = Fair (marginal; meeting only minimum requirements)
5 = Poor (below standard and unacceptable; improvement required or termination will result)

Factors for Review

Job Knowledge   Rating: 4
Degree to which the employee knows and understands his/her job and its functions

Bernie has met the minimum job requirements in terms of her understanding of her job and its functions, although she has not put too much effort into applying herself to learn more and to use past experience to handle new situations as they arise.

Quality of Work   Rating: 5
Accuracy, presentability, attention to detail, etc.

Overall, her work quality has been poor. See next comments.

Quantity of Work   Rating: 5
Amount of work consistently produced within requirements of the position

Bernie has not been very successful in finding and making appropriate placements for employees seeking help in finding other positions. Her success rate stands currently at about 45 percent, which is much too low. Many people have complained that she has not shown much interest in their cases and that they are frequently left to their own devices, rather than being able to rely on her for adequate assistance. Additionally, she submits reports late and incomplete.

146

Work Interest   Rating: 4

Employee's attitude toward his/her work, specialized knowledge of the job, receptivity to new work assignments, efforts to acquire new or broader job knowledge

Bernie often seems to be overwhelmed when new elements are added to her job. She is unable to take on additional responsibilities and has indicated that lately she has become bored and disinterested in what she is doing.

Initiative   Rating: 5

Ability to act independently without specific instructions

She has shown no signs of being motivated to do anything more than what she has to do.

Judgment   Rating: 5

Ability to evaluate situations, draw conclusions, and make sound decisions

This is not one of Bernie's strengths at all. She has made some unwise decisions on her own, and as a result has to be monitored frequently to ensure that she is following established protocol. This has made her nervous about even the smallest decisions, which she now runs by me at all times.

Interpersonal/Communication Skills   Rating: 4

Tact, courtesy, self-control, discretion, ability to communicate verbally and in writing

She has sometimes been tactless in her remarks to employees, and occasionally has offended coworkers with inappropriate remarks.

Dependability   Rating: 3

Punctuality, regular attendance at meetings, overall reliability

Bernie has generally been punctual and has shown up at department meetings in a timely manner, although rarely contributes anything to meetings.

Organizational Skills   Rating: 5

Ability to plan and organize work, make efficient use of work time, adhere to estab-
lished rules and procedures, and follow through

> Bernie is easily flustered when her workload gets intense. Her time-man-
> agement skills are weak, and her desk is often sloppy and disorganized.
> Files cannot be located in her absence.

Growth Potential   Rating: 4

Ability to progress to higher level work and assume more responsible duties

> She is currently not ready to move on to a higher work level.

OVERALL RATING

Since employee's last appraisal, his/her performance has: ____ Improved
                                                             ____ Maintained same level
                                                             _X_ Declined

COMMENTS

Noteworthy performance strengths:

> At the present time, there are no noteworthy performance strengths. In
> the past, Bernie's strengths have been in the areas of cooperation and
> attentiveness to detail, but she has slipped considerably and needs to pull
> herself back up again.

Areas needing improvement:

> Just about all of the areas listed above require improvement. I would par-
> ticularly like to see her take more of an interest in what she is doing and
> take some initiative to improve her own situation, rather than relying solely
> on management to do it for her. These efforts cut both ways, and we are
> more than ready to meet her halfway, but she has to be willing to take on
> responsibility for making the changes necessary that will result in a better
> review next time.

Plan of action:

> Bernie has been experiencing a number of personal problems at home that
> have had a direct effect on her job performance. We have been allowing
> her a certain amount of leeway because of these problems, but are now
> requesting her to put some effort back into improving her performance.

EMPLOYEE'S COMMENTS

Employee's signature: _____ Date: _____

Evaluator's signature: _____ Date: _____

PROGRAM DEVELOPMENT COORDINATOR
—POOR LEVEL
Interim Review

Name: Mimi Kawolski

Date: July 6, 20XX

Performance Rating

On a scale of 1-10, your overall performance rating is a 4. Your job performance has largely been inconsistent, with adequate work done one week
and poor achievements the next week. You often seem to be fatigued and
bored with your job. I know you are involved in theater work and that that
interests you more than this job does. However, you must try to understand
that while you are being paid for the work you are doing here, you must
dedicate yourself to that work and its successful completion. The programs on which you are supposed to be working have been suffering due to
your lack of attention and apparent inability to stir up any interest in
them.

Strengths

You have very strong interpersonal skills and get along well with all people,
regardless of their social or cultural background. Additionally, you are
creative and innovative and have the ability to spark other people's imagi-
nations. I would like to see you apply these strengths to ideas that may
strengthen our overall programs and give you more of an opportunity to be
creative on the job.

Weaknesses

You have poor organizational skills and have a hard time prioritizing your
work. Your main weakness appears to be your lack of interest in your job. As
we have discussed, I wonder whether this is the right line of work for you.

Goals and Directions

Your fundamental goals should be focused on program development and
working on ways to improve your overall job performance. We have already
discussed specifics such as organization, prioritization, and what might be

done to incite your interest and creativity. We will review where you stand in three months' time.

Employee Comments

Employee's signature: _____ Date: _____

Evaluator's signature: _____ Date: _____

PERFORMANCE EVALUATION
(Mediator—Poor Level)

Performance evaluation for: Yvonne Merriweather

Date: March 1, 20XX

JOB FACTORS:

1. Job Knowledge

   (weak) 1 <u>2</u> 3 4 5 (superior)

   Comments:

   Yvonne has been experiencing consistent failure in the successful resolution of disputes that she mediates, and I think a large part of that is due to her lack of job knowledge in the appropriate areas. She fails to educate herself adequately about the backgrounds and experiences of the parties involved in the disputes and has not done a thorough job on acquainting herself with all aspects of the way the company is run and how the different units interact, which is crucial to her job.

2. Productivity

   (weak) 1 <u>2</u> 3 4 5 (superior)

   Comments:

   Her productivity rate is well below average. She often has dispute cases pending, and many have never been brought to proper closure.

3. Quality of Results

   (weak) 1 <u>2</u> 3 4 5 (superior)

   Comments:

   Overall quality of her results has been weak due to her failure to bring adequate closure to so many cases. I have received numerous complaints of her inattention and unresponsiveness.

4. Initiative

   (weak) 1 <u>2</u> 3 4 5 (superior)

   Comments:

   She has demonstrated little to no initiative in her approach to her work.

5. Teamwork

   (weak) 1 <u>2</u> 3 4 5 (superior)

Comments:

Yvonne has made some friends within the company, but largely keeps to herself. Rather than take advantage of the experience of others and seeking help when it's needed, she will often just let a situation ride in the hope that it will resolve itself. She seems to be reluctant to use the resources that are available to her within the department and acts as a "lone gun" more often than she should.

6. Decision Making

   (weak) 1 <u>2</u> 3 4 5 (superior)

   Comments:

   Yvonne has made some rash decisions that have resulted in clean-up work on the part of others to correct the situation. She is not capable of independent judgment at this time and has been advised to pass all major decisions by me prior to their implementation.

7. Problem Solving

   (weak) 1 <u>2</u> 3 4 5 (superior)

   Comments:

   This is a very weak area for Yvonne. Her lack of ability to make sound judgments makes it difficult for her to be an effective problem solver, which is crucial in the kind of work she is doing.

8. Organization

   (weak) 1 <u>2</u> 3 4 5 (superior)

   Comments:

   She is below company standards for organizational skills. She has a difficult time managing her schedule, and her office is often too disorganized and messy, presenting a poor image.

9. Communication

   (weak) 1 <u>2</u> 3 4 5 (superior)

   Comments:

   She is too reticent to seek help and struggles with self-expression, both verbally and in writing.

10. Receptiveness to Criticism

    (weak) 1 <u>2</u> 3 4 5 (superior)

Comments:

Yvonne tends to be hypersensitive to criticism and more often than not reacts defensively when she feels she is being attacked. This has made it difficult to work with her to help her improve her job performance, as one never knows how she is going to react to being critiqued.

OVERALL RATING:

_X_ Needs improvement in job performance
___ Meets job requirements
___ Exceeds job requirements

1. *Work over the past six months:*
   Overall, Yvonne's work has been very poor, and despite efforts to help her improve, it has gotten worse. She is very unhappy with the current state of affairs, as are we.

2. *Goals for the coming six months:*
   Efforts are now underway to find Yvonne another job within the company with which she would feel more comfortable.

EMPLOYEE COMMENTS

Employee's signature: _____ Date: _____

Evaluator's signature: _____ Date: _____

6

Model Evaluations for Customer Service and Related Support Workers

This group consists of skilled and semi-skilled workers who act as the first line of contact with your customers. Typically these are service rather than sales contacts. They may meet the public face to face or through the telephone, the Internet, or other media. They are likely to work alone or in small, same-task groups. Their job titles include:

- Customer Service Representative
- Member Services Representative
- Order Desk
- Information Desk
- Complaint Department
- Box Office
- Product Information Line
- E-mail Service Representative
- Web-Site Service Representative

Gauging Performance

The work these employees perform is characterized by flexibility and responsiveness to the people with whom they come into contact. Because individuals in these positions work closely with other people, they must be adaptable and creative in all interpersonal relationships. Their communication skills are very important. Since many of those with whom they deal may be angry or unhappy, they need to be able to handle conflict and confrontation without allowing it to bother them on a personal level.

Cheerful and responsive individuals who have the ability to listen to and interact well with others are highly sought in these positions. Innovation in the overall design of their work is seldom expected from these workers, but they must be unceasingly innovative in their handling of the people with whom they work.

The key issues in these positions usually revolve around the ability to represent the company to the outside world in such a way that all contacts result in positive feelings toward the company. The ability to be part of a task group and to cooperate on achieving group goals is important. It is often also important that these workers be able to work independently and maintain their composure without too much support from others.

Performance Indicators

The top-level performer

- Has a high degree of appropriate knowledge; these people need to know the most about the company in a generalized way
- Has a track record of maintaining excellent relations with the public
- Is able to work quickly and with consistency, but without seeming rushed
- Is highly dependable
- Demonstrates a consistently cooperative manner and outstanding interpersonal abilities
- Demonstrates a high level of sensitivity to cultural diversity and individual special needs
- Shows appropriate initiative and ability to work independently
- Is punctual and regular in attendance
- Adapts well to changing situations and demands

- Is well organized
- Is comfortable and receptive to appropriate criticism

The good performer

- Has an acceptable degree of appropriate knowledge and a willingness to learn
- Has a track record of maintaining good relations with the public
- Is usually able to work quickly without seeming rushed
- Is usually dependable
- Demonstrates a generally cooperative manner and acceptable interpersonal abilities
- Demonstrates an acceptable level of sensitivity to cultural diversity and individual special needs
- Shows adequate initiative and independence
- Has acceptable attendance
- Usually adapts to changing situations and demands
- Is adequately organized
- Is usually comfortable and receptive to criticism

The poor performer

- Has a less than acceptable degree of appropriate knowledge
- Has a weak record for maintaining good relations with the public
- Is unable to work quickly enough or may seem rushed and fragmented
- Is less than dependable
- Demonstrates at times an uncooperative manner and unacceptable interpersonal abilities
- Demonstrates an unacceptable level of sensitivity to cultural diversity and individual special needs
- Shows inadequate initiative and independence
- Has unacceptable attendance
- Usually does not adapt to changing situations and demands
- Is poorly organized
- Is not consistently comfortable and receptive to criticism

Sample Reviews for Top-level Performers

PERFORMANCE EVALUATION

Name: Lee Chen   Title: Technical-Support Rep
Date: November 30, 20XX_   Interim   Annual X

I. JOB FACTORS: RATING:

1. Job knowledge   (poor) 1 2 3 4 <u>5</u> (excellent)
2. Quality of work   (poor) 1 2 3 4 <u>5</u> (excellent)
3. Productivity   (poor) 1 2 3 4 <u>5</u> (excellent)
4. Responsiveness to customers   (poor) 1 2 3 4 <u>5</u> (excellent)
5. Dependability   (poor) 1 2 3 4 <u>5</u> (excellent)
6. Interpersonal skills/Teamwork   (poor) 1 2 3 4 <u>5</u> (excellent)
7. Adaptability   (poor) 1 2 3 4 <u>5</u> (excellent)
8. Organizational skills   (poor) 1 2 3 4 <u>5</u> (excellent)
9. Communication skills (verbal/written)   (poor) 1 2 3 4 <u>5</u> (excellent)
10. Analytic skills   (poor) 1 2 3 4 <u>5</u> (excellent)
11. Professionalism   (poor) 1 2 3 4 <u>5</u> (excellent)
12. Punctuality   (poor) 1 2 3 <u>4</u> 5 (excellent)

Overall Rating   (poor) 1 2 3 4 <u>5</u> (excellent)

II. SUMMARY/COMMENTS

Lee is a superb tech-support representative and a real asset to this company. He has numerous abilities and talents that serve him well, chief among them being his communication and analytical skills. He has a gift for being able to pinpoint the source of a customer's computer problems and being able to talk him or her through a solution. In the process, he is usually able to help customers reach a higher understanding of the computer's internal workings so that they might be able to diagnose and cure their own problems in the future. He is lucid and logical in his approach to each solution and has an easygoing, affable manner with everybody he talks to. It is very rare that a need will arise to send a technician out into the field to assist a customer; most times, Lee is able to take care of things over the telephone to the customer's satisfaction. He has drawn high praise for his abilities, and we have numerous letters of appreciation on file from satisfied customers. His efforts have added significantly to the company's reputation for high-quality service.

Lee also draws high marks within the office. He is always willing to help out others when needed, and is a frequent source for advice and information. "Let's ask Lee" has, in fact, become the department's motto and is used whenever there is a particularly sticky problem to be solved. His knowledge of computers and applications programs is outstanding, and he stays on top of all trends and new-product developments.

There has been a minor problem with punctuality, but overall Lee's work quality and contributions to this company and its customers have outweighed all other considerations. I am recommending him for the standard cost-of-living increase, as well as a 5-percent merit increase in salary.

III. GOALS FOR NEXT REVIEW

It is difficult to establish goals for Lee, when he continues to surpass himself every time. I have had a couple of discussions with him regarding his professional development and future career directions. He has real leadership potential and should be giving some consideration to managerial work. He has indicated that he is comfortable in his present position and enjoys it so that he wonders about the different responsibilities and the added stress of being a manager. He has agreed to think about it, however, and we will periodically review where he is and when he might consider entering a management training program. In the meantime, he is to continue as he has been doing, and he will continue to earn the company's gratitude for his efforts.

IV. EMPLOYEE COMMENTS

Employee's signature: _____ Date: _____

Evaluator's signature: _____ Date: _____

PERFORMANCE EVALUATION
Customer Service

Name: Leonard Lewison   Title: Customer Service Representative
Date: October 10, 20XX

Job Knowledge

Len is an outstanding representative who works hard to keep well informed about all aspects of his job. He works hand in hand with sales representatives to get feedback on how the product line is being received and what the typical complaints are so that he can anticipate and plan for problems down the road. He also collects feedback from customers regarding how the product line is being received and used, in order to provide valuable information to marketing for upgrades and new-product development. His attention to details and ability to learn and disseminate appropriate information makes him one of our most valuable representatives.

Quality of Work

As indicated above, Len's work is top-drawer. He is thorough, accurate, and neat in everything he does and maintains a professional approach to his work at all times.

Productivity/Timeliness

His productivity is superb. With few exceptions (depending on the nature of the problem), all calls are completed within 24 hours, and all correspondence is answered within 48 hours. Daily reports are never late. He is quick, efficient, and timely with all tasks assigned to him.

Organizational Skills

Some improvement might be made in this area. Reports and call sheets usually end up in a pile on his desk, and it is sometimes weeks before he gets around to filing. Finding files in his absence can be difficult, due to the disorganization of his desk.

Courtesy/Responsiveness

This is undoubtedly one of Len's strong suits. He gets along well with people, and it is a point of honor to him to take care of a customer complaint or concern immediately. Customers will ask for him by name when they call because they know they are going to get top-notch service from him.

Communication Skills

Len generally expresses himself well, although sometimes he can confuse a customer by getting too technical when explaining something. He needs to stick to the basics of what he is talking about. Writing skills are somewhat weak, but pass muster for his purposes. He uses standard formats for most letters he writes and asks others to proofread his correspondence when he is writing about a particularly difficult problem that requires a more detailed explanation. He thus does an excellent job of overcoming one of his few deficiencies.

Interpersonal Skills/Teamwork

Len works well as part of our team. He has an easygoing attitude and doesn't allow himself to become upset by overbearing or irate customers. He also relates well with the other staff and will provide backup when needed, without being asked. His willingness to pitch in whenever and wherever he is needed is one of his greatest strengths.

Adaptability/Dependability

He adapts well to new situations and is thoroughly conscientious and dependable.

Attendance/Punctuality

Unless traffic problems hold him up, Len is always on time and has maintained an excellent attendance record.

Goals for Next Review

Len is to create a cleaner, more organized work space and try to get things filed promptly, without undue delay. I would also like to see him contribute more at staff meetings, as his experience and creativity can undoubtedly be beneficial to the department.

Employee Comments

Employee's signature: _____ Date: _____

Evaluator's signature: _____ Date: _____

PERFORMANCE EVALUATION
Customer Service

Name: Patricia Binford   Title: Technical-Training Rep
Date: Sept. 25, 20XX   Interim   Annual X

I. JOB FACTORS: *RATING:*

1. Job knowledge   (poor) 1 2 3 4 <u>5</u> (excellent)
   Comments:

   Pat continues to improve her knowledge and overall understanding of our
   differing photocopiers, particularly the color machines. Her expertise, along
   with her willingness to learn even more than is required for basic cus-
   tomer-training purposes, makes her the best trainer of all our reps. She has
   received high marks time and again from satisfied customers who were
   impressed by her extensive knowledge of the product and her ability to
   answer all their questions.

2. Quality of work   (poor) 1 2 3 4 <u>5</u> (excellent)
   Comments:

   Pat's thoroughness and attention to detail yield a quality job performance
   that has enhanced the company's reputation for good service.

3. Productivity   (poor) 1 2 3 <u>4</u> 5 (excellent)
   Comments:

   Because she is a perfectionist who wants to make sure that the customer
   has learned everything necessary for understanding and operating our
   machines, Pat takes longer in conducting training sessions than other reps
   do. This occasionally results in delays and sometimes in rescheduled
   appointments, as a customer waits for a training session. Most customers
   have been understanding and reported that the wait was worth it after
   Pat's visit. However, I would like to see her find ways to use her time more
   effectively in order to ensure that the training session takes place as soon
   as possible after delivery of the machine.

4. Responsiveness to customers   (poor) 1 2 3 4 <u>5</u> (excellent)
   Comments:

   Pat remains available to answer customer questions by phone even after
   the completion of training.

5. Dependability   (poor) 1 2 3 4 <u>5</u> (excellent)
   Comments:

   She is a conscientious worker whose dedication and thorough attention to customer needs makes her our most dependable training rep.

6. Interpersonal skills   (poor) 1 2 3 4 <u>5</u> (excellent)
   Comments:

   Pat has a great personality and has won many fans among our customers. In addition, she works very well with company staff and often helps other trainers when they are struggling to learn a new machine.

7. Adaptability   (poor) 1 2 3 4 <u>5</u> (excellent)
   Comments:

   She learns the ins and outs of new models in no time and adjusts well to any sort of change.

8. Organizational skills   (poor) 1 2 3 <u>4</u> 5 (excellent)
   Comments:

   Pat is generally very well organized, although she has occasionally left demonstrations materials behind at a client's office or has arrived at client training sessions without all the materials needed to demonstrate a particular feature of the machine. However, she has a remarkable ability to "wing it," so this has not been a huge problem. Still I would like to see her take more care in packing up when she leaves an office so as to avoid extra trips to retrieve materials.

9. Communication skills (verbal/written) (poor) 1 2 3 4 <u>5</u> (excellent)
   Comments:

   As should be made clear by the above comments, Pat's communication skills are an important part of her success in training our customers. She has an easy ability to explain things well, so that clients clearly understand the technicalities of their new machine. This is no mean feat.

10. Analytic skills   (poor) 1 2 3 4 5 (excellent)
    Comments:

    Not a major job criteria.

11. Professionalism   (poor) 1 2 3 <u>4</u> 5 (excellent)

Comments:

Pat has a very earthy sense of humor, which she occasionally "lets rip" during a training session. In the past six months, two customers complained that she was "not very serious." On the other hand, most clients appear to appreciate the wit she inserts into their sessions. I have talked to Pat about working to gauge a customer's reactions to her jokes and to check herself if it's clear that she is not being received well. Other than this small complaint, Pat's professional deportment is excellent.

12. Punctuality   (poor) 1 2 3 <u>4</u> 5 (excellent)

Comments:

See #3.

Overall Rating   (poor) 1 2 3 4 <u>5</u> (excellent)

II. SUMMARY/COMMENTS

Although there are a few minor glitches in her job performance, as described in comments above, I have to give Pat top marks overall. She is unquestionably our best trainer and has invariably received praise from the customers she has trained in the use of our photocopying equipment. Her efforts have generated a high rate of customer satisfaction and contributed to word-of-mouth approval of both our machines and our service that in turn has contributed to higher sales achieved in the last year. Pat's excellent work cannot be praised highly enough.

III. GOALS FOR NEXT REVIEW

I would like to see improvement in the areas mentioned above—specifically, better management of her time to ensure a more punctual schedule for training sessions with customers—and improved ability to pack up and ensure she has all necessary materials before leaving a client area. In addition, I am recommending that Pat's willingness to help other trainers be put to better use by making her an in-house trainer—in essence, the training staff's in-house expert and troubleshooter. Pat has indicated that her preference is for working in the field with customers, but she is willing to divide her time between field and office to see how she likes her additional responsibilities. We have agreed upon six months as the time frame for this experiment, and if it works out, Pat will be moved into a more responsible position on a full-time basis.

IV. EMPLOYEE COMMENTS

Employee's signature: _____ Date: _____

Evaluator's signature: _____ Date: _____

PERFORMANCE EVALUATION
Customer Service

Name: Stephen Ayochuk   Title: Customer Service Rep
Date: June 30, 20XX   Interim   Annual X

I. JOB FACTORS: RATING:

1. Job knowledge   (poor) 1 2 3 <u>4</u> 5 (excellent)
   Comments:

   Stephen carefully reviews and familiarizes himself with all product information that is passed out to the staff. He has also been taking computer
   courses to enhance his skills in that area.

2. Quality of work   (poor) 1 2 3 4 <u>5</u> (excellent)
   Comments:

   He is a superb worker who focuses on customer satisfaction and achieves
   excellent results.

3. Productivity   (poor) 1 2 3 4 <u>5</u> (excellent)
   Comments:

   He handles all calls quickly, efficiently, and courteously. He answers correspondence within 48 hours of receipt.

4. Responsiveness to customers   (poor) 1 2 3 4 <u>5</u> (excellent)
   Comments:

   Many customers ask for him by name because they know they will get
   excellent service from Stephen.

5. Dependability   (poor) 1 2 3 4 <u>5</u> (excellent)
   Comments:

   He is our hardest-working rep, and I depend on him to provide support and
   assistance to the other reps when I am in a meeting or otherwise preoccupied. He is also the designated manager whenever I am away from the
   office.

6. Interpersonal skills/Teamwork   (poor) 1 2 3 4 <u>5</u> (excellent)
   Comments:

   He gets along well with his fellow C.S. reps, as well as with other company
   employees. His friendly, easygoing manner and excellent sense of humor
   brighten our office!

7. Adaptability   (poor) 1 2 3 <u>4</u> 5 (excellent)
    Comments:

    He sometimes struggles when a new procedure is introduced or we experi-
    ence a rapid growth in our product line that requires us to learn a great
    deal at once, but he adjusts quickly and manages to adapt quite well to
    new situations as they arise.

8. Organizational skills   (poor) 1 2 <u>3</u> 4 5 (excellent)
    Comments:

    My one complaint about Stephen is that he keeps the messiest desk I have
    ever seen. While he claims that he can work with the disarray of his work
    area, it is difficult to find anything if a problem that he has been han-
    dling comes up in his absence and we need to get our hands on the paper-
    work. On some occasions I have had to call him at home to inquire as to
    the whereabouts of a particular file. I would like to see him take extra
    care to keep his desk clean and his files and in-baskets neatly labeled.

9. Communication skills (verbal/written) (poor) 1 2 3 <u>4</u> 5 (excellent)
    Comments:

    He has occasional problems with grammar and spelling; otherwise, Stephen
    has excellent communication skills.

10. Analytic skills   (poor) 1 2 3 4 <u>5</u> (excellent)
    Comments:

    His ability to analyze problems and to piece together the puzzle of what-
    went-wrong-where is one of Stephen's strengths. He bolsters this with the
    ability to reason out the best solution that keeps both customer and man-
    agement happy.

11. Professionalism   (poor) 1 2 3 4 <u>5</u> (excellent)
    Comments:

    Stephen maintains a very professional manner, while at the same time
    ensuring that we never lose our sense of humor.

12. Punctuality   (poor) 1 2 <u>3</u> 4 5 (excellent)
    Comments:

    He has trouble arriving on time in the morning, but makes up for it by stay-
    ing later at night. Still, I would like to see him arrive when he is supposed
    to. There has been improvement recently.

Overall Rating   (poor) 1 2 3 <u>4</u> 5 (excellent)

II. SUMMARY/COMMENTS

Except for the punctuality problem and the condition of his work area, Stephen's total score would undoubtedly be a 5. He is a real asset to the company and to me personally, as his expertise, interpersonal skills, and level-headed approach to his work has enabled me to trust him with additional responsibilities and with the care of the department when I am away. For this reason, I am strongly recommending that the title of Assistant Customer Service Manager be created for Stephen, with the appropriate salary increase to recognize his abilities and contributions to the department and to the company.

III. GOALS FOR NEXT REVIEW

Clean and organize work area immediately, then keep it neat and well organized. Improve punctuality problems. Take on new responsibilities as Assistant C.S. Manager, when approved.

IV. EMPLOYEE COMMENTS

Employee's signature: _____ Date: _____

Evaluator's signature: _____ Date: _____

PERFORMANCE EVALUATION
Order-Processing/Customer Service

Name: Connie Stephenson   Title: Order Representative

Date: April 1, 20xx   Interim   Annual X

I. JOB FACTORS: RATING:

1. Job knowledge   (poor) 1 2 3 4 <u>5</u> (excellent)
   Comments:

   Connie stays on top of all the new-product information and is able to answer most customer questions as they are placing their orders.

2. Quality of work   (poor) 1 2 3 4 <u>5</u> (excellent)
   Comments:

   She is quick, efficient, courteous, and attentive to details.

3. Productivity   (poor) 1 2 3 4 <u>5</u> (excellent)
   Comments:

   Excellent turnaround time on phone calls. On average, she handles 8–10 more calls per day than the other reps.

4. Responsiveness to customers   (poor) 1 2 3 4 <u>5</u> (excellent)
   Comments:

   Many customers have chosen to do repeat business with us because they enjoy talking to her so much and receive such excellent service from her.

5. Dependability   (poor) 1 2 3 4 <u>5</u> (excellent)
   Comments:

   Connie is dedicated to her work and does not allow herself to get distracted by outside influences when she is at her desk. She can also be counted on to make good decisions when responding to customer questions and knows when to hand off a call to a supervisor.

6. Interpersonal skills/Teamwork   (poor) 1 2 <u>3</u> 4 5 (excellent)
   Comments:

   She is more of a loner than most of the other reps, and also a fierce perfectionist who sometimes critiques the work of other reps more than she should, rather than leaving correction to a supervisor. This has caused some friction between her and at least two of the others. On the other hand, she works very well with the Customer Service representatives in the resolution of problems, appeasement of customers, etc.

7. Adaptability   (poor) 1 2 3 <u>4</u> 5 (excellent)
   Comments:
   She is comfortable in any situation that is directly related to the performance of her job. She has a harder time with social interactions.

8. Organizational skills   (poor) 1 2 3 4 <u>5</u> (excellent)
   Comments:
   Superb.

9. Communication skills (verbal/written) (poor) 1 2 3 4 <u>5</u> (excellent)
   Comments:
   Connie has excellent powers of expression, is always clear and concise.

10. Analytic skills   (poor) 1 2 3 4 <u>5</u> (excellent)
    Comments:
    She has often anticipated and resolved problems before they happen, saving much time and effort for Customer Service.

11. Professionalism   (poor) 1 2 3 4 <u>5</u> (excellent)
    Comments:
    Connie is a dedicated professional in her approach to every aspect of her job.

12. Punctuality   (poor) 1 2 3 4 <u>5</u> (excellent)
    Comments:
    She is punctual every day and doesn't abuse break time.

Overall Rating   (poor) 1 2 3 4 <u>5</u> (excellent)

II. SUMMARY/COMMENTS

It should be clear from the above that Connie is a top-notch order representative. She knows what is required of her and is thoroughly focused on what she is doing. Her product knowledge is superb, enabling her to analyze whether or not it will meet the customer's needs. In addition, she has increased sales by bringing additional items to a customer's attention. In this respect, she exercises excellent judgment by determining whether the additional sale is in the customer's best interests, but she isn't pushy and always respects the customer's decision. Her telephone manners are superb. All in all, she has been a great asset to the company.

Connie's only problem seems to be her interactions with other order-entry reps. She expects them to meet the same high standards she sets for herself, and this has frequently caused confrontations that are better handled by a supervisor's mediation. She has agreed to "back off" from now on and to bring matters of customer protocol to the supervisor's attention rather than causing any more friction between herself and the others. It is interesting that this happens at all, given her otherwise courteous and respectful interactions with other company staff, especially those with whom she works in Customer Service.

In fact, Connie has expressed an interest in moving on to Customer Service, which I support wholeheartedly.

III. GOALS FOR NEXT REVIEW

Connie will be making the transition to Customer Service within the next 2–3 months. As this will bring her into contact with Marketing and Sales, I would like to see her continue to broaden her knowledge of our product line by spending a bit of time in each of those departments.

She has the capacity to move into a supervisory position eventually, although I would be concerned about her treatment of subordinates due to her perfectionism and high expectations of others. I have suggested that she take one or two seminars to improve her interpersonal skills. As we see improvement in her interactions with peers, we will examine the probability of training for advancement into a key role.

IV. EMPLOYEE COMMENTS

Employee's signature: _____ Date: _____

Evaluator's signature: _____ Date: _____

Sample Reviews for Mid-level Performers

INTERIM PERFORMANCE EVALUATION
Customer Service

Name: Mark Johnson

Title: Customer Support Rep

Date: June 30, 20XX

Interim X   Annual

I. JOB FACTORS:

RATING:

1. Job knowledge — (poor) 1 2 <u>3</u> 4 5 (excellent)
2. Quality of work — (poor) 1 2 <u>3</u> 4 5 (excellent)
3. Productivity — (poor) 1 2 <u>3</u> 4 5 (excellent)
4. Responsiveness to customers — (poor) 1 2 <u>3</u> 4 5 (excellent)
5. Dependability — (poor) 1 2 <u>3</u> 4 5 (excellent)
6. Interpersonal skills/Teamwork — (poor) 1 2 3 <u>4</u> 5 (excellent)
7. Adaptability — (poor) 1 2 <u>3</u> 4 5 (excellent)
8. Organizational skills — (poor) 1 <u>2</u> 3 4 5 (excellent)
9. Communication skills (verbal/written) — (poor) 1 <u>2</u> 3 4 5 (excellent)
10. Analytic skills — (poor) 1 2 <u>3</u> 4 5 (excellent)
11. Professionalism — (poor) 1 2 <u>3</u> 4 5 (excellent)
12. Punctuality — (poor) 1 2 <u>3</u> 4 5 (excellent)

Overall Rating — (poor) 1 2 <u>3</u> 4 5 (excellent)

II. SUMMARY/COMMENTS

I am pleased with your overall progress, which has improved since your last interim review. Punctuality has improved, and you have applied yourself to gaining a better understanding of how to talk to a customer on the telephone—that is, how to ask the right questions, make the right interpretations, and provide the right advice. As you well know, this is not an easy thing to do. All in all, it is quite evident that you have a good working knowledge of computer systems and are competent in handling the most basic of calls. However, you are still experiencing difficulties with leading a customer through solving more complicated system problems. The sticking point is not your understanding of what the customer is trying to say, but the customer's understanding of what <u>you</u> are trying to say. You mustn't try so hard to impress the client with your superior technical knowledge; talk in language that he or she can understand. In addition, I have occasionally heard a note of impatience in your voice as you have coped with these more difficult calls—and if I can hear it, the customer can certainly hear it. You must try to remember that most people you talk to are well aware of the fact that they are not so skilled or knowledgeable as you are. They may even be intimidated by you. It is your job to put them at their ease and to help them through their problem so that they emerge with a better understanding of their computer, as well as with a lot more confidence. This makes you part psychologist as well as customer support rep, but it's not so difficult as it may sound. You have already made considerable improvement in handling basic customer calls in a fast and efficient manner. Now we need to zero in on the specific areas in which you are still having problems and teach you some tricks for handling a situation so that the customer ends up less intimidated and more satisfied with the assistance you've provided.

I have only one other concern, and that has to do with your organizational skills. Your call reports are still poorly filled out and frequently misfiled. I recommend you get at least one desk organizer and spend some time with Lisa to pick up some hints on how you might be able to keep your desk in better order. I would also like to see your call reports typed rather than handwritten.

Do not take the above criticism too negatively. I want to stress again how well you've done in the last three months. The improvement you've made is noteworthy, and I want to see it continue!

III. EMPLOYEE COMMENTS

Employee's signature: _____ Date: _____

Evaluator's signature: _____ Date: _____

PERFORMANCE EVALUATION

Name: Manuel DeLuca   Title: Concierge
Date: August 18, 20XX   Interim   Annual X

I. JOB FACTORS: *RATING:*

1. Job knowledge   (poor) 1 2 3̲ 4 5 (excellent)
   Comments:

   Manny is an able concierge who possesses sufficient skills and job knowledge for providing basic assistance to hotel guests.

2. Quality of work   (poor) 1 2 3̲ 4 5 (excellent)
   Comments:

   Generally good. Manny meets the criteria set for the job. However, I would like to see him extend himself a little more by trying to think of creative ideas for improving the services provided by the Concierge Desk.

3. Productivity   (poor) 1 2 3̲ 4 5 (excellent)
   Comments:

   Productivity is difficult to judge, since no two days are alike, and as a result some days will be more productive than others. In fact, Manny rarely has a day when he is not productive in some way.

4. Responsiveness to guests   (poor) 1 2 3 4̲ 5 (excellent)
   Comments:

   He has a friendly, responsive manner with our guests and is almost always able to handle their questions or find the right person to help them if their requests are not within the specific definition of his duties.

5. Dependability   (poor) 1 2 3 4̲ 5 (excellent)
   Comments:

   Manny is a dependable employee who does his best when on the job.

6. Interpersonal skills/Teamwork   (poor) 1 2 3̲ 4 5 (excellent)
   Comments:

   He works well with other members of the hotel staff and will do whatever is asked of him, but he does not extend himself to volunteering for anything that is outside the scope of his job.

7. Adaptability   (poor) 1 2 <u>3</u> 4 5 (excellent)

Comments:

Manny has the sort of job that requires him to constantly be adapting to changing situations, different personality types, and so forth. In this regard, he is fine, and meets the job criteria.

8. Organizational skills   (poor) 1 2 <u>3</u> 4 5 (excellent)

Comments:

He keeps the Concierge Desk neat and orderly and is good about keeping all forms and leaflets filed or displayed in their appropriate locations.

9. Communication skills   (poor) 1 2 <u>3</u> 4 5 (excellent)

Comments:

His basic communication skills are fine, although I have noticed that he sometimes has trouble providing directions. I have recommended that he write down directions to the locations that he is most frequently asked about, and if any location is within walking distance, he should draw a map to accompany his directions. This should help to alleviate some of the strain involved in assisting a guest to find his or her way around the city.

10. Analytic skills   (poor) 1 2 3 4 5 (excellent)

Comments:

Not a job criteria.

11. Professionalism   (poor) 1 2 <u>3</u> 4 5 (excellent)

Comments:

Manny maintains a good professional attitude when he is on the job and assisting our guests. I am mildly concerned about his behavior when he goes off duty but remains in the hotel—particularly when he hangs out in the bar after his shift has ended. He tends to become loud and boister-ous, which can be annoying to other guests in the bar and which can, in turn, reflect poorly on the hotel. I have spoken to him about this and have asked him to moderate his behavior when he is off duty.

12. Punctuality   (poor) 1 2 <u>3</u> 4 5 (excellent)

Comments:

There have been a few occasions of tardiness, but he is generally punctual.

Overall Rating   (poor) 1 2 <u>3</u> 4 5 (excellent)

II. SUMMARY/COMMENTS

Overall, Manny has been doing fine in the job. He does exactly what is expected of him, but I would like to see him stretch himself a bit and surprise us from time to time by going the extra distance on his own. I have explained to him that opportunity for advancement lies in his ability to show some initiative and creativity in the performance of his duties and that he should not feel so bound to doing things strictly "by the book." I think Manny has the potential to become really outstanding in his job if he just applies himself a bit more. His off-duty behavior is the only point that concerns me, and he has agreed to work on this.

III. GOALS FOR NEXT REVIEW

(1) Present at least three new ideas for improving services provided by the Concierge Desk and, if approved, take charge of implementing those ideas, including the training of other staff, if necessary. (2) Improve ability to assist guests by having written directions and/or maps prepared. (3) Demonstrate more initiative in the overall performance of duties.

IV. EMPLOYEE COMMENTS

Employee's signature: _____ Date: _____

Evaluator's signature: _____ Date: _____

PERFORMANCE EVALUATION

Name: Meredith Feingold   Title: Order Representative
Date: January 31, 20XX   Interim   Annual X

I. JOB FACTORS: RATING:

1. Job knowledge   (poor) 1 2 <u>3</u> 4 5 (excellent)
2. Quality of work   (poor) 1 2 <u>3</u> 4 5 (excellent)
3. Productivity   (poor) 1 2 <u>3</u> 4 5 (excellent)
4. Responsiveness to customers (poor) 1 2 <u>3</u> 4 5 (excellent)
5. Dependability   (poor) 1 2 3 <u>4</u> 5 (excellent)
6. Interpersonal skills/Teamwork (poor) 1 <u>2</u> 3 4 5 (excellent)
7. Adaptability   (poor) 1 <u>2</u> 3 4 5 (excellent)
8. Organizational skills   (poor) 1 2 3 <u>4</u> 5 (excellent)
9. Communication skills (verbal/written) (poor) 1 2 <u>3</u> 4 5 (excellent)
10. Analytic skills   (poor) 1 2 <u>3</u> 4 5 (excellent)
11. Professionalism   (poor) 1 <u>2</u> 3 4 5 (excellent)
12. Punctuality   (poor) 1 2 <u>3</u> 4 5 (excellent)

Overall Rating   (poor) 1 2 <u>3</u> 4 5 (excellent)

II. SUMMARY/COMMENTS

Meredith has had her ups and downs in the past year, and mainly downs due to the death of her father and a personal situation that seriously affected the quality of her work and forced her to take a three-month leave of absence after her last performance review. In the eight months since she has returned, there has been gradual improvement, which leads me to believe that she is capable of achieving more and making a significant turnaround for herself in the year to come. Currently, she is working on an average level, with some problem areas requiring work on her part if she hopes to continue on her road to improved productivity and a higher quality of work.

Specifically, the professionalism that she brings to the job has been undermined by her inability to adapt to changing situations and new developments in the work environment, as well as her difficulties in working as part of a team. She prefers to function as a sole unit within the department and tends to stay aloof from her coworkers; she has sometimes offended others with her attitude and becomes defensive in the face of criticism. Rather than turning to others for support and assistance, or passing a complaint along to Customer Service, she will struggle alone with a problem until she has worked it out. This slows her down and affects her productivity. She has been taking fewer orders on a daily basis as a result.

On the plus side, she is dependable in that she is earnest about her job and has demonstrated a sincere desire to do well. She also has very good organizational skills and maintains a clean, neat desk, with all the information she needs close at hand.

III. GOALS FOR NEXT REVIEW

Meredith needs to work primarily on her interpersonal skills. She tends to get snappish or sarcastic with others (although not with customers), and I would like to see her reduce this tendency and work on nurturing more of a team-player attitude. While it is fine for her to continue to deal with simple problems that can be handled quickly and easily, she is to pass the more difficult problems and complaints on to Customer Service for handling. I will be monitoring this to ensure that it is happening. I would also like to see an overall improvement in attitude; I have recommended to Meredith that she lighten up a bit and not feel quite so deadly serious about her job. It is my feeling that if she relaxed more and weren't so hard on herself all the time, she might find it easier to improve in all areas of her job.

IV. EMPLOYEE COMMENTS

Employee's signature: _____ Date: _____

Evaluator's signature: _____ Date: _____

179

INTERIM PERFORMANCE EVALUATION
(Customer Service Representative)

Performance evaluation for: Daniel Halverson

Date: June 30, 20XX

JOB FACTORS:

1. Productivity (amount of satisfactory work completed)

    (weak) 1 2 <u>3</u> 4 5 (superior)

    Comments:

    You adequately meet the daily requirements of your job.

2. Quality of work (accuracy, thoroughness, attention to detail)

    (weak) 1 2 <u>3</u> 4 5 (superior)

    Comments:

    Although you are doing well overall, you occasionally overlook some details when filing reports of calls handled that can affect follow-up later if the particular problem arises again. It is important that you report all aspects of a call and how it was handled, no matter how trivial the details may seem to you.

3. Job knowledge (skills and knowledge necessary for the job)

    (weak) 1 2 <u>3</u> 4 5 (superior)

    Comments:

    You seem to do all right when you are supplied with the information needed to do your job, but when new situations arise that are not covered by your training, you tend to doubt yourself and your abilities. You need to make more of an effort to trust your basic skills and to draw upon your prior experience in order to deal with the more unusual problems that customers may present to you.

4. Responsiveness to customers (timeliness)

    (weak) 1 2 3 <u>4</u> 5 (superior)

    Comments:

    You are cheerful and maintain a helpful attitude, even with difficult customers. You do your best to answer a question as quickly as possible, although you are sometimes slowed down by self doubts.

180

5. Dependability (perseverance and conscientiousness)

(weak) 1 2 3 4̲ 5 (superior)

Comments:

There is no doubt that you are trying very hard to make improvements. This has been noticed, and your efforts are appreciated.

6. Teamwork (ability to work with others)

(weak) 1 2 3̲ 4 5 (superior)

Comments:

Expectations are met. As you attempt to improve your performance, try talking to other C.S. representatives and learn from their experiences.

7. Adaptability (resourcefulness, problem solving, learning)

(weak) 1 2̲ 3 4 5 (superior)

Comments:

You are still finding it difficult to cope with new situations (see #3).

8. Organization

(weak) 1 2 3̲ 4 5 (superior)

Comments:

You maintain your work area and files according to department standards. Don't be afraid to suggest organizational methods that you feel may improve your efficiency. Your ideas may save time and money.

9. Communication skills (verbal and written)

(weak) 1 2 3̲ 4 5 (superior)

Comments:

You work well with customers and speak clearly and concisely on the telephone. However, your written correspondence tends to have too many grammatical or spelling errors and needs to be checked before transmitting, which is time-consuming. You may want to look into an English class at a local college and also make better use of the spell checker on your computer. There is also a dictionary by my desk if you need it.

10. Attendance and punctuality

(weak) 1 2 3 4̲ 5 (superior)

Comments:

Your attendance record is excellent, and your initial problem with punctuality seems to have cleared up since we talked about it. Good work!

OVERALL RATING:

___ Needs improvement in job performance

_x_ Meets job requirements

___ Exceeds job requirements

1. *Work over the past six months:*

   Generally you have improved, although you have a way to go yet. Your biggest problem seems to be self-confidence. You seem to find it necessary to have everything written down for you and have a hard time coping with situations that are not covered by the written material. You do seek out help, and this is good. You also persevered through some rough patches when every call you handled seemed to go wrong. Your patience in dealing with difficult customers works to your credit. Keep applying your skills in this area.

2. *Goals for the coming six months:*

   Continue to use others as a resource for learning and improving your job performance. Find out how other C.S. reps have handled particularly difficult problems. Before coming to me with something you think you can't handle, try to think of a solution or two that you can present to me along with the problem, which will enable us to hone your instincts. Come up with new ideas for organizing your work area and for improving current procedures used.

3. *Additional comments:*

   You have definitely made progress and have the potential to work with a minimum of direction once you feel more confident in your abilities. Don't give up on yourself.

Employee Comments

Employee's signature: _____ Date: _____

Evaluator's signature: _____ Date: _____

PERFORMANCE EVALUATION
Customer Service

Name: May Sanderson   Title: Complaints Clerk
Date: December 9, 20XX

Job Knowledge

May possesses adequate knowledge for the successful performance of her duties. Her job does not require her to know everything about our product line, but enough to be able to field inquiries and complaints and point people in the right direction. Her duties also require her to have strong people skills and the ability to handle a certain amount of stress due to being in a front-line, "direct-fire" position. She has these skills and abilities in abundance and is generally a good, solid worker.

Quality of Work

The overall quality of her work is good, although she has shown a tendency to be easily distracted from her work due to her sociability. She gets into long conversations with callers and others, often resulting in people being kept waiting. In addition, she has taken too long at breaks, leaving other clerks and customer service representatives with the added burden of taking care of a portion of her workload. When she is on the job and attending to customers, she does well.

Productivity/Timeliness

As indicated above, this is a problem area that needs work. Her productivity is affected by the amount of time she spends being sociable, both with callers and with coworkers.

Organizational Skills

This is a weak area for May. She is often behind on filing and allows papers to pile up for too long, making it difficult to find necessary documents when they are needed. Time-management skills are also a weakness.

Courtesy/Responsiveness

Again it is primarily her sociability that keeps her from being more responsive to customers. Otherwise, she is well liked for her courtesy and friendliness.

Communication Skills

May is not called upon to do much in the way of correspondence or reports, and in fact her writing skills are weak. However, her primary responsibility requires her to communicate verbally with others, and in that she excels. She has a friendly, easygoing manner that immediately puts people at ease, and she can handle the most irate customer with skill and bring calm and peace back into a situation due to her ability to be sympathetic and concerned. She rarely has a problem "connecting" with somebody.

Interpersonal Skills/Teamwork

In addition to communicating well with customers, May gets along well with her coworkers—perhaps a little too well at times, as she likes to spend a lot of time visiting and socializing with others. She gets along well enough with her coworkers, however, so that she is willing and able to provide assistance to others when called upon to do so. She is clearly a dedicated team member.

Adaptability/Dependability

May is highly adaptable to new experiences and situations, and except for the problem of leaving her post too often, is generally dependable.

Attendance/Punctuality

She has occasionally taken time off without adequate notice and frequently arrives at the office later than she should. This is an area to be improved.

Goals for Next Review

May is to work on sticking closer to her desk and taking breaks within the prescribed time period, no longer. She also needs to monitor the length of her phone calls and resolve issues with more due speed in order to keep other customers from waiting too long for a response. Attendance and punctuality problems also need to be addressed, and she will be closely monitored for arrival and departure times for the next six months.

Employee Comments

Employee's signature: _____ Date: _____

Evaluator's signature: _____ Date: _____

PERFORMANCE EVALUATION

Name: James Hansen   Title: Technical-Support Rep

Date: March 30, 20XX   Interim   Annual X

I. JOB FACTORS:

RATING:

1. Job knowledge   (poor) 1 2 3 <u>4</u> 5 (excellent)
2. Quality of work   (poor) 1 2 <u>3</u> 4 5 (excellent)
3. Productivity   (poor) 1 2 <u>3</u> 4 5 (excellent)
4. Responsiveness to customers   (poor) 1 <u>2</u> 3 4 5 (excellent)
5. Dependability   (poor) 1 2 <u>3</u> 4 5 (excellent)
6. Interpersonal skills/Teamwork   (poor) 1 2 <u>3</u> 4 5 (excellent)
7. Adaptability   (poor) 1 2 <u>3</u> 4 5 (excellent)
8. Organizational skills   (poor) 1 2 <u>3</u> 4 5 (excellent)
9. Communication skills (verbal/written) (poor) 1 2 <u>3</u> 4 5 (excellent)
10. Analytic skills   (poor) 1 2 <u>3</u> 4 5 (excellent)
11. Professionalism   (poor) 1 2 <u>3</u> 4 5 (excellent)
12. Punctuality   (poor) 1 <u>2</u> 3 4 5 (excellent)

Overall Rating   (poor) 1 2 <u>3</u> 4 5 (excellent)

II. SUMMARY/COMMENTS

Jim is a competent representative of Technical Support who does not push himself to be anything more than competent. That is to say, he comes in every day and does what is required of him, but he doesn't take much initiative to expand the scope of what he could be doing. This is troublesome, given that he is working in a field that is always changing, and therefore he should be making more of a concerted effort to stay on top of current developments. While he does spend a lot of time with other reps learning new techniques and enhancements from them and turns to others frequently for assistance when he comes up against a problem he can't handle, I want to see him sign up for more structured classes and workshops to enable him to be more independent in fielding computer-related questions and resolving problems for our in-house clients.

He is basically a dependable worker, but I would like to see him improve his response time to customers. He is good about answering emergency calls immediately, but the standard, nonemergency requests in his job queue often have a turnaround time of anywhere from two days to two weeks. He needs to prioritize his time better to enable him to respond to all requests within a reasonable time frame. He should also let clients know that he has received their request and a reasonable estimate of when to expect him to respond.

Jim has a problem with punctuality, often arriving at a job up to an hour late, and he also spends a little too much time on breaks. This is hard to monitor, as he spends most of his time in the field and doesn't check in with the Support Desk as often as he should. I would therefore like to see him take a more responsible approach to his job in terms of timeliness.

III. GOALS FOR NEXT REVIEW

- Attend more courses, workshops, and demonstrations to increase working knowledge of computer technology, systems, and applications.
- Improve client relations by acknowledging requests received and providing estimate of response time. If delayed for any reason, keep clients informed of when to reasonably expect service for their requests.
- Improve punctuality and time spent on breaks to ensure maximum use of time.
- Increase check-in times with the home office to report on whereabouts and jobs completed as well as to obtain any new requests that have come in.

IV. EMPLOYEE COMMENTS

Employee's signature: _____ Date: _____

Evaluator's signature: _____ Date: _____

187

Sample Reviews for Poor Performers

PERFORMANCE EVALUATION
Customer Service

Name: Talia Valbiro   Title: Concierge

Date: July 2, 20xx

Job Knowledge

Talia is generally able to provide basic assistance to hotel guests but often fails to keep herself informed and updated on all services provided by the Concierge Desk. She frequently forgets the existence of special offers and services given by the hotel and is inattentive at staff meetings.

Quality of Work

Overall, the quality of her work is poor. She tried very hard when she first began working, but found herself overwhelmed by the demands of the job, even though they are minimal. She gets flustered easily and on several occasions has been overheard giving incorrect directions to guests. She has made some useful suggestions regarding flyers and brochures, but tends to get moody and upset when some of her ideas are not always accepted. Her failure to accept the occasional "no" to her suggestions has a detrimental effect on her job interest, and work quality generally suffers until her mood picks up again.

Strengths

Talia has displayed a certain amount of initiative with the suggestions she has made for informational materials and ways of making the Concierge Desk more presentable and attractive to guests. She is articulate and creative and interacts well with hotel guests.

Weaknesses

Her weakest trait is her inconsistency in behavior. On some days she is cheerful and interested, on others days she appears to be down and moody. This seems to stem from her failure to take criticism well and to her belief that when an idea of hers is turned down, it is a direct attack on her. She needs to learn that a "no" is not always a judgment of her and that there are often sound reasons when an idea of hers is rejected. We do not want to discourage Talia from continuing to make contributions toward the betterment of the Concierge Desk; therefore, I have had several talks with her about attitude and understanding the whys and wherefores of management decisions.

Courtesy/Responsiveness

Talia is unfailingly courteous and respectful of all hotel guests. However, she frequently fails to extend that same consideration to her supervisors, with whom she has become insubordinate on several occasions. She is clearly interested and willing, but has a strong independent streak that makes her chafe under authority and become defensive and discourteous. This is true only of her interactions with other hotel staff. She does not experience similar problems with guests, with whom she is always responsive and willing to help.

Communication/Interpersonal Skills

Talia's interpersonal skills are generally good, except when she is in a defensive mode, as described above. She communicates her ideas effectively and usually interacts well with hotel guests, providing answers to questions, guidance on things to see and do in the city, and so on.

Adaptability/Dependability

Talia can be depended upon to do a good job in all her interactions with hotel guests. However, she is often inflexible regarding the running of the Concierge Desk and prefers a set routine with set people with whom she has developed a good working relationship. Any deviation from this routine and setup tends to throw her, and she has a hard time making the adjustment.

Attendance/Punctuality

She has occasionally been late for work, but no real problems have been noted.

Goals for Next Review

Talia's overall evaluation is borderline poor. She has the capacity to improve, particularly if she can change her attitude and learn to adapt to new situations and people. She also needs to be less defensive about criticism and not buck authority so much. By the time of her next review, there should be a noticeable change in attitude and flexibility. Additionally, she should continue offering suggestions for new services and opportunities at the Concierge Desk, as this demonstrates strong initiative and creativity, which should be encouraged.

Employee Comments

Employee's signature: _____ Date: _____

Evaluator's signature: _____ Date: _____

PERFORMANCE EVALUATION

Employee's Name: Gus Kaliades   Review Period: From 1/XX to 12/XX
Job Title: Customer-Support Assistant Interim Annual X
Department: Customer Services
Name and Title of Evaluator: Bill MacKenzie, C.S. Supervisor

Performance Guide:

A — Consistently exceeds job requirements
 Performance is exceptional, above and beyond what is expected
B — Meets job requirements
 Does a good job; meets and sometimes exceeds requirements capably and competently
C — Improvement needed to meet job requirements
 Is not performing at satisfactory level; extra supervision is required
O —Other
 Not applicable to this area of evaluation

1. Job Knowledge   Grade: C
 Understands and effectively utilizes job-related information, procedures, and skills
 Comments:

 Although Gus has spent a considerable amount of time in training sessions and working under close personal supervision, he still has a hard time effectively using and expanding any job knowledge outside the computer. In fact, he frequently avoids his responsibilities by assisting other people with computer problems not directly related to his job. His willingness to help notwithstanding, he should be focusing his computer skills on developing our World Wide Web site as a means of responding to customer needs and providing valuable information about the company and its products, which means he has to concentrate on becoming an expert in the information-providing area.

2. Quality of Work   Grade: C
 Completes assignments accurately and efficiently in accordance with department standards
 Comments:

 As above. He has more than once failed to complete projects assigned to him to enhance customer support services over the Internet. He is also considerably behind on the writing of job aids to cover features of the Web site not included in our policies-and-procedures manual.

3. Timeliness   Grade: C

Finishes assignments within a reasonable or better time frame

Comments:

As above. He has not stayed on top of the timely completion of his normal work duties.

4. Work Habits   Grade: C

Plans and organizes work well, follows procedures, and makes efficient use of work time

Comments:

Whatever Gus does, he does it well. As is made clear by the above, the problem is that he does not focus on his own responsibilities but allows himself to be too easily distracted by others. He also appears to be more interested in the graphics and overall look of the Web page than in developing the information in it, making it more complete and accessible to the customer.

5. Initiative and Resourcefulness   Grade: B

Demonstrates ability to work without direction and offer suggestions; can come up with creative solutions

Comments:

When his mind is on his own work, Gus can be quite innovative and resourceful.

6. Decision Making   Grade: N/A

Evaluates situations, draws conclusions, and makes sound decisions

Comments:

7. Adaptability and Flexibility   Grade: B

Adjusts to new ideas and situations and is receptive to new or additional work assignments

Comments:

The ability is there, and in fact he takes more of an interest in his job when new challenges are thrown his way, particularly as regards anything of a technical nature to do with the computer.

192

8. Customer Responsiveness   Grade: C

Is immediately responsive to customer requests and concerns and anticipates customer needs

Comments:

This is the most crucial part of his job, yet it is what he neglects the most. As indicated above, he is supposed to be focusing on anticipating what a customer is likely to need or want to know when contacting us through the Internet. He has preferred to take questions received and pass them on to a Customer Service rep to handle by phone or e-mail. He has only occasionally utilized those questions in his work on the Web site, thereby missing a valuable resource for that part of his duties. While he has taken information provided by others and incorporated it into the site, he has failed to expand the scope of his own knowledge in order to be more responsive to the customer on a direct basis.

9. Punctuality and Dependability   Grade: C

Can be relied upon to be punctual and to do what is required without follow-up

Comments:

Gus is always punctual, although he takes a while to settle down at his desk. Dependability is another issue, as is clear from the above.

10. Use of Resources   Grade: N/A

Cares for and maintains equipment; conserves and economizes office resources

Comments:

11. Communication Skills   Grade: B

Communicates with others clearly and effectively

Comments:

He is quite effective in dealing with other personnel regarding their computer problems, which is why he is called upon so often to provide assistance in that area. He has an excellent way of helping people to understand their computers. I just wish he would transfer that same effectiveness to his dealings with customers.

12. Interpersonal Skills   Grade: B

Interacts well with others; demonstrates courtesy, patience, diplomacy, discretion, and self-control; works well with a team

Comments:

Gus is very popular and has excellent people skills.

193

13. Supervisory Skills   Grade: N/A

Supervises employees effectively; maintains sound working relationships

Comments:

14. Professional Growth   Grade: B

Works to develop new skills and takes advantage of opportunities for training and development

Comments:

See comments below.

SUMMARY

Summarize employee's performance level since last review; indicate any improvement or decline.

Gus has not shown any appreciable improvement in terms of accomplishing the goals and objectives of his job, particularly as regards adequate customer support. However, other skills have risen to the surface, which seem to show that he missed his true calling. His ease on the computer and his ability to quickly and easily help others resolve computer-related problems make it evident that he really should be in Technical Support. In this way, his customer-service skills can be utilized more effectively and in an area in which he would clearly find more personal satisfaction. I have made this recommendation to Gus, and he is enthusiastic about making such a change. I suspect that the quality of his performance reviews will rise considerably when that happens.

GOALS/OBJECTIVES FOR THE NEXT 12 MONTHS

Indicate whatever goals or criteria the employee must meet for the next review period.

Gus will meet with Bob Daniels to discuss the transfer to Technical Support when a position becomes available. I have spoken to Bob myself, and he indicates that Gus will have to go through a certain amount of training and take some courses to enhance the skills he will be needing to utilize in Tech Support, as well as to make him more qualified. I have agreed to let Gus spend one day a week in Bob's department to pursue these objectives.

In the meantime, I am expecting Gus to still focus a good portion of his energies on doing what is required of him in his current position. In particular, I would like to see him utilize in-house resources on improving the Web site to make it more accessible and useful to external customers.

EMPLOYEE'S COMMENTS

Employee's signature: _____ Date: _____

Evaluator's signature: _____ Date: _____

Department Head's Signature: _____ Date: _____

PERFORMANCE EVALUATION
Customer Service

Name: MacDonald Cameron   Title: Order-Entry Representative

Date: March 24, 20XX

Job Knowledge

Mac has now been working in the Order-Entry Department for a year, in which time he has failed to grasp sufficient understanding of our product line and services. Time and again he has put calls on hold while he has sought for answers from others or in the piles of papers on his desk. At this point, he should be more fully aware of what he needs to know to do an effective and responsive job.

Quality of Work

Work quality has been poor overall. His work area is sloppy and disorganized, and he frequently loses important information, such as price lists. He has had a difficult time adapting to the new computerized order-entry system and frequently doubles his efforts by writing down orders before entering them into the computer. By doing this, he sometimes misses certain information he should have asked of the customer and has to call back to get that information. There have also been numerous reports of misplaced files and insufficient log entries for the daily tally of orders.

Productivity/Timeliness

His productivity record is poor due to his inability to organize himself and have relevant data close at hand whenever a customer calls. It takes Mac twice as long to handle an order as it does for any other order representative. The number of times he has to put a customer on hold while he looks up a price or an order code not only slows him down, it also irritates the customer.

Organizational Skills

As already described, his organizational and time-management skills must be improved.

Courtesy/Responsiveness

While Mac is always polite and friendly, his responsiveness to customers needs improvement for the reasons stated above.

Communication Skills

Although courteous and respectful toward callers, Mac's communication skills could be improved, particularly when he is called upon to explain anything regarding the product line. Without any information immediately at hand, he may get tongue-tied or provide erroneous information.

Interpersonal Skills/Teamwork

Mac's interpersonal skills are generally fine, and he works well with other order-entry reps. He seems to function best in a team situation, and it is important for him to be close by other people for backup, rather than having to act independently.

Adaptability/Dependability

Mac has difficulty adjusting to any changes in procedure or additions to the product line that require him to learn new information. He is dependable as long as he has strict parameters within which to work.

Attendance/Punctuality

There have been no attendance or punctuality problems noted.

Goals for Next Review

This job has been a struggle for Mac from the start. The lack of organization in his area probably provides the biggest problem for him and could be the root cause of his difficulties in learning what he needs to know for the job and in responsiveness to customers. He will devote the next three months to straightening out and organizing his work area in such a way that he has relevant materials close at hand and is able to improve his productivity and responsiveness. In addition, he is to spend one hour each day in the marketing department to learn more about the product line,

197

features, prices, etc. He will have an interim review in three months' time to see what progress he is making toward improving his overall job performance.

Employee's Comments

Employee's signature: _____ Date: _____

Evaluator's signature: _____ Date: _____

PERFORMANCE EVALUATION

Name: Gladys Day   Department: Operations
Title: Customer Service Representative   Supervisor: Andrea MacIntyre
Date of hire: March 22, 20XX   Review period: From 3/XX to 2/XX

Ratings: Employee is to be rated on a scale of 1 to 3, as described below.
  1: Below expectations: Performance is substandard and requires improvement.
  2: Meets expectations: Performance fully meets and occasionally exceeds standards.
  3: Exceeds expectations: Performance consistently exceeds set standards.
N/A: Not applicable. Lack of sufficient knowledge to evaluate the performance factor.

Section I: Basic Job Skills

	Below	Meets	Exceeds	N/A
Job knowledge	1	2	3	N/A
Quality of work	1	2	3	N/A
Productivity/Timeliness	1	2	3	N/A
Dependability	1	2	3	N/A
Work habits	1	2	3	N/A
Organizational skills	1	2	3	N/A
Resourcefulness	1	2	3	N/A
Problem solving	1	2	3	N/A
Care of office equipment	1	2	3	N/A

Comments:

Numerous attempts have been made to work with Gladys to improve her job performance and to impress upon her the importance of her position. Nevertheless, she seems to find it too difficult to handle both the order-processing and the customer service aspects of her job. She does better with rote jobs that don't require too much thinking; therefore, I have attempted to give her primarily order-processing tasks and to split the bulk of the customer service calls between myself and John. Nevertheless, John and I have found that a too-large portion of the C.S. calls we have handled have involved errors made by Gladys in the course of her order-entry duties. For example, in one case, a customer who had ordered 100 hammers received 1,000 instead. The cost to us of straightening out this error, crediting the customer, and arranging the return shipment was bad

199

enough; but such goofs affect our reputation with our customers and put us into an embarrassing position we can ill afford for a company of our size.

Section II: Personal Attributes

	Below	Meets	Exceeds	N/A
Attendance/Punctuality	1	<u>2</u>	3	N/A
Ability to take direction	<u>1</u>	2	3	N/A
Initiative	<u>1</u>	2	3	N/A
Cooperativeness	<u>1</u>	2	3	N/A
Adaptability	<u>1</u>	2	3	N/A
Receptiveness to criticism	<u>1</u>	2	3	N/A
Communication skills	<u>1</u>	2	3	N/A
Interaction with coworkers	1	<u>2</u>	3	N/A
Courtesy/Hospitality	<u>1</u>	2	3	N/A

Comments:

Although Gladys gets along fine with John and with other clerks in the office, she has a real problem with authority, and there has been friction between her and me. From the start, she has not taken direction very well, and she does not do a good job of retaining what she has learned. She seems to regard my attempts to go over her errors with her as a personal attack on her, and our meetings are characterized too often by an atmosphere of combativeness. I have attempted to deal with the problem she has with me personally by bringing in Bill Jones to mediate our meetings. However, she regards this as management's "ganging up" on her, and Bill has had as little success with her as I have. As for her errors, she refuses to be accountable for any mistake she has made, always insisting that she hadn't been properly informed, so how was she to know, or providing an excuse for her negligence. Her inability to take any responsibility for her actions is a source of great frustration for me.

Section III: Strengths and Weaknesses

Describe employee strengths:

None.

Describe areas for improvement:

As is clear from the above, all areas require improvement.

Describe goals for next performance review and means by which goals will be achieved:

See comments below.

Section IV: Comments

Evaluator:

Gladys's job performance has steadily declined since she was hired a year ago. I have made every attempt to work out the problems with her and to ease her job responsibilities in order to accommodate her limited skills. Although it was evident that there were problems early on, my awareness of her status as a single mother and my desire to do what I could to help her outweighed other considerations. I believe the difficulties of her personal life have a direct bearing on the general sloppiness of her work, her inability to learn and retain what she has learned, and her problems with authority figures. I twice made the recommendation that she seek counseling, but she rejected this.

At this point, the company cannot afford to continue bearing the consequences of her repeated and costly errors. Gladys has received several verbal warnings and two written warnings. Her failure to improve either her attitude or her job performance makes it necessary to terminate her from her position. She has been informed that she will receive one month's severance pay in lieu of notice.

Employee:

Employee's signature: _____ Date: _____

Evaluator's signature: _____ Date: _____

PERFORMANCE EVALUATION
Customer Service

Name: Joseph Rispoli   Title: Customer Support Representative

Date: January 4, 20XX

Job Knowledge

Joe's job knowledge continues to be weak. He has failed to stay current with new advances in either the product line or the services we offer to support our new products. He seems unable to absorb new information or to apply prior experience to new situations as they arise.

Quality of Work

Quality of work is poor. Joe does not seem to have much interest in his job or in taking responsibility for his errors, which are numerous and have, in fact, multiplied in recent months. The rise in errors has also resulted in a rise in customer irritability.

Productivity/Timeliness

Joe fails to produce at the expected rate. Other customer-support reps have frequently had to take up the slack for him and help him with his backlog. His call reports are invariably late.

Organizational Skills

Joe's work area is sloppy and disorganized. He has often misplaced files and does not return materials to their proper location. His failure to have necessary materials close at hand has made it difficult for him to respond to customer calls in an efficient manner.

Courtesy/Responsiveness

Joe has been overheard to snap at customers on several occasions. He has been impatient and rude too often and—despite several verbal warnings—has failed to change his attitude and monitor himself for rudeness to customers.

Communication Skills

He communicates in a poor fashion and rarely makes himself clear. Writing skills are also bad; letters must be proofread by others before they can be sent.

Interpersonal Skills/Teamwork

Joe tends to be a loner. He does not interact much with his coworkers and has sometimes antagonized others with a sarcastic attitude and inappropriate jokes.

Adaptability/Dependability

He adapts well to new circumstances and the introduction of new products or procedures, but otherwise cannot be depended on to be consistent and productive at all times.

Attendance/Punctuality

He frequently arrives late and leaves early and has taken a considerable amount of time off without adequate notice or preparation for how his position is to be covered in his absence.

Goals for Next Review

No goals have been established. Joe has expressed a grave amount of unhappiness with his job, and a mutual decision was made that he should start looking for another position immediately. He will be kept on in his current position until he finds another job elsewhere.

Employee's Comments

Employee's signature: _____ Date: _____

Evaluator's signature: _____ Date: _____

INTERIM REVIEW: COMMENTS

Employee name: Betty Stone   Date: May 1, 20XX
Job Title: Customer Service Representative

Overall appraisal for the last three months:

You have not met our expectations for the job. Overall, performance has been extremely weak and disappointing. Although you initially expressed enthusiasm for the job, you don't seem to be taking too much of an interest in it.

Strengths and weaknesses demonstrated during the last three months:

You have not demonstrated any appreciable strengths. Weaknesses: You are often inattentive when receiving instructions or information, which has resulted in having to repeat things to you more than once. I have provided you with detailed checklists and informational sheets so that you have something to refer to in answering customer inquiries, yet you have not been motivated to study or use them. Your telephone manner needs significant improvement; you do not speak clearly, and you often sound bored and uninterested, which is the wrong attitude to take with customers. In fact, boredom seems to be your problem overall.

Skills, abilities, or tools needed to improve or enhance job performance:

See goals and objectives section.

Barriers to job satisfaction:

The biggest barrier is your attitude. If you do not like what you are doing here and cannot improve how you feel about it, it may be time to start looking for another job.

Goals and objectives for the next three months:

First and foremost, your attitude must be improved, and at once. Second, you must work on studying all data that have been provided to you to improve your knowledge of company products and policies and thus be better equipped to service the customer. Finally, I want you to demonstrate a genuine interest in your job and willingness to apply yourself harder to acquiring the skills and knowledge you need to do it effectively.

Additional comments:

We seem to be at an impasse. If immediate improvement is not seen, you will be terminated, prior to the next three-month review, if necessary.

Employee's comments:

Employee's signature: _____ Date: _____

Evaluator's signature: _____ Date: _____

PERFORMANCE EVALUATION

Name: David Hope   Title: Customer Service Rep
Date: June 30, 20XX   Interim   Annual X

I. JOB FACTORS: *RATING:*

1. Job knowledge   (poor) 1 <u>2</u> 3 4 5 (excellent)
2. Quality of work   (poor) 1 <u>2</u> 3 4 5 (excellent)
3. Productivity   (poor) <u>1</u> 2 3 4 5 (excellent)
4. Responsiveness to customers   (poor) 1 <u>2</u> 3 4 5 (excellent)
5. Dependability   (poor) 1 <u>2</u> 3 4 5 (excellent)
6. Interpersonal skills/Teamwork   (poor) <u>1</u> 2 3 4 5 (excellent)
7. Adaptability   (poor) 1 <u>2</u> 3 4 5 (excellent)
8. Organizational skills   (poor) <u>1</u> 2 3 4 5 (excellent)
9. Communication skills (verbal/written) (poor) 1 2 <u>3</u> 4 5 (excellent)
10. Analytic skills   (poor) 1 <u>2</u> 3 4 5 (excellent)
11. Professionalism   (poor) 1 2 <u>3</u> 4 5 (excellent)
12. Punctuality   (poor) 1 <u>2</u> 3 4 5 (excellent)

Overall Rating   (poor) 1 <u>2</u> 3 4 5 (excellent)

II. SUMMARY/COMMENTS

David's overall job performance has been poor. He has some strengths, which include an innate sense of professionalism that exists despite the problems he has had with the job, and he has good communication skills, especially in writing. His primary problem may be in his interactions with others. He works best on an independent basis and has trouble relating to other reps; he tends to get defensive at any implied criticism and refuses to go to any of the others for assistance. He is generally disorganized, although he seems to be able to find what he needs or wants in the mess on his desk. Nonetheless, his general sloppiness makes it difficult for anybody else to find important materials in his absence. Customer responsiveness has also been poor, as he has frequently left customers "hanging" for several days while he researches a problem and tries to effect a solution. He needs to bring up his productivity rate considerably.

III. GOALS FOR NEXT REVIEW

David's overall rating is very poor, but we are not yet ready to give up on him. He will be closely monitored over the next three months to see demonstrable improvement made in all areas. He has to be willing and interested enough in his position and his future with the company. I will be working closely with him to go over problem areas and teach the techniques he will need to make the appropriate improvement, particularly focusing on his interactions with others and the importance of acting as part of a team rather than as a lone gun. His progress will be reviewed again in three months' time.

IV. EMPLOYEE COMMENTS

Employee's signature: _____ Date: _____

Evaluator's signature: _____ Date: _____

7

Model Evaluations for Salespeople

This group consists of workers who sell your organization, service, or product to the public. They usually work one-on-one, but are often part of sales teams. Objective data resulting from the financial success of their sales work is usually easy to track and often part of their incentive system. Their efforts not only sell your company's product or service, but also your organization, in terms of repeat business and long-term customer satisfaction; tracking those parts of their performance may be more difficult. Their job titles include:

- Sales Assistant
- Member-Outreach Clerk
- Development Assistant
- Telemarketer
- Promotions Supervisor
- Subscription Sales
- Group Sales
- Banquet and Special-Event Sales
- Sales/Product Representative
- Rental Manager
- New-Product Sales
- Special-Account Representative

Gauging Performance

The work these employees perform primarily involves interacting with people. Energy, cheerfulness, and an optimistic outlook are important character traits for these workers. Their communication skills are crucial to their success. The nature of sales is that a good deal of the time the sale doesn't happen, even when the worker has done a good job. Thus, it is essential that poor sales cycles do not defeat a successful worker's personal attitudes about his or her job.

Individuals with the ability to listen to and react well with others are highly effective in these positions. Innovation in the overall design of their work is seldom expected from these workers, but they must be unceasingly innovative in their approaches to people, especially potential customers.

A high degree of product knowledge is a real asset to these workers. In an everchanging world, this means flexibility and a continuous energy for mastering new materials.

The key issues in these positions usually center on the ability to turn knowledge and people skills into products sold. These workers often work in teams for group goals, in addition to being recognized for individual competitive efforts.

Performance Indicators

The top-level performer

- Has a high degree of appropriate knowledge and keeps that knowledge up to date
- Has excellent people skills and maintains good relations with the public
- Works with energy and cheerfulness
- Is highly dependable
- Can "close" without seeming pushy
- Demonstrates a consistently cooperative manner and outstanding interpersonal abilities
- Demonstrates a high level of sensitivity to cultural diversity and individual special needs
- Shows appropriate initiative and works independently
- Is punctual and regular in attendance
- Adapts well to changing situations and demands

- Is well organized
- Is comfortable and receptive to appropriate criticism

The good performer

- Has an acceptable degree of appropriate knowledge and usually keeps that knowledge up to date
- Has acceptable people skills and relations with the public
- Usually works with energy and cheerfulness
- Is generally dependable
- Can "close" most of the time without seeming pushy
- Usually demonstrates a cooperative manner and good interpersonal abilities
- Demonstrates an adequate level of sensitivity to cultural diversity and individual special needs
- Usually shows appropriate initiative and works independently
- Is generally punctual and regular in attendance
- Usually adapts well to changing situations and demands
- Is adequately organized
- Is generally comfortable and receptive to appropriate criticism

The poor performer

- Has difficulty maintaining an acceptable degree of appropriate knowledge
- Sometimes has difficulty in dealing with the public and demonstrates poor people skills
- Has an uneven flow of energy and cheerfulness
- Is not dependable
- Has difficulty "closing"
- Has difficulty maintaining a cooperative manner and good interpersonal abilities
- Demonstrates an inadequate level of sensitivity to cultural diversity and individual special needs
- Does not always show appropriate initiative
- Has inadequate attendance
- Has difficulty adapting to changing situations and demands
- Is poorly organized
- Has difficulty with criticism

Sample Reviews for Top-level Performers

PERFORMANCE REVIEW
Sales/Marketing

Name: Susan Glanzman   Type of Evaluation:

Job Title: Sales Representative   Interim   Annual X

Date: October 10, 20XX

Evaluation Guide

1 = Excellent (exceptional; exceeds expectations)

2 = Good (consistently meets, and frequently exceeds, usual expectations)

3 = Satisfactory (conforms to standards; meets expectations)

4 = Fair (marginal; meeting only minimum requirements)

5 = Poor (below standard and unacceptable; improvement required or termination will result)

Factors for Review

Sales   Rating: 1

Achieves quarterly and yearly sales quotas; improves growth of territory

Job Knowledge   Rating: 1

Degree to which the employee knows and understands his/her job and its functions

Work Quality/Organizational Skills   Rating: 1

Effective planning and organization, follow-up, etc.; effective use of time

Written and Oral Communication   Rating: 2

Ability to present information and ideas to others in an articulate and effective manner, as well as to listen effectively, comprehend, and respond to the ideas of others clearly and concisely

Judgment/Decision Making   Rating: 1

Ability to reason through problems, review alternative solutions, reach sound conclusions, and modify decisions when necessary

Interpersonal Skills   Rating: 1

Tact, courtesy, self-control, patience, loyalty, and discretion; ability to work harmoniously with others

Adaptability   Rating: 1

Ability to learn new skills, concepts, and processes; resourcefulness; flexibility in thinking

Persuasiveness   Rating: 1
Ability to negotiate, argue persuasively, use influence on others to achieve goals

Initiative   Rating: 1
Ability to act independently without specific instructions

Customer Responsiveness   Rating: 2
Timely response to customer questions, concerns, and problems

Stability Under Pressure   Rating: 1
Mental and emotional balance under stress due to pressure of work

Dependability   Rating: 2
Attendance at meetings, timeliness in meeting appointments, conscientiousness

Fiscal Management   Rating: 2
Ability to work within specified budget

OVERALL RATING: 1

EVALUATOR'S COMMENTS

Summarize your overall evaluation of the employee's performance, noting any strengths and weaknesses. Provide goals and plan for further development and current estimate of the employee's capacity and ambition for future growth.

Sue has been an exceptional sales representative from the beginning of her association with our company. She consistently achieves high standards, often setting her own quotas above those established for her by management. She has a full understanding of our product line and is able to answer all questions authoritatively, as well as to emphasize the strongest selling points. She researches her customers with care and is able to tailor sales presentations according to an individual client's specific needs and desires. She works both ends of her job—sales and customer service—with terrific efficiency and attention to details. She is well organized, manages her busy calendar with little to no difficulty, and keeps the main office well informed of her schedule and whereabouts at all times. Her only real drawback in this area is that she sometimes schedules appointments too close together, which causes her to arrive late at a customer's office on occasion. She is attempting now to allow more time on her calendar for getting from one appointment to another.

Sue does a very able job of prospecting for new customers and always has potential new clients in the pipeline, while maintaining and servicing her

213

current customer list. She closes on most new sales within three months, an excellent record for our market and product line. Her skills in persuasion, communication, and initiative are evident in her sales record, which consistently exceeds her quarterly quota by anywhere from 5 to 20 percent. Her attention to the sales end of her work sometimes prevents her from returning customer service-related calls quickly, although when she does, she follows through on problems and does everything in her power to reassure the customer that she is working in his or her best interests.

Her travel expenses sometimes exceed her budget, and she has occasionally overspent on sending out promotional materials, but otherwise she manages to keep control of her financial responsibilities. Finally, while she communicates well verbally, she has weak writing skills and has sometimes sent out letters to customers that have not been proofed carefully for grammar or spelling, or are vague and unresponsive. She needs to take more care with her correspondence and ensure that her words and ideas are as clear on paper as they are when she is speaking. I have suggested that she write her letters exactly as if she were talking to somebody, forgetting any formalities, then go back over them for grammar, spelling, and punctuation. My secretary has indicated a willingness to help Sue with her correspondence, particularly when a large account is in the balance.

OTHER ACTION TO BE TAKEN

Sue will be taking over Ron Trotter's territory as of October 15. This move will probably help her manage her schedule better, as it keeps the range of her new territory closer to her home base. Sue will have her work cut out for her, as performance in Ron's territory has slipped dramatically in the last year, but I fully expect she will be up to the challenge and will soon bring sales back to an excellent level.

EMPLOYEE'S COMMENTS

Employee's signature: _____ Date: _____

Evaluator's signature: _____ Date: _____

INTERIM PERFORMANCE EVALUATION

Sales: Telemarketing
Performance evaluation for: Mario Villanucci
Date: July 1, 20XX

JOB FACTORS:

1. Job Knowledge   (weak) 1 2 3 4 <u>5</u> (superior)
   Comments:

   Your overall understanding of our cable service and that of our competitors is superb. You are always well prepared to provide in-depth information about channels and programming as well as the different options a potential customer has to choose from. You keep yourself updated on all changes and advances and thus are always prepared for each prospecting call you make. Good work!

2. Productivity   (weak) 1 2 3 4 <u>5</u> (superior)
   Comments:

   You have succeeded in besting your previous record for total number of calls made in one day. Your desire to excel presents a good example to the rest of the staff.

3. Sales Achievements   (weak) 1 2 3 4 <u>5</u> (superior)
   Comments:

   New cable subscriptions have gone up by 30 percent in the last six months, due in great part to your efforts. In addition, your thorough follow-up calls to new customers to ensure their satisfaction with their cable service have reinforced our reputation as "the cable company that cares."

4. Initiative/Decision Making   (weak) 1 2 3 <u>4</u> 5 (superior)
   Comments:

   You have come up with some excellent ideas for tele-promotion and have also shown enormous enterprise in your pursuit of customer satisfaction.

5. Organizational Skills   (weak) 1 2 3 <u>4</u> 5 (superior)
   Comments:

   You keep your work area in good order and file reports quickly and efficiently.

6. Communication Skills   (weak) 1 2 3 4 <u>5</u> (superior)
   Comments:

   This is your strongest suit. Your telephone manner is pleasant and sincere, and you have an excellent ability to "hook" most potential customers within the first two minutes of the call. You also have an excellent ability to determine when a customer doesn't want to talk and it is better to discontinue the call. You never stray too far from the prepared script, but you are able to establish an unscripted rapport that helps to cement the sale. This is a remarkable talent.

7. Persuasiveness   (weak) 1 2 3 4 <u>5</u> (superior)
   Comments:

   See #6. Clearly you are a very persuasive individual.

8. Courtesy   (weak) 1 2 3 4 <u>5</u> (superior)
   Comments:

   Your courteous telephone manner has received high and well-deserved praise.

9. Adaptability   (weak) 1 2 3 4 <u>5</u> (superior)
   Comments:

   None.

10. Professionalism   (weak) 1 2 3 4 <u>5</u> (superior)
    Comments:

    There is no question of your highly professional attitude, both with customers and with your office coworkers.

OVERALL RATING:

___ Needs improvement in job performance
___ Meets job requirements
_X_ Exceeds job requirements

1. Work over the past three months:

   Your work has obviously been highly impressive, and I can't praise you enough. Of all the telemarketing reps I've trained over the years, nobody has learned his or her job quite so quickly as you have, nor understood the importance of telephone manners quite so well as you instinctively do. You have demonstrated patience, tact, discretion, and the utmost courtesy in your cold calls. This is especially important when dealing with customers who resent being called. Your ability to control the call has frequently enabled you to sway a once disinterested customer into at least considering your proposal and then into agreeing to the 30-day trial. Your subsequent follow-up calls to measure customer satisfaction and answer questions have been highly successful, resulting in the decision to remain with our service 95 percent of the time. Bravo!

2. Goals for the coming three months:

Continue as you have been doing. In addition, I would like to utilize your experience instincts in the training of new telemarketing representatives. Therefore one day of each week will be set aside for this purpose. I am also putting you on track for eventual promotion to the sales management staff.

3. Additional comments:

You have proven to be a valuable asset to the company. Keep up the good work!

EMPLOYEE COMMENTS

Employee's signature: _____ Date: _____

Evaluator's signature: _____ Date: _____

PERFORMANCE EVALUATION
Salesperson

Employee's Name: Candy Sutton   Review Period: From 8/XX to 8/XX
Job Title: Sales Assistant (Cosmetics)   Interim   Annual X
Name and Title of Evaluator: Bette Niven, Floor Manager

Performance Guide:

A — Consistently exceeds job requirements
   Performance is exceptional, above and beyond what is expected
B — Meets job requirements
   Does a good job; meets and sometimes exceeds requirements capably and compe-
   tently
C — Improvement needed
   Is not performing at satisfactory level; extra supervision is required
O — Other
   Not applicable to this area of evaluation

1. Job Knowledge   Grade: A
   Understands and can clearly explain the product or service; Effectively uses train-
   ing and experience to enhance job knowledge
   Comments:

   Although Candy had no sales experience prior to joining our store, her long-
   standing interest in cosmetics gave her a good foundation (pun not intend-
   ed) for learning the product and its advantages over competitors'. Her
   fashion sense and unerring eye for color, combined with a relaxed and
   friendly manner, has made her very popular with customers who come for
   advice and has helped to increase sales by 20 percent over the last six
   months.

2. Customer Service   Grade: A
   Is attentive to customers and handles all questions and complaints quickly and
   courteously; does not keep customers waiting
   Comments:

   Candy treats customers as she herself would want to be treated. She is
   unfailingly patient and ensures that no customer is kept waiting for too
   long. Her popularity has created a base of repeat customers, and word-of-
   mouth has brought in numerous new customers. There has never been a
   single complaint lodged against her.

3. Work Habits   Grade: A

   Is neat and well organized; can handle multiple tasks easily and efficiently

   Comments:

   Candy frequently finds herself dealing with two or three customers at a time. Different needs and different demands can create a stressful situation. Candy handles it with equanimity, and if unable to get assistance, can convince certain customers to return when it is less busy. She is meticulous with paperwork and is always on top of her sales receipts.

4. Initiative and Resourcefulness   Grade: A

   Demonstrates ability to work without direction and offers new ideas and solutions

   Comments:

   Candy took over the decorations and theme displays of the cosmetics counter six months ago and has demonstrated striking imagination and verve since then. Her eye-catching displays have played a key role in the attraction of new customers.

5. Decision Making   Grade: N/A

   Evaluates situations, draws conclusions, and makes sound decisions

   Comments:

   Candy is not currently in a position to make decisions.

6. Adaptability and Flexibility   Grade: A

   Is willing to work extra hours or in other departments when needed; works well under stressful conditions; can accommodate customer needs

   Comments:

   Candy is always accommodating and does her best wherever she works.

7. Accountability   Grade: N/A

   Is willing to accept responsibility for job-related decisions and actions

   Comments:

8. Interpersonal Skills   Grade: A

   Interacts well with others; demonstrates courtesy, patience, diplomacy, discretion, and self-control; communicates clearly and effectively

   Comments:

   Candy's abilities in this area should be self-evident from comments in other areas. She is clearly enthusiastic about her work, and she conveys her enthusiasm to her coworkers. There is a great esprit de corps in and around the cosmetics counter thanks to Candy.

9. Personal Appearance   Grade: A

   Presents a neat and attractive appearance in clothing, hair, makeup, etc.

   Comments:

   Candy practices what she preaches to customers.

10. Sales Quotas   Grade: A

    Meets or exceeds sales goals for product/service

    Comments:

    As already mentioned, sales at the cosmetics counter have increased 20 percent over the last six months. I believe a large part of that, if not the largest part, is due to Candy's winning personality and innovative ideas as well as a thorough knowledge of her product.

SUMMARY

Summarize employee's performance level since last review; indicate any improvement or decline.

This is Candy's first annual review, and it should be evident from my comments that I think very highly of her. She has poise, confidence, and intelligence, and she has created a booming business at the cosmetics counter. It is my belief that she would do well in whatever department she is placed; she is truly management material. I recommend a 10 percent pay increase for Candy, who should be placed into a management training program as soon as possible—for the store's benefit, as well as hers.

GOALS/OBJECTIVES FOR THE NEXT 12 MONTHS

Indicate whatever goals or criteria the employee must meet for the next review period.

Increase participation in other departments to gain an overall knowledge of the store and its products. Begin management training upon approval.

EMPLOYEE'S COMMENTS

Employee's signature: _____ Date: _____

Evaluator's signature: _____ Date: _____

PERFORMANCE EVALUATION
Sales/Marketing

Name: Curt Mandelbaum   Title: Subscription-Sales Representative
Date: 4/19/XX

Sales Achievements

Curt has done an outstanding job of boosting magazine subscriptions and more than doubling his sales quota over the past year. He has more than met all the goals set for him and has achieved record sales for every magazine we represent. He has the best success rate in cold calls over all other sales reps in the department. He has built an extensive client list, and his follow-up is top-notch, resulting in the highest rate of subscription renewals.

Job Knowledge

Curt is a master of product knowledge. He knows the contents and selling points of every magazine we represent and how to tailor those selling points to the individual needs of the clients he contacts. He has built up a useful database of facts and figures concerning the various journals that is often tapped by other sales reps in the department. His understanding of the different markets we sell to and their clients helps him to evaluate and create individualized sales pitches. He has a storehouse of information in his head at all times and is quite remarkable in his ability to draw out what he needs to close a sale.

Work Quality/Productivity

As is evidenced by his sales achievements, Curt's productivity rate is superb. He tackles everything he does with an eye to excellence, and the overall quality of his work is top-notch.

Organizational Skills/Time Management

Curt is highly organized, keeps his files in order and his desk neat and clean, and manages to juggle all aspects of his schedule effectively. He spends a great deal of his time on the telephone making cold calls and follow-up calls, but also manages to stay on top of his paperwork and e-mail. He keeps a cool, collected head on his shoulders, even when working under great stress and pressure.

Decision Making/Problem Solving

The nature of Curt's work does not make this a large factor in his evaluation. However, he has sound judgment and the ability to make reasonable, rational decision at all times.

Interpersonal/Communication Skills

Curt has superb interpersonal skills. He is usually able to grab a potential customer's attention within the first 30 seconds of the person's picking up the telephone. He can clearly articulate the pertinent details of the magazine he is selling and has a knack for closing a sale within anywhere from five to ten minutes of first introducing himself. He is well spoken, polite, and very attentive to what the customer might want or need. He is keenly attuned to a customer's tone of voice and knows how he is being received and whether or not it is worth his while to continue. He rarely errs in his judgment of sales potential, and his superb interactive skills service him well.

Persuasiveness/Salesmanship

Curt's salesmanship skills are remarkably good and effective. See above comments.

Initiative/Dependability

Curt is extraordinarily dedicated to his job, and highly dependable. He took it upon himself to create the informational database we are now using, in addition to providing a list of sales tips to other reps who have struggled a bit more with the difficulties of selling by telephone. He has frequently altered his sales script to suit the situation. When faced with a problem, he is quick to work out a solution on his own and is never fazed by obstacles.

Summary and Goals for Next Review

Curt continues to excel and has also proven himself to be a leader among his fellow sales reps, providing advice and encouragement, as well as effective tips for selling. His strong abilities as well as his communication skills have combined to make him the rep on whom I depend the most. He is being promoted to assistant manager of the department and will be put in charge of training programs for all new sales representatives, as well as of the development of new sales programs, which will increase our customer base and provide greater opportunities to expand.

Employee's Comments

Employee's signature: _____ Date: _____

Evaluator's signature: _____ Date: _____

PERFORMANCE EVALUATION

Name: Suzanne Winston   Title: Sales Assistant

Date: January 28, 20XX

Ratings: Employee is to be rated on a scale of 1 to 3, as described below.

   1: Below expectations: Performance is substandard and requires improvement.

   2: Meets expectations: Performance fully meets and occasionally exceeds standards.

   3: Exceeds expectations: Performance consistently exceeds set standards.

N/A: Not applicable. Lack of sufficient knowledge to evaluate the performance factor.

Section I: Basic Job Skills

	Below	Meets	Exceeds	N/A
Job knowledge	1	2	3	N/A
Quality of work	1	2	3	N/A
Customer service	1	2	3	N/A
Dependability	1	2	3	N/A
Work habits	1	2	3	N/A
Resourcefulness	1	2	3	N/A
Problem solving	1	2	3	N/A
Care of register, counters	1	2	3	N/A

Comments:

Suzanne is tailor-made for sales work. Whatever department she is assigned to, she becomes familiar with the product quickly and can talk about it like the expert she has become. This is a remarkable ability; whether it's refrigerators, televisions, men's clothing, or children's toys, she manages to memorize the salient features and answer customer questions easily and satisfactorily. She is rarely stymied, and when she comes up against a question she can't answer (which is rare), she is quick to find the answer elsewhere without keeping the customer waiting too long.

Section II: Personal Attributes

	Below	Meets	Exceeds	N/A
Attendance/Punctuality	1	2	3	N/A
Ability to take direction	1	2	3	N/A
Initiative	1	2	3	N/A
Cooperativeness	1	2	3	N/A
Adaptability	1	2	3	N/A
Communication skills	1	2	3	N/A
Interaction with coworkers	1	2	3	N/A
Courtesy/Hospitality	1	2	3	N/A

Comments:

Suzanne always has a smile on her face, even with the most trying of customers. She explains products and services so well that there is rarely a question once she is through with a customer. She is extremely reliable, never takes an unscheduled day off, and, as indicated above, she is remarkably adaptable. For these reasons, she has become our "fail-safe mechanism." She fills in for absent or tardy employees and acts as a resource or backup when some departments become busier than usual. She frequently offers useful and informed suggestions for improving department displays and customer service. She has earned the respect of her fellow sales assistants and has no problems supervising others when asked to.

Section III: Strengths, Weaknesses, Goals

Describe employee strengths:

Suzanne's strengths are made clear by the comments above. She is an exceptional employee whose talents should be utilized to the fullest.

Describe areas for improvement:

None at this time.

Describe goals for next performance review and means by which goals will be achieved:

She has agreed to enter a management-training program with the goal of becoming a Sales Manager and obtaining official responsibilities and salary commensurate with her talent and abilities.

Section IV: Additional Comments

Evaluator:

It should be clear that I think highly of Suzanne. I am recommending a 5 percent salary increase at this time, with an additional 5 percent increase to be implemented upon her promotion to Sales Manager.

Employee:

Employee's signature: _____ Date: _____

Evaluator's signature: _____ Date: _____

PERFORMANCE REVIEW

Name: Bruce Dangerfield
Job Title: Promotions Supervisor
Date: July 12, 20xx

Type of Evaluation:
Interim   Annual   X

Evaluation Guide

1 = Excellent (exceptional; exceeds expectations)
2 = Good (consistently meets, and frequently exceeds, usual expectations)
3 = Satisfactory (conforms to standards; meets expectations)
4 = Fair (marginal; meeting only minimum requirements)
5 = Poor (below standard and unacceptable; improvement required or termination will result)

Factors for Review	*Rating*
Job Knowledge	1
Work Quantity	1
Work Quality	1
Creativity/Resourcefulness	2
Communication Skills	2
Judgment/Decision Making	2
Interpersonal Skills/Teamwork	1
Organizational Skills	1
Adaptability	1
Initiative	2
Analytic Skills	2
Resilience/Stability Under Pressure	1
Dependability	1
Supervisory Skills	2

Overall Rating: 1

COMMENTS/GOALS:

Bruce has been a superb supervisor of promotions since taking over the position nine months ago. Prior to that, he had worked as a marketing coordi-

227

nator and had already proven his talent for promotions in that capacity. Over the course of his working life, he has acquired extensive knowledge of various types of promotions, the markets they are geared toward, and how they can be made to fit particular products. He uses this knowledge, along with his extensive knowledge of our product line, to come up with suitable and successful promotions that are cost-effective and sales effective. His responsibilities encompass both low-budget advertising campaigns and in-store promotions, and he does an excellent job in both areas. He was especially brilliant in the campaign he devised for the AutoWidget Thingie-Do, which was colorful and eye-catching and boosted sales in every store where a display was set up.

Bruce's organizational skills are superb. He manages a staff of 20 people and has numerous projects he is working on at one time, yet keeps his schedule in order and is able to relate the status of each project in an instant. He works well under pressure and has yet to miss a deadline.

He is still getting accustomed to the job and has a few areas in which some improvement might be made. While he can be very creative in terms of design, he often repeats certain ideas in his promotions a little too often and does not act on new ideas as quickly as he should—that is to say, he sometimes rejects fresh ideas in favor of the "tried and true" and doesn't seem willing to take any risks. I believe that because he is so new to his position and has not been a supervisor for too long, he may feel threatened by certain people who may be more qualified in some areas than he is, as well as perhaps who are more creative. He should not allow this to concern him, but rather should take advantage of the skills and opportunities that his staff may have to offer him, to better utilize their resources and their ideas and give them the appropriate recognition. By making them feel more a part of the creative process rather than just using them to carry out his ideas, he will undoubtedly go even further in his success and create more ways of promoting our products and boosting our sales. This is true not just in terms of the design and execution of a promotion, but in all the analyses and decision making that takes place before a promotion gets off the ground.

Bruce should therefore concentrate on his supervisory abilities and make better use of the resources both inside and outside his department in order to improve the overall teamwork that goes into making a successful promotion. His leadership is crucial to our success, and I feel certain that he will earn even higher marks at his next performance evaluation.

EMPLOYEE'S COMMENTS

Employee's signature: _____ Date: _____

Evaluator's signature: _____ Date: _____

PERFORMANCE EVALUATION: SALES

Name: Paul Adkins   Title: Automobile Salesperson

Date: 6/24/xx

Sales Achievements

Paul has set new records for sales in each of the last three quarters. Since starting with XYZ Automotive three years ago, he has more than tripled his quotas and recently was named Salesperson of the Year by the Tri-County Association of Cars and Trucks. Profits are high, and that is due in large part to Paul's superb abilities as a salesman. He has been especially successful in his sales of minivans and sports-utility vehicles.

Job Knowledge

Paul's understanding of the market and his knowledge of every vehicle we sell stands alone. He rarely needs to look up details, but is able to produce facts and figures as needed off the top of his head. He has excellent negotiation skills and interpersonal abilities that allow him to hone in on what a potential customer needs and how we can best suit those needs, both in terms of the vehicle itself and the appropriate financial arrangements. When he doesn't know the answer to a question (which is rare), he knows where to go to get the answer. His resourcefulness and all-around capabilities are enormous.

Work Quality/Productivity

His sales achievements provide the best evidence of the quality of Paul's work and his productivity. He works quickly and efficiently, with the best interests of both the company and the customer firmly in mind, and this attention to both sides of his sales transactions have played a large role in his extraordinary productivity.

Communication Skills

His communication skills are excellent, being both pleasant and articulate. He has a strong ability to interpret what a customer is looking for, then to

230

make a sales presentation that explains the advantages of the vehicle he is selling clearly and concisely, and emphasizing those points that are of the biggest concern to the customer. This skill is extremely advantageous.

Judgment/Decision Making

He is strong on all counts, well able to determine what a customer wants and what we have to sell that would best suit the situation. He always makes sound decisions regarding financial arrangements.

Interpersonal and Communication Skills (Persuasiveness)

This is probably the key to Paul's success. He almost always strikes a responsive chord with potential customers, who are taken with his ability to communicate and persuade, as well as with the clear feeling of honesty and trustworthiness that he conveys. He has the ability to show the utmost in and concern for his customers as well as a patience and lack of pushiness that makes a good impression on those who consider all salespeople to be overly pushy. All in all, his good appearance, professional demeanor, and empathy with his customers have empowered Paul with strong people skills that have enhanced his ability to close a sale.

Initiative/Dependability

He can and does work independently, with no supervision or need for supervision. He is highly dependable—rarely out sick and willing to come in and work on days when other reps are unexpectedly absent. He exceeds all criteria for initiative.

Customer Responsiveness

As is evident from other comments, Paul is attentive to customer concerns and provides superb service in every respect.

Summary and Goals for Next Review

Our faith in Paul and his abilities is boundless. His skills are outstanding in every respect, and he continues to outperform himself with every sales

231

quarter. I believe he will do well in a managerial capacity, and to that end he will shortly enter a management-training program, concurrent with his salesman duties. He is an extraordinary individual who already acts as a leader among the staff, and he will be able to tackle any future responsibilities with the same ease and capability with which he is now handling his current workload.

Employee's Comments

Employee's signature: _____ Date: _____

Evaluator's signature: _____ Date: _____

Sample Reviews for Mid-level Performers

PERFORMANCE EVALUATION
Sales Representative/Manager

Employee's Name: Joseph Valentine   Review Period: From 9/XX to 3/XX

Job Title: Salesperson: Territory 1   Interim   X   Annual

Name and Title of Evaluator: Alan Jones, Sales Manager

Performance Guide

A — Consistently exceeds job requirements

    Performance is exceptional, above and beyond what is expected

B — Meets job requirements

    Does a good job; meets and sometimes exceeds requirements capably and competently

C — Improvement needed

    Is not performing at satisfactory level; extra supervision is required

O — Other

    Not applicable to this area of evaluation

1. Achievement of Sales Quotas   Grade: B

   Meets or exceeds quotas set for territory on a quarterly basis; achieves sales quotas efficiently and in accordance with company standards

   Comments:

   Standard performance. See #2.

2. Territory Growth   Grade: C

   Successfully recruits new customers and increases sales volume

   Comments:

   Since taking over Territory 1 in September, you have adequately maintained the customer base. However, you have not demonstrated sufficient initiative to seek out new customers and expand your base.

3. Job Knowledge   Grade: B

   Understands and effectively utilizes job-related information, procedures, and skills

   Comments:

   Although I know you study the materials that are sent to you and stay on top of all product upgrades, we are not getting any feedback from you as

233

to your customers' questions and concerns. As you know, customer feedback is crucial to product development and is part of honing your own job skills.

4. Timeliness   Grade: C
   Completes sales visits and follow-up calls within a reasonable or better time frame; files sales reports on a timely basis
   Comments:

   It is evident that improvement is needed in this area. Your tardiness in following up on sales calls nearly resulted in the loss of orders from two major customers. The company cannot afford this, and neither can you. In addition, continued delays in filing your sales reports cannot be permitted.

5. Work Habits   Grade: C
   Plans and organizes schedule well, follows procedures, and makes efficient use of time between road and office
   Comments:

   This is an area where your challenges must be met promptly and decisively. Your difficulty in managing your schedule directly affects your ability to fulfill all the requirements of your job. I recommend talking to some of the other sales reps about how they manage their time, then coming back to me with your planned schedule for the next month so that I can make suggestions on how to better organize your schedule. Although you are past the training stage, I will also be accompanying you on two or three upcoming sales calls.

6. Initiative and Resourcefulness   Grade: C
   Demonstrates ability to work without direction and offer new ideas for making sales quotas
   Comments:

   The direction and training you received when you were first hired should have prepared you for what you were about to face on the road. Your experiences in the last three months should have given you a base for identifying areas that were problematic or had potential for increased profitability. You need to analyze your customers and listen to what they're telling you in order to determine what they really need and what you need to know to service them better. Do not rely solely on instructions from management for innovative ways to attract and keep customers.

7. Decision Making   Grade: C
   Evaluates situations, draws conclusions, and makes sound decisions

Comments:

See #6. The same principle applies.

8. Adaptability and Flexibility   Grade: B

   Is able to adjust to market changes, customer demands, additional accounts, etc.

   Comments:

   You are doing an adequate job in this area, but could use some improvement.

9. Accountability   Grade: B

   Is willing to accept responsibility for job-related decisions and actions

   Comments:

   It is clear you want to learn, and you are quick to admit when you have been in error or have "screwed up." Now try to learn from your mistakes.

10. Customer Responsiveness   Grade: B

    Is able to answer all client questions and work with Customer Service to handle all concerns, complaints, and problems

    Comments:

    You have been generally good in responding to established customers concerning problem orders or questions regarding product upgrades. You need to demonstrate that same responsiveness with potential new customers. You also need to improve your call-back time. Customer calls should be returned within two hours or less of receipt of their message.

11. Interpersonal Skills   Grade: B

    Interacts well with others; demonstrates courtesy, patience, diplomacy, discretion, and self-control; communicates with both customers and home base clearly and effectively

    Comments:

    You have a good attitude, and people like you. Obviously this can and should be used to your advantage. Your "people skills" are your strongest asset.

12. Professional Growth   Grade: C

    Works to develop new skills and takes advantage of opportunities for training and development to improve sales/customer service skills

    Comments:

    Don't wait for required seminars or training sessions to improve yourself. Your willingness to ask questions, seek help from other sales reps or from me,

235

and sign up for additional workshops in sales techniques will help you to raise your score at your next evaluation.

SUMMARY

You began this job six months ago with a very enthusiastic attitude. That has dampened somewhat as the realities of the job have hit you, but you shouldn't allow it to discourage you altogether. Despite any doubts you may have, you do have the ability to become a good sales representative. It will simply take a lot of hard work and determination to apply yourself to both your personal and your sales goals. However, be forewarned that if significant improvement is not seen within the next three months, we will have to reevaluate your suitability as a sales rep.

GOALS/OBJECTIVES FOR THE NEXT 12 MONTHS

- Devise and maintain a time-management schedule that maximizes effective contact with both current and potential customers. Review it with me.
- Demonstrate improvement in response time to customer calls as well as follow-up of initial new sales calls.
- Seek out additional training opportunities for improving job skills.
- Five-percent growth in Territory 1 sales by July 1.

EMPLOYEE'S COMMENTS

Employee's signature: _____ Date: _____

Evaluator's signature: _____ Date: _____

PERFORMANCE EVALUATION
Sales: Telemarketing

Name: Bette Washington   Date: March 1, 20XX

JOB FACTORS:

1. Job Knowledge   (weak) 1 2 3 <u>4</u> 5 (superior)
   Comments:

   Bette has demonstrated a good grasp of the company's basic and premium cable services as well as the cable market at large, in order to do an effective job as a telemarketer. She keeps all necessary reference materials close at hand and stays up to date on changes and upgrades in pricing and different levels of service. She is generally able to answer all questions put to her and to present our company's offerings clearly and effectively.

2. Productivity   (weak) 1 2 <u>3</u> 4 5 (superior)
   Comments:

   Bette meets the criteria for productivity, although I believe she is capable of doing better. She sells on average 10 new cable subscriptions per week.

3. Sales Achievements   (weak) 1 2 <u>3</u> 4 5 (superior)
   Comments:

   She does good, steady work and meets the quotas that have been established for her. As a result, we will be upping her quotas (see Goals, below).

4. Initiative/Decision Making   (weak) 1 2 <u>3</u> 4 5 (superior)
   Comments:

   Once again, she maintains a steady performance. She does not quite excel, in that she doesn't apply herself to doing anything outside of her established script for making calls. I would like to see her take more of a risk by departing from the script when the situation seems to call for it, and attempting to sell a customer on a subscription using more innovative and original methods.

5. Organizational Skills   (weak) 1 2 3 <u>4</u> 5 (superior)
   Comments:

   She keeps her work area in good order and files reports on time.

6. Communication Skills   (weak) 1 2 <u>3</u> 4 5 (superior)
   Comments:

237

She has a clear, pleasant voice and a good telephone manner. My one observation has been that she tends to read her script too much like a script. I have been encouraging her to memorize and even change the wording occasionally in an effort to make herself sound more conversational. Customers tend to respond better to people who talk to them as people, and not as an audience for some lines written on a piece of paper.

7. Persuasiveness   (weak) 1 2 <u>3</u> 4 5 (superior)
   Comments:

   Bette employs the skills she has learned to make an effective presentation, although it may be too much by rote. Once again, I feel she should inject more of her own personality into her sales pitch in order to make it more personal to the prospective customer.

8. Courtesy   (weak) 1 2 <u>3</u> 4 5 (superior)
   Comments:

   She meets the standards for courtesy and respect.

9. Adaptability   (weak) 1 2 <u>3</u> 4 5 (superior)
   Comments:

   Bette has little problem adapting to change, and in fact seems to welcome it as relief from the same old routine.

10. Professionalism   (weak) 1 2 3 <u>4</u> 5 (superior)
    Comments:

    All criteria are met. Bette maintains a good professional manner, both on the telephone and off. She gets along well with other telemarketers and responds well to direction and to criticism. She has a good, strong work ethic.

OVERALL RATING:

___ Needs improvement in job performance

_X_ Meets job requirements

___ Exceeds job requirements

EMPLOYEE'S COMMENTS:

Employee's signature: _____ Date: _____

Evaluator's signature: _____ Date: _____

INTERIM REVIEW: COMMENTS

Employee name: Fred Beradinis   Date: February 29, 20XX
Job Title: Promotions Supervisor

Overall appraisal for the last six months:

On the whole, you've been doing a consistently excellent job. You've come up with some original ideas for promotions and implemented them in a cost-effective manner. I especially liked the creative graphics you produced for the displays promoting our new line of artist's color markers. You have worked out an efficient schedule for planning and executing new promotions in conjunction with the marketing staff and for changing displays in the various stores every few weeks. You've also managed your staff efficiently and have worked well with store managers in keeping them informed about and involved in upcoming promotions. My only real complaint is that you should do a better job of keeping me informed. I'm still not seeing your weekly reports in a timely manner, nor am I made aware of what you may be working on at any given time or when your schedule has changed. I frequently stop by your office to talk to you, only to discover that you are out in the field and have not left word on where you can be reached. While I admire your initiative, I do not appreciate it when Mr. Baron knows of one of your ideas before I do, since you should be clearing all ideas with me first. I also do not want to hear of meetings that have been scheduled without consulting my calendar first. I must not only be in the loop, I should be first on your list to be informed about any new promotion and where it is in the planning stages, as well as any and all meetings regarding your projects.

Strengths and weaknesses demonstrated during the last six months:

Your major strengths are your creativity and your initiative. As you have gained confidence in yourself, you have been bolder about implementing your ideas. However, this may prove to be a weakness if you continue to leap before you look. Your ideas and successful management of your staff are getting you noticed. Don't blow it by becoming overconfident, which can sometimes lead to a superior attitude that can and will offend others. It should be clear by this and other comments that I have not been pleased by your failure to keep me informed. I am, however, very pleased that you are clearly one of the company's rising stars and am interested in seeing that you attain the professional goals you have set for yourself.

Skills, abilities, or tools needed to improve or enhance job performance:

A more diplomatic and politically conscious approach to the reporting structure within the company is your first start. I want a weekly progress report and your schedule on my desk by noontime every Monday, or a reasonable explanation of its delay. You are not to schedule any meetings without first checking with my secretary to determine that I can make it; and I want a full report on all meetings that I am unable to attend.

Barriers to job satisfaction:

You can be held back by your own impression that others are holding you back. This is certainly not the case. You are in charge of your own destiny, and your talent will really take you places. You know this already; the danger is in blaming others when something has not gone the way you wanted it to, as well as in being a little too smug about your abilities.

Goals and objectives for the next six months:

You have ten major promotions coming up in the next six months. I am certain you will plan and execute them with your usual attention to detail and excellence.

Additional comments:

I know you have come away from our recent conversations with the feeling that I am trying to keep you from advancement. I have tried to assure you that in fact I am proud of what you have accomplished and the successful direction in which you are headed. I am merely trying to restrain you from what I feel is a "bull-in-a-china-shop" attitude on your part. I will help you if you allow me to help, and I will be fully supportive of you when an opportunity arises for your promotion. I am simply asking that you demonstrate some respect for my position as your supervisor and keep me informed at all times.

Employee's comments:

Employee's signature: _____ Date: _____

Evaluator's signature: _____ Date: _____

PERFORMANCE REVIEW

Name: Alice Tsakonis_

Job Title: Salesperson

Date: November 15, 20XX

Type of Evaluation:

Interim   Annual   X

Evaluation Guide

1 = Excellent (exceptional; exceeds expectations)

2 = Good (consistently meets, and frequently exceeds, usual expectations)

3 = Satisfactory (conforms to standards; meets expectations)

4 = Fair (marginal; meeting only minimum requirements)

5 = Poor (below standard and unacceptable; improvement required or termination will result)

Factors for Review	Rating
Sales	3
Job Knowledge	2
Work Quality	3
Communication Skills	2
Judgment/Decision Making	3
Interpersonal Skills	3
Adaptability	3
Persuasiveness	3
Initiative	3
Customer Responsiveness	2
Stability Under Pressure	3
Dependability	3

OVERALL RATING: 3

COMMENTS/GOALS:

Alice has been a steady, reliable salesperson for True Blue Automotive Sales. Although she has not had any outstanding quarters in sales, she has consistently met the goals that have been established for her. She has a very pleasant but assertive personality that conveys a good impression of someone who is honest and knowledgeable. She has had her work cut out for her because of her gender and the erroneous impression many people have that a woman cannot possibly know so much about cars as a man. In fact, she has had to deal with customers who deliberately snub her in favor of talking to a male representative. However, Alice is a level-headed individual who does not allow such behavior to bother her. The fact that she has still managed to meet her sales quotas is evidence of her ability to overcome such prejudice, and in fact many customers are impressed with her knowledge of cars.

Alice's greatest skill is her ability to effectively communicate with customers, determine what they're looking for, and steer them to the car that best meets their needs. She does this in a friendly, unassuming manner that puts most customers at ease. Sometimes, however, her quiet manner can work to her detriment, particularly when she is talking to a man who wants to impress her with his own superior knowledge and does so in an aggressive manner that runs contrary to her own style. She has learned to handle this type of problem by steering the customer to another male rep. Nevertheless, I would like to see Alice become more assertive herself and learn some better techniques for handling the "rougher" element of customer. This is not to disparage her style, which clearly works; but she is in a business in which assertiveness is an asset, therefore she should be working on this area.

Overall, Alice has done well, and I firmly believe she can and will do better. As a challenge, her sales quota has been increased by 10 percent for each of the next two quarters.

EMPLOYEE'S COMMENTS

Employee's signature: _____   Date: _____

Evaluator's signature: _____   Date: _____

PERFORMANCE EVALUATION
Salesperson

Employee's Name: Carlie Popjoy   Review Period: From 6/xx to 5/xx

Job Title: Sales Assistant (Bridal Registry)   Interim   Annual x

Name and Title of Evaluator: Rupert Smith, Department Manager

Performance Guide

A — Consistently exceeds job requirements

Performance is exceptional, above and beyond what is expected

B — Meets job requirements

Does a good job; meets and sometimes exceeds requirements capably and competently

C — Improvement needed

Is not performing at satisfactory level; extra supervision is required

N/A — Other

Not applicable to this area of evaluation

1. Job Knowledge   Grade: B

Understands and can clearly explain the product or service; effectively uses training and experience to enhance job knowledge

Comments:

Carlie has a good understanding of the products and services offered through the bridal registry. She is able to answer almost all questions regarding the different makes and styles of china, crystal, and table settings, plus patterns, etc. When she doesn't immediately know the answer, she is able to use computer resources to look it up.

2. Customer Service   Grade: A

Is attentive to customers and handles all questions and complaints quickly and courteously; does not keep customers waiting

Comments:

Carlie has strong people skills and is well suited to this sort of sales work, in that she loves to help in the planning of weddings and in finding the right pattern and other needs for a couple.

3. Work Habits   Grade: B

Is neat and well organized; can handle multiple tasks easily and efficiently

Comments:

She keeps the desk area clean and neat so that it is always presentable for customers when she sits with them. She sometimes gets a little flustered when there are numerous demands on her; she has a clear preference for doing one thing at a time, and doing it thoroughly before moving on to something else.

4. Initiative and Resourcefulness   Grade: B

Demonstrates ability to work without direction and offers new ideas and solutions

Comments:

She does reasonably well and rarely wobbles when forced to handle the registry alone for any period of time. She has displayed some resourcefulness, but generally prefers to work according to instructions and not to deviate from known methods of salesmanship.

5. Decision Making   Grade: B

Evaluates situations, draws conclusions, and makes sound decisions

Comments:

She is able to make simple decisions and to act according to previously learned experience and the dictates of the situation. She leaves major decisions to me and will not take the risk of making an error. Her caution is good, but not always necessary, especially if it might mean keeping a customer waiting for an answer on something.

6. Adaptability and Flexibility   Grade: B

Is willing to work extra hours or in other departments when needed; works well under stressful conditions; can accommodate customer needs

Comments:

Carlie meets the criteria for the most part, although she has been a bit resistant to working extra hours during the busiest wedding seasons and will do it only when asked. She has sometimes been asked to help out in other departments, and has done so, although it is clear that she would far rather stay in the bridal registry.

7. Accountability   Grade: B

Is willing to accept responsibility for job-related decisions and actions

Comments:

This is not a major factor in Carlie's evaluation, although it should be noted that she does take responsibility for any error in judgment she

244

might make or any mistake or offense to a customer (the latter being rare).

8. Interpersonal Skills   Grade: A

Interacts well with others; demonstrates courtesy, patience, diplomacy, discretion, and self-control; communicates clearly and effectively

Comments:

This is Carlie's strength. She is friendly and personable and is well liked by customers. She is interested in weddings and in the choices being made, and is encouraging and extremely helpful when assisting a couple to make their decisions. Many times she is dealing with nervous, uncertain people, and she has a knack for putting them at their ease and getting them to enjoy the selection process.

9. Punctuality/Dependability   Grade: B

Can be relied upon to be timely and to meet or exceed expectations

Comments:

Except for occasional mild grumbling when asked to help out elsewhere, Carlie is generally a dependable employee who makes the most of her work in the bridal registry. There have been occasional moments of tardiness, but nothing too serious.

10. Sales Quotas   Grade: B

Meets or exceeds sales goals for product/service

Comments:

Carlie has met and sometimes exceeded her quarterly quotas. Given her demonstrated strengths in selling, it is possible for her to do better. I believe she fails to exceed quotas more often because she is exceedingly respectful of customer feelings and does not wish to appear too pushy by suggesting more than they might want or need. Nevertheless, I feel she should take more initiative in pointing out other possibilities to customers in case she is able to light on something they hadn't thought about but would in fact be willing to consider.

SUMMARY

Summarize employee's performance level since last review; indicate any improvement or decline.

Carlie's previous review noted her tentativeness and lack of self-confidence in dealing with customers. She has improved immeasurably in this area, and I am delighted to see her doing so much better overall, especially in that she is meeting sales goals so well for the most part. She continues to be somewhat tentative when it comes to initiative and resourcefulness, and to expanding possible sales by making alternative suggestions (see #10). As she continues to grow in her job, I anticipate that she will become even more confident in her abilities and get past some of the personal issues that have been holding her back.

GOALS/OBJECTIVES FOR THE NEXT 12 MONTHS

Indicate whatever goals or criteria the employee must meet for the next review period.

Carlie is to work on improving her initiative and willingness to take more risks. I would like to see a 10-percent increase in sales generated by her over the next six months.

EMPLOYEE'S COMMENTS

Employee's signature: _____ Date: _____

Evaluator's signature: _____ Date: _____

PERFORMANCE REVIEW
Sales/Marketing

Name: Ronald Trotter

Job Title: Sales Representative

Date: October 5, 20XX

Type of Evaluation:

Interim   Annual   X

Evaluation Guide

1 = Excellent (exceptional; exceeds expectations)

2 = Good (consistently meets, and frequently exceeds, usual expectations)

3 = Satisfactory (conforms to standards; meets expectations)

4 = Fair (marginal; meeting only minimum requirements)

5 = Poor (below standard and unacceptable; improvement required or termination will result)

Factors for Review

Sales   Rating: 4

Achieves quarterly and yearly sales quotas; improves growth of territory

Job Knowledge   Rating: 2

Degree to which the employee knows and understands his/her job and its functions

Work Quality/Organizational Skills   Rating: 4

Effective planning and organization, follow-up, etc.; effective use of time

Written and Oral Communication   Rating: 3

Ability to present information and ideas to others in an articulate and effective manner, as well as to listen effectively, comprehend, and respond to the ideas of others clearly and concisely

Judgment/Decision Making   Rating: 3

Ability to reason through problems, review alternative solutions, reach sound conclusions, and modify decisions when necessary

Interpersonal Skills   Rating: 4

Tact, courtesy, self-control, patience, loyalty, and discretion; ability to work harmoniously with others

Adaptability   Rating: 5

> Ability to learn new skills, concepts, and processes; resourcefulness; flexibility in thinking

Persuasiveness   Rating: 4

> Ability to negotiate, argue persuasively, use influence on others to achieve goals

Initiative   Rating: 2

> Ability to act independently without specific instructions

Customer Responsiveness   Rating: 4

> Timely response to customer questions, concerns, and problems

Stability Under Pressure   Rating: 4

> Mental and emotional balance under stress due to pressure of work

Dependability   Rating: 3

> Attendance at meetings, timeliness in meeting appointments, conscientiousness

Fiscal Management   Rating: 4

> Ability to work within specified budget

OVERALL RATING: 3.5

EVALUATOR'S COMMENTS

Summarize your overall evaluation of the employee's performance, noting any strengths and weakness. Provide goals and plan for further development and current estimate of the employee's capacity and ambition for future growth.

Ron has long been one of our most faithful and reliable sales reps, having started with the company 12 years ago this month. Due to the depth of his knowledge and experience, we have depended on him to provide our strongest showing in the field and to be the rep who all other reps should emulate. He has consistently met and exceeded expectations throughout the years, both in territory sales growth and in support provided to the home office by way of customer feedback, leads for new product development, and interaction with the Customer Service Department.

It is therefore a disappointment that his performance has slipped so dramatically within the last 12 months. Sales in his territory have dropped by

15 percent, and relations with certain longtime customers have deteriorated, due primarily to his increasing failure to return calls or respond to complaints in a timely fashion. Furthermore, he has signed up no new accounts since March of this year—a first for Ron. He has also been tardy in filing sales reports and frequently allows weeks to go by before reporting in to the home office.

This behavior is highly unusual for Ron, and we recently had a number of meetings to discuss the problem and determine how corrective action could be taken. It turns out that Ron has suffered a number of personal setbacks that have directly affected his ability to concentrate on his job. He did not confide in me prior to this because he has been seeking counseling and making a serious attempt to overcome certain emotional difficulties that have been inhibiting his job performance. However, it is clear that he is not succeeding. In recent weeks he has been working to win back some key customers that we had lost, and in fact he is on the verge of re-signing the Dornback account. However, overall he has not been able to stay on top of all of his job responsibilities, and it seems clear that a change is in order, for the sake of both Ron and the company.

ACTION TO BE TAKEN

As of October 15, Sue Glanzman will be taking over Ron's territory. Ron has requested a three-month leave of absence (unpaid), during which time he plans to move and get his personal life more settled. When he returns to the company, he will work in the home office for at least another three months, primarily to assist the telemarketing staff and to assist me with the planned reorganization of territories, as well as the next five-year sales plan. A determination will then be made as to whether Ron should return to the field or take a full-time office job, instead.

EMPLOYEE'S COMMENTS

Employee's signature: _____ Date: _____

Evaluator's signature: _____ Date: _____

Sample Reviews for Poor Performers

INTERIM PERFORMANCE EVALUATION
Telemarketing

Performance evaluation for: Bert Wooster

Date: 6/24/XX

JOB FACTORS:

1. Productivity (amount of satisfactory work completed)
   (weak) <u>1</u> 2 3 4 5 (superior)
   Comments:
   I cannot put it any other way: You are not meeting the required daily quota of calls. You seem to be easily distracted, and you are also spending too much time on the calls you do make in discussing areas that do not focus on selling our service.

2. Job Knowledge (skills and knowledge necessary for the job)
   (weak) 1 <u>2</u> 3 4 5 (superior)
   Comments:
   This is not an area where I feel much more growth is possible for you.

3. Dependability (perseverance and conscientiousness)
   (weak) 1 <u>2</u> 3 4 5 (superior)
   Comments:
   The challenge here is to focus more on what you are doing and the goals you are supposed to be meeting.

4. Initiative (motivation and determination)
   (weak) <u>1</u> 2 3 4 5 (superior)
   Comments:
   Frankly, I'm concerned here. At our weekly meetings, you offer no input on your experiences with calls, what you learned from them, and how others may benefit from your experiences; nor do you seem to be interested in what others have to say. Take the time to think about what you are doing, how you might be doing better, and the steps you need to take to actively demonstrate your interest in the job.

5. Cooperation (ability to work with others)

(weak) <u>1</u> 2 3 4 5 (superior)

Comments:

You have perhaps been too aloof from your fellow telemarketers, and this isolation does not help you to learn from their experiences or to solicit assistance when you need it.

6. Attendance and Punctuality

(weak) <u>1</u> 2 3 4 5 (superior)

Comments:

You are late getting to work 3–4 days out of each week and have frequently missed the start of our weekly meetings. You have also been absent from work far too often. This pattern must change immediately.

7. Adaptability (resourcefulness, problem solving, learning)

(weak) 1 <u>2</u> 3 4 5 (superior)

Comments:

You have a difficult time accepting new procedures when they are introduced and seem to balk at changes.

8. Organization

(weak) <u>1</u> 2 3 4 5 (superior)

Comments:

You approach your calls in a haphazard manner and do not fill out your call sheets logically or file them on time.

9. Receptiveness to Criticism

(weak) <u>1</u> 2 3 4 5 (superior)

Comments:

Your attitude when your work is criticized is often sullen and defensive. I believe you can be more open to suggestions.

OVERALL RATING:

<u> X </u> Needs improvement in job performance

___ Meets job requirements

___ Exceeds job requirements

1. *Work over the past three months:*

   When you first started, you seemed to be keen on what you were doing and eager to learn your job, in addition to being careful about the organization of your desk and attentive to details. However, as time has gone on, your attitude has become increasingly lackadaisical, and you have demonstrated a decreasing lack of interest and motivation in what you are doing. You often stray from the purpose of your calls; remember, you are calling people for a business reason, not a social one.

2. *Goals for the coming three months:*

   First and foremost, you must achieve your daily quota of calls, beginning this week. This is crucial if you wish to continue your employment here. Second, I would like to see you take a more active role in department operations, and in particular in weekly meetings. I believe you should be supplying at least one suggestion per meeting, as your colleagues do.

3. *Additional comments:*

   You are evidently unhappy with your job, and this concerns me. You cannot work productively if this unhappiness continues. I would like you to examine why you are dissatisfied and to let me know what can be done to make you feel more motivated about what you are doing, if anything. Let's meet on a weekly basis to discuss how things are going. You are also welcome to come and talk to me if you need to express yourself at a time other than our regularly scheduled meetings.

EMPLOYEE'S COMMENTS:

Employee's signature: _____ Date: _____

Evaluator's signature: _____ Date: _____

PERFORMANCE REVIEW

Name: Larry Kingman
Job Title: Promotions Supervisor
Date: May 15, 20XX

Type of Evaluation:
Interim   Annual   X

Evaluation Guide

1 = Excellent (exceptional; exceeds expectations)
2 = Good (consistently meets, and frequently exceeds, usual expectations)
3 = Satisfactory (conforms to standards; meets expectations)
4 = Fair (marginal; meeting only minimum requirements)
5 = Poor (below standard and unacceptable; improvement required or termination will result)

Factors for Review	Rating
Job Knowledge	4
Work Quantity	4
Work Quality	4
Creativity/Resourcefulness	4
Communication Skills	3
Judgment/Decision Making	4
Interpersonal Skills/Teamwork	3
Organizational Skills	4
Adaptability	4
Initiative	4
Analytic Skills	4
Resilience/Stability Under Pressure	4
Dependability	4
Supervisory Skills	5

OVERALL RATING: 4

COMMENTS/GOALS:

Larry has failed overall to meet most criteria and goals for his job. This is unfortunate, as he has managed to work his way up through the ranks to his current position of Promotions Supervisor and we had high expectations of his success. However, there have been numerous problems from the start of his taking over the position. Primarily, he is unable to be an effective manager of people and has had to cope with a number of personnel crises that have preoccupied his time and attention to the exclusion of all other aspects of his work. These crises included a higher-than-average turnover rate and a number of clashes between employees, as well as a failure for them to accept Larry's hard-won authority as their supervisor. The end result was that, in lieu of coordinating promotion campaigns, he was forced to train new personnel, mediate disputes, and defend himself against a number of attacks.

The end result of all this was that Larry could not focus on the real purpose of his work, nor was he successful in settling the numerous staff disputes and crises. He fell behind on deadlines continuously, was unable to explore new ideas, and was forced to recycle old ones in order to get promotions off the ground. His inability to take control of his staff and failure to complete several important projects combined to give him the low ratings cited in this evaluation.

I have had several talks with Larry about the situation, and he wishes to have one more opportunity to make amends and prove what he is capable of doing, especially now that he has solved many of his personnel problems. To that end, he is on three months' probation to make visible improvements in all his job factors. Results will be evaluated based on the stability in his department and any rise in sales that come about due to a fresh and original promotion campaign. If he continues to fall short in the performance of his duties, a less stressful position will be found for him elsewhere within the company.

EMPLOYEE'S COMMENTS

Employee's signature: _____ Date: _____

Evaluator's signature: _____ Date: _____

PERFORMANCE REVIEW
Sales/Marketing

Name: Burton Wolinsky

Job Title: Marketing Representative

Date: 4/19/XX

Type of Evaluation:

Interim   Annual X

Evaluation Guide

1 = Excellent (exceptional; exceeds expectations)

2 = Good (consistently meets, and frequently exceeds, usual expectations)

3 = Satisfactory (conforms to standards; meets expectations)

4 = Fair (marginal; meeting only minimum requirements)

5 = Poor (below standard and unacceptable; improvement required or termination will result)

Factors for Review

Sales   Rating: N/A

Achieves quarterly and yearly sales quotas; improves growth of territory

Job Knowledge   Rating: 4

Degree to which the employee knows and understands his/her job and its functions

Work Quality/Organizational Skills   Rating: 4

Effective planning and organization, follow-up, etc.; effective use of time

Written and Oral Communication   Rating: 4

Ability to present information and ideas to others in an articulate and effective manner, as well as to listen effectively, comprehend, and respond to the ideas of others clearly and concisely

Judgment/Decision Making   Rating: 4

Ability to reason through problems, review alternative solutions, reach sound conclusions, and modify decisions when necessary

Interpersonal Skills   Rating: 4

Tact, courtesy, self-control, patience, loyalty, and discretion; ability to work harmoniously with others

Adaptability   Rating: 5

    Ability to learn new skills, concepts, and processes; resourcefulness; flexibility in thinking

Persuasiveness   Rating: 4

    Ability to negotiate, argue persuasively, use influence on others to achieve goals

Initiative   Rating: 4

    Ability to act independently without specific instructions

Customer Responsiveness   Rating: N/A

    Timely response to customer questions, concerns, and problems

Stability Under Pressure   Rating: 4

    Mental and emotional balance under stress due to pressure of work

Dependability   Rating: 5

    Attendance at meetings, timeliness in meeting appointments, conscientiousness

Fiscal Management   Rating: 5

    Ability to work within specified budget

OVERALL RATING: 4

EVALUATOR'S COMMENTS

Summarize your overall evaluation of the employee's performance, noting any strengths and weakness. Provide goals and plan for further development and a current estimate of the employee's capacity and ambition for future growth.

    Burt has been an inconsistent and unproductive marketing representative for some time and has been unable to meet the established goals and criteria for his position. Although he has been with the company long enough to have a good grasp of our product lines, he still has not been able to come up with viable marketing strategies of any sort. He has been unable to organize or follow through on any plans resulting from strategic meetings with the sales department, and in fact has often missed many of those meetings. His frequent absences, inattention to the work at hand, apparent lack of interest in what he is doing, and failure to respond to repeated warnings to improve his work have all led to the inescapable conclusion that he is not up to the demands of the position.

ACTION TO BE TAKEN

Burt has been dismissed from his position as of the date of this evaluation.

EMPLOYEE'S COMMENTS

Employee's signature: _____ Date: _____

Evaluator's signature: _____ Date: _____

PERFORMANCE EVALUATION
Salesperson

Employee's Name: Kristine Ardinger   Review Period: From 2/XX to 7/XX

Job Title: Sales Assistant   Interim   Annual X
      (Household Appliances)

Name and Title of Evaluator: Harold Hicks, Department Manager

Performance Guide

A — Consistently exceeds job requirements

    Performance is exceptional, above and beyond what is expected

B — Meets job requirements

    Does a good job; meets and sometimes exceeds requirements capably and competently

C — Improvement needed

    Is not performing at satisfactory level; extra supervision is required

N/A — Other

    Not applicable to this area of evaluation

1. Job Knowledge   Grade: C

   Understands and can clearly explain the product or service; effectively uses training and experience to enhance job knowledge

   Comments:

   Kris has not done an effective job of learning the details of the various appliances that we sell. She is unable to distinguish among brand names, and although she has received extensive training, she cannot speak to customers with any authority about the features of different makes and models, no matter what the appliance.

2. Customer Service   Grade: C

   Is attentive to customers and handles all questions and complaints quickly and courteously; does not keep customers waiting

   Comments:

   She has met none of the criteria. She seems almost to be afraid of dealing with customers, if only because her lack of authority will be exposed. She prefers to handle straight sales transactions with customers who have made up their minds, rather than attempting to sell.

258

3. Work Habits   Grade: C

   Is neat and well organized; can handle multiple tasks easily and efficiently

   Comments:

   Although she has never failed to be neat and presentable in appearance and attitude, in all respects of her work habits Kris has been severely lacking. She can handle only the simplest of tasks and tends to be overwhelmed when there are several things to do, and especially when there are several customers who all require attention at the same time. Her fear and hesitancy have affected the overall quality of her work.

4. Initiative and Resourcefulness   Grade: C

   Demonstrates ability to work without direction and offers new ideas and solutions

   Comments:

   She is unable to work without instruction or supervision. She has demonstrated no signs of resourcefulness.

5. Decision Making   Grade: C

   Evaluates situations, draws conclusions, and makes sound decisions

   Comments:

   Kris avoids making decisions of any sort and when put to the test will look to others for assistance.

6. Adaptability and Flexibility   Grade: B

   Is willing to work extra hours or in other departments when needed; works well under stressful conditions; can accommodate customer needs

   Comments:

   Although she has not proven herself capable of working in pressurized circumstances in our department, she has been willing to be loaned out to other departments on occasion, where she has shown more of an aptitude and ability to be more of a real salesperson. This strengthens my opinion that she has simply been put into the wrong department and would fare better dealing with merchandise that did not intimidate her and cause her to question her skills and abilities. (See goals and objectives.)

7. Accountability   Grade: N/A

   Is willing to accept responsibility for job-related decisions and actions

   Comments:

   Kris has not really placed herself into any position or situation where she has to be accountable for what she does. Most times she simply avoids taking on the responsibility.

8. Interpersonal Skills   Grade: C

Interacts well with others; demonstrates courtesy, patience, diplomacy, discretion, and self-control; communicates clearly and effectively

Comments:

She has been too shy and hesitant about expressing her evident unhappiness with her position. She needs to become more assertive. She is actually a lovely individual with plenty to offer, but no real opportunity to prove her stuff. Having been thrown into the fire, as it were, she has withdrawn into herself and makes no real effort to interact with others or to seek assistance.

9. Punctuality/Dependability   Grade: B

Can be relied upon to be timely and to meet or exceed expectations.

Comments:

She has to be credited for showing up on time and not taking unscheduled absences. She does make some attempt to fulfill expectations, even when those attempts end up being weak and ineffectual.

10. Sales Quotas   Grade: C

Meets or exceeds sales goals for product/service.

Comments:

She has made a few sales, mainly with customers who already knew what they were looking for or made their purchasing decision based solely on price or manufacturer. However, she has not been able to meet monthly or quarterly quotas.

SUMMARY

Summarize employee's performance level since last review; indicate any improvement or decline.

Kris has struggled through in our department for the last six months. She is interested in exploring opportunities in retail sales, but was clearly placed into the wrong position. She is not suited to anything having to do with appliances or hardware, and it is clear to me that she would be happier and probably more effective in another department. She has lacked any proper guidance, and her shyness prevented her from taking up the matter with Human Resources. She is to be commended for her efforts to struggle it out, but I for one hate to see her continue being so unhappy, in addition to which our sales have suffered due to her inability to meet quotas.

Thus, I arranged for Kris to meet with the appropriate representative in Human Resources, and a transfer to the Children's Clothing department will take place immediately. I wish Kris well in her efforts to find a more suitable milieu that will enable her to show what she is capable of doing.

GOALS/OBJECTIVES FOR THE NEXT 6 MONTHS

Indicate whatever goals or criteria the employee must meet for the next review period.

None for this department. See above.

EMPLOYEE'S COMMENTS

Employee's signature: _____ Date: _____

Evaluator's signature: _____ Date: _____

PERFORMANCE REVIEW
Sales/Marketing

Name: Barry Hunsacker
Job Title: Sales Representative
Date: November 11, 20XX

Type of Evaluation:
Interim   Annual X

Evaluation Guide

1 = Excellent (exceptional; exceeds expectations)
2 = Good (consistently meets, and frequently exceeds, usual expectations)
3 = Satisfactory (conforms to standards; meets expectations)
4 = Fair (marginal; meeting only minimum requirements)
5 = Poor (below standard and unacceptable; improvement required or termination will result)

Factors for Review

Sales   Rating: 5
> Achieves quarterly and yearly sales quotas; improves growth of territory

Job Knowledge   Rating: 3
> Degree to which the employee knows and understands his/her job and its functions

Work Quality/Organizational Skills   Rating: 4
> Effective planning and organization, follow-up, etc.; effective use of time

Written and Oral Communication   Rating: 4
> Ability to present information and ideas to others in an articulate and effective manner, as well as to listen effectively, comprehend, and respond to the ideas of others clearly and concisely

Judgment/Decision Making   Rating: 4
> Ability to reason through problems, review alternative solutions, reach sound conclusions, and modify decisions when necessary

Interpersonal Skills   Rating: 4
> Tact, courtesy, self-control, patience, loyalty, and discretion; ability to work harmoniously with others

Adaptability   Rating: 5

Ability to learn new skills, concepts, and processes; resourcefulness; flexibility in thinking

Persuasiveness   Rating: 4

Ability to negotiate, argue persuasively, use influence on others to achieve goals

Initiative   Rating: 4

Ability to act independently without specific instructions

Customer Responsiveness   Rating: 4

Timely response to customer questions, concerns, and problems

Stability Under Pressure   Rating: 4

Mental and emotional balance under stress due to pressure of work

Dependability   Rating: 3

Attendance at meetings, timeliness in meeting appointments, conscientiousness

Fiscal Management   Rating: 4

Ability to work within specified budget

OVERALL RATING: 4

EVALUATOR'S COMMENTS

Summarize your overall evaluation of the employee's performance, noting any strengths and weakness. Provide goals and plan for further development and current estimate of the employee's capacity and ambition for future growth.

Barry's job performance has gone increasingly downhill, and despite repeated meetings and warnings that he was not living up to expectations, he has failed to demonstrate any reasonable improvement in most aspects of his job. His primary failing has been in his ability to prospect. His market research is weak, and he puts little initiative into exploring new opportunities for potential clients. He has also failed to develop new sales presentations; he has been using the same tired old materials for the past two years, and it is looking worn around the edges, both literally and figuratively. He hasn't come up with any new ideas for a while and doesn't show any interest in his job or his customers. We have lost several major customers due primarily to Barry's not returning calls or following up on complaints or concerns in a timely fashion.

Barry has demonstrated little to no powers of independent judgment and resourcefulness. He has largely seemed indifferent to the fact that sales have slipped so dramatically and that his own job performance is lacking. In discussing this review with him, he disputed many of the low marks I gave him, specifically those in persuasiveness and communication. Nevertheless, I stand by my ratings. I believe that Barry has allowed personal concerns to creep into his job, and although he was once a reliable and effective sales representative, he has not proven himself equal to any of his appointed tasks for some time.

As a result of his failure to meet job criteria and expectations, sales in his territory are down by nearly 30 percent. A continued downslide cannot be tolerated.

ACTION TO BE TAKEN

Because of his past record with the company, and as a result of several meetings that I have had with him, Barry has been given six months to work on bringing his territory's performance back up to snuff. Specifically, he needs to be turning the major portion of his attention on prospecting for new clients and on closing the amount of time between identifying a hot prospect and closing on the sale. He also needs to demonstrate improvement in all areas on which he was rated poorly. He is to come to me for clarification of the improvements that we expect to see and for guidance, as needed.

EMPLOYEE'S COMMENTS

Employee's signature: _____ Date: _____

Evaluator's signature: _____ Date: _____

PERFORMANCE EVALUATION
Sales/Marketing

Name: Darlene Carmicheal
Title: Telemarketing Fundraiser
Date: March 3, 20XX

Sales Achievements

Darlene has achieved only 50 percent of her goals for new commitments in support for our station. This is a drop of nearly 30 percent from what she was achieving a year ago; therefore her sales record has declined significantly.

Job Knowledge

Technically, her job knowledge is adequate. She has been with the station long enough that she knows what is expected of her, how to conduct her calls, and how to deal with basic questions. She is still experiencing difficulty when more complex issues arise and she can't answer inquiries regarding financial arrangements that might be made for large donors or the occasional complaint regarding programming.

Work Quality/Productivity

As her sales record indicates, Darlene has not been meeting standards for productivity. The number of calls she makes on a daily basis has declined, as has the number of sales she has closed. She has developed a very lackadaisical attitude toward her work and has not reacted either positively or negatively to criticism or attempts to help her improve. Overall, the quality of her work has degenerated significantly, and she has offered no explanation or concern about why this has happened.

Organizational Skills/Time Management

Darlene's organizational and time-management skills are very poor. The setup of her work station does not allow for easy access to forms and reference materials, nor does she keep her paperwork properly filed. Reports are always submitted late, and she cannot keep on top of either her call schedule (on average, only 15-20 calls per day, as opposed to the required 35) or her correspondence (letters answered within two weeks as opposed to two days).

Decision Making/Problem Solving

She is unable to make decisions or solve problems and is most likely to hand any difficult calls or correspondence over to somebody else for handling.

Interpersonal/Communication Skills

Once again, this is an area that has experienced a significant decline. When she first started, she always sounded interested and friendly on the telephone. At this point, she has clearly become bored and reads her script in a droning fashion, conveying an attitude that does not convince potential donors of the importance of giving. Her writing skills are poor, and her correspondence must be checked before it is sent out.

Initiative/Dependability

Because of her poor production record and apathetic attitude, Darlene cannot be considered to be a dependable employee. She has provided no evidence of any initiative to improve her job performance.

Attendance/Punctuality

She has frequently been late getting to work and has taken too many days off without advance notice.

Summary and Goals for Next Review

Darlene has clearly not been able to meet established standards. Her overall performance has slipped from par to drastically subpar. She has lost all motivation and desire to work and has not responded to repeated attempts to work with her on her problems and improve her sales record. I have not been able to determine the root cause of this decline and her evident unhappiness and dislike for the work, nor have I been able to work out an equitable solution with her. Having done all that can possibly be done, it seems to have become necessary to let Darlene go. She has been informed of her dismissal and been given three weeks' pay in lieu of notice.

Employee's Comments

Employee's signature: _____ Date: _____

Evaluator's signature: _____ Date: _____

8

Model Evaluations for Engineers, Programmers, and Other Technical Specialists

This group consists of highly trained, technically oriented individuals. They are likely to work alone or in small, temporary project teams. Their job titles include:

- Project engineer
- Process engineer
- Research scientist/technician
- Process scientist/technician
- Plant engineer
- Manufacturing engineer
- Maintenance specialist
- Skilled manufacturing operator
- Regulatory compliance specialist
- Quality-assurance engineer
- Lab technician
- Industrial engineer
- Programmer

- Management information specialist
- Manufacturing control-system programmer
- Manufacturing control-system technician

Gauging Performance

The work these employees perform is characterized by a high level of expertise, thoroughness, and attention to detail. Individuals in these positions must be able to plan and execute project-oriented work. They may be weakest in delegation and communication skills.

A team member with superior technical skills and strong interpersonal communication skills often proves to be an extraordinary asset to the organization. While innovation from these team members is certainly welcome, in most cases that innovation must be accompanied by exhaustive analytical work. The pace of global business competition limits the number of complex, technically demanding initiatives that can repeatedly "go back to the drawing board."

Because of the high price of failure and the high cost of proving unique concepts, the vast majority of the work undertaken by this type of worker is derivative, that is, based on proven concepts and techniques. In most cases, a risk-taking personality is not a standard profile for success in these jobs.

The key issues in these positions usually center on what can be demonstrated to work in the real world. Typically, projects and new products must proceed to implementation with both speed and accuracy, which are two competing motivations. This places a premium on technical competence and careful, consistent execution.

Performance Indicators

The top-level performer

- Is considered one of the "in-house experts" in field of expertise
- Can competently perform in other related technical areas
- Plans and executes projects independently
- Assembles project documentation with an eye to operator accessibility

- Shows understanding of operating assumptions and troubleshooting techniques
- Anticipates problems, plans contingency measures
- Should be identified as a leader due to strong interpersonal and communication skills
- Should instill confidence, respect, and motivation on the part of others through personal actions and communications

The good performer

- Is technically competent in field of expertise
- Plans and executes projects with minimal supervision
- Recognizes potential problems and proposes solutions
- Assumes project documentation responsibilities easily
- Addresses design assumptions and troubleshooting instructions with little or no trouble
- Has interpersonal and communication skills that allow effective participation in project-review meetings
- Is capable of directing others on elements of project execution
- Should be capable of leading in-house project teams

The poor performer

- Does not display minimum required technical competency
- Shows little or no commitment to improving skills, or to learning with enthusiasm and understanding
- Plans and executes projects with difficulty, even with appropriate supervision in areas of particular difficulty or sensitivity
- Has trouble documenting projects logically and clearly
- Has difficulty with interpersonal and communication skills
- Is late with updates and other information for project-review meetings
- Has difficulty interacting with appropriate individuals during project execution
- Has trouble with other company personnel and departments when placed in a support role

Sample Reviews for Top-level Performers

PERFORMANCE EVALUATION

Name: Cheryl Simmons

Title: Quality Assurance Engineer

Date of hire: 2/15/XX

Department: Manufacturing

Supervisor: Havrilla Stevens

Review period: From 2/XX to 2/XX

Ratings: Employee is to be rated on a scale of 1 to 3, as described below.

    1: Below expectations: Performance is substandard and requires improvement.

    2: Meets expectations: Performance fully meets and occasionally exceeds standards.

    3: Exceeds expectations: Performance consistently exceeds set standards.

N/A: Not applicable. Lack of sufficient knowledge to evaluate the performance factor.

Section I: Basic Job Skills

	Below	Meets	Exceeds	N/A
Job knowledge	1	2	<u>3</u>	N/A
Quality of work	1	2	<u>3</u>	N/A
Productivity/Timeliness	1	<u>2</u>	3	N/A
Dependability	1	2	<u>3</u>	N/A
Work habits	1	2	<u>3</u>	N/A
Organizational skills	1	<u>2</u>	3	N/A
Resourcefulness	1	2	<u>3</u>	N/A
Problem solving	1	2	<u>3</u>	N/A

Comments:

Cheryl is a valued employee and one of the best Q/A engineers we have in the plant. She is particularly strong in applying her imagination and problem-solving skills in averting problems and developing creative solutions. Her knowledge of the job is excellent, and her accuracy and attention to detail are superb. The area to which Cheryl should direct her attention is in becoming better organized in order to raise her level of productivity just a bit.

Section II: Personal Attributes

	Below	Meets	Exceeds	N/A
Attendance/Punctuality	1	2	<u>3</u>	N/A
Ability to take direction	1	2	<u>3</u>	N/A
Initiative	1	2	<u>3</u>	N/A
Cooperativeness	1	2	<u>3</u>	N/A
Adaptability	1	2	<u>3</u>	N/A
Receptiveness to criticism	1	2	<u>3</u>	N/A
Communication skills	1	<u>2</u>	3	N/A
Interaction with coworkers	1	2	<u>3</u>	N/A

Comments:

In all personal attributes Cheryl is clearly a strong performer. She is very serious and very "on task," and this attitude makes it easy for her coworkers to accept her decisions even when the decision must be to reject product at times. There are times when her expertise and focus get in the way of her understanding how much care she must take in communicating her decisions to others. She always has her facts well in hand but could make a better effort to explain the results clearly to less technically proficient coworkers.

Section III: Strengths and Weaknesses

Describe employee strengths:

Cheryl is a true expert and is recognized as such widely throughout the plant. Her understanding of the product requirements and the customer difficulties that result when those requirements have not been met make her a tremendous asset to our overall productivity and success.

Describe employee weaknesses:

Cheryl's strengths are also her weaknesses. Her carefulness and attention to detail sometimes result in a slower production rate than might be desired. The trick is, of course, to keep the quality level undiminished while raising productivity just a bit. Further, when communicating with coworkers Cheryl needs to remind herself that others may not be quite so technically proficient and needs to focus on communicating in a less technical way.

Describe goals for next performance review:

As indicated above:

1. Try, through a more highly organized approach, to keep the quality level undiminished while raising productivity.

2. Make real efforts to accommodate the needs of her coworkers in all job communications. Be cognizant of the many levels of expertise in the workers to whom she must relate.

Section IV: Comments

Evaluator:

Cheryl is a strong and valuable asset to our business. In a crucial position she is clearly knowledgeable and reliable. We can hardly do better than that. Any areas requiring attention are certainly matters of "gilding the lily" and should be viewed as suggestions for growth, not serious job deficiencies. It's important to note this, for Cheryl is as demanding of herself as she is careful about our manufacturing quality. Any suggestions for improvement must be understood within the context of overall performance excellence.

Employee:

Employee's signature: _____ Date: _____

Evaluator's signature: _____ Date: _____

PERFORMANCE EVALUATION
Management Information Specialist

Name: Jeanne Hansen
Date: August 3, 20XX

Performance Rating 1–10

Jeanne earns an overall 9 rating. She has company-wide acceptance as "the expert" on all of our information systems. She has increased the productivity of every member of the staff through improved systems and thorough training programs that have increased end-user confidence and comfort.

Strongest Work Elements

Jeanne is always ahead of the curve when it comes to all three areas of her job. In hardware, she attends product seminars and is always on top of the best equipment available to do the job we need at the most cost-effective level. In software, she is also knowledgeable and negotiates with potential providers for unique software solutions for our particular needs. In end-user training and support, Jeanne is always aware of the positive benefits we can gain from learning new technologies. She is also aware, however, of the cost in time, energy, and employee effort and good will that such improvements exact.

Weakest Work Elements

Now and then supervisors have had to assist Jeanne in wearing the appropriate clothes and hairstyle for her type of job. She is very focused on the nuts-and-bolts parts of her job and has energy and enthusiasm to spare. But sometimes her supervisors have had to intervene and ask Jeanne to go home and change her clothes. I have talked with Jeanne about this, and she is understanding.

What We Expect

We have grown to count on Jeanne's expertise and knowledgeable service to the rest of the staff. I am sure the little peculiarities that require attention will be easy to bring into line. Jeanne is an excellent MIS and we look forward to an excellent future.

Forecast

Jeanne has an excellent future with our company, and she will be considered for promotion to supervisor and/or trainer.

Employee Comments

Employee's signature: _____ Date: _____

Evaluator's signature: _____ Date: _____

PERFORMANCE EVALUATION—TOP LEVEL

Name: Ramon Morales   Department: Condominium Services
Title: Maintenance Administrator   Supervisor: Lance Powers
Date of hire: 2/15/XX   Review period: From 2/XX to 2/XX

Ratings: Employee is to be rated on a scale of 1 to 3, as described below.

  1: Below expectations: Performance is substandard and requires improvement.

  2: Meets expectations: Performance fully meets and occasionally exceeds standards.

  3: Exceeds expectations: Performance consistently exceeds set standards.

N/A: Not applicable. Lack of sufficient knowledge to evaluate the performance factor.

Section I: Basic Job Skills

	Below	Meets	Exceeds	N/A
Job knowledge	1	2	<u>3</u>	N/A
Quality of work	1	2	<u>3</u>	N/A
Productivity/Timeliness	1	2	<u>3</u>	N/A
Dependability	1	<u>2</u>	3	N/A
Work habits	1	2	<u>3</u>	N/A
Organizational skills	1	<u>2</u>	3	N/A
Resourcefulness	1	2	<u>3</u>	N/A
Problem solving	1	2	<u>3</u>	N/A

Comments:

Ramon is a very hard worker, and he knows how to do his job well. He has particular magic with rebellious plumbing, and that is a real bonus. He always understands what needs to be done and what steps must be taken to accomplish the goal. Sometimes he could be a bit better organized about how he allocates work to others so that more work can be accomplished overall. He sometimes has to do more work himself because he has not organized the work of others as efficiently as he might. He has also been missing from work a few times without notice. This is probably related to his difficulty in communicating on the telephone.

Section II: Personal Attributes

	Below	Meets	Exceeds	N/A
Attendance/Punctuality	1	<u>2</u>	3	N/A
Ability to take direction	1	2	<u>3</u>	N/A
Initiative	1	2	<u>3</u>	N/A
Cooperativeness	1	2	<u>3</u>	N/A
Adaptability	1	2	<u>3</u>	N/A
Receptiveness to criticism	1	2	<u>3</u>	N/A
Communication skills	1	<u>2</u>	3	N/A
Interaction with coworkers	1	<u>2</u>	3	N/A

Comments:

Ramon is an excellent worker and a positive workplace influence. All of his coworkers and all of the residents like him and enjoy having him around. It is important that Ramon continue to work on his language skills. All of the areas in which he is measured less than "3" are probably the result of reluctance to appear foolish on Ramon's part or misunderstanding on the part of others. But mastering the language in which he must communicate at work is important for Ramon. He has such strong skills it would be a shame to have his future limited through language deficiency. This is particularly apparent in his avoidance of using the telephone.

Section III: Strengths and Weaknesses

Describe employee strengths:

Ramon is skilled and has a fine way with coworkers and residents. He makes a fine appearance and his cheerfulness and industriousness win him many friends. His "expert" understanding of all the mechanical and landscape needs of the complex make working or living here much better for everyone.

Describe employee weaknesses:

Ramon must be sure to be present at work or call his manager and give adequate notice of his planned absence. Excessive absence is not the problem, but failure to communicate with his manager when absence is necessary is. Further, Ramon must continue to work at improving communication in English. He was hired with the clear understanding that effective English language communication was a job requirement. He has improved a great deal but must continue to work on this.

278

Describe goals for next performance review:

As noted above:

1. Be sure to notify the manager if an absence is necessary.
2. Continue to improve English language skills.
3. Work at being better organized in applying the skills of other workers.

Section IV: Comments

Evaluator:

Ramon and I have worked together to be sure that language skills do not stand in the way of his success. This is a difficult matter for him to deal with, and he must be encouraged to keep working on it. On the other hand, his skills and his attitude are so excellent that I feel it is definitely worth the effort to keep him "on task" in addressing that issue. I hope Ramon will continue to give his excellent support to the running of this complex. He makes a big difference here.

Employee:

Employee's signature: _____ Date: _____

Evaluator's signature: _____ Date: _____

PERFORMANCE EVALUATION
Heating-Equipment Technician

Name: Waymon Hayes   Date: Dec. 30, 20XX

Quality of Work

Waymon scores a perfect "10" for the overall quality of his work. He has demonstrated tremendous mechanical talent and is able to install any kind of furnace and heating system quickly and flawlessly. He also has the technical know-how to perform routine maintenance and repairs that keep heating equipment running smoothly. He is able to diagnose mechanical and operating problems with great accuracy and comes up with effective solutions that are almost always permanent. He stays on top of his workload and is responsive to customers. All in all, he has a strong work ethic, maintaining consistently high standards of excellence in every aspect of his job.

Job Knowledge

Waymon's expertise is superb in every way. As already mentioned, he has excellent diagnostic ability and can get to the heart of any problem quickly and accurately. He stays on top of current developments on the field and is able to make informed recommendations to customers who are looking to replace or upgrade their heating systems. His all-around knowledge of all types of machinery, systems, and parts make him the expert to go to.

Strongest Work Elements

Without question Waymon's strongest talent is his diagnostic ability. In addition to this, he is able to effect both installations and repairs in record time. He knows how to economize his time so that he uses every minute on the job to its maximum, enabling him to finish up quickly and move on to the next job. Customers appreciate his speed and thoroughness, as well as his willingness to stop and explain how their heating system works and/or what they need to do to keep it well maintained. He keeps his van in good order, and his tools are neatly organized and in good condition. Overall, Waymon pays attention to the details and applies quality to everything he does.

280

About the only aspect of his job that Waymon seems to dislike is routine inspections. He tends to put these off for as long as possible, preferring to focus his attention on the challenges posed by installations or figuring out the cause of a problem and repairing it. He usually needs reminders of when inspections are due, especially in the summertime.

Customer Responsiveness

Waymon has an excellent rapport with customers. He stays on top of service calls, checking in with the main office upon completion of each call to see what else has come in, and then checking ahead with the customer to let him/her know when he will be there. He treats each customer with respect, taking care to listen with his full attention and is also very patient about explaining things such as the cause of a particular problem and how it might be avoided in the future. He is courteous and professional at all times, and we have received many compliments about his friendly manner and the strong sense of competence that he conveys.

Dependability

Waymon is completely dependable in every respect, as all the above comments make clear.

Forecast/Goals

Waymon's overall performance has been nothing short of superb. He has notable strengths and talents in every area, and this includes his ability to lead and instruct other technicians. He is frequently sent out on job sites where other technicians are having difficulties in order to effect a quick solution and to provide proper technical guidance and instruction. He is liked and respected by customers and coworkers alike. It is clear that in addition to his many skills and abilities described here, he also has talents in the managerial arena. For that reason, we are entering him into a management-training program, with an eye toward eventually putting him into a direct supervisory and training capacity over the entire team of technicians. Waymon has agreed to do this only if he is also able to keep his hand in the installation-and-repair end of things as well. We hope to work out an appropriate solution that will accommodate Waymon's personal desires as well as our own desire to make the most of his extraordinary talents.

Employee's Comments

Employee's signature: _____ Date: _____

Evaluator's signature: _____ Date: _____

PERFORMANCE EVALUATION

Name: Elma Martin   Department: Underwriting
Title: Computer Programmer   Supervisor: Amy Lowell
Date of hire: 3/15/XX   Review period: From 3/XX to 3/XX

Ratings: Employee is to be rated on a scale of 1 to 3, as described below.

1: Below expectations: Performance is substandard and requires improvement.

2: Meets expectations: Performance fully meets and occasionally exceeds standards.

3: Exceeds expectations: Performance consistently exceeds set standards.

N/A: Not applicable. Lack of sufficient knowledge to evaluate the performance factor.

Section I: Basic Job Skills

	Below	Meets	Exceeds	N/A
Job knowledge	1	2	3	N/A
Quality of work	1	2	3	N/A
Productivity/Timeliness	1	2	3	N/A
Dependability	1	2	3	N/A
Work habits	1	2	3	N/A
Organizational skills	1	2	3	N/A
Resourcefulness	1	2	3	N/A
Problem solving	1	2	3	N/A

Comments:

Elma is embarrassing to evaluate because one finds oneself feeling one must "find something to criticize." I will not make that effort. Elma is perhaps excessively self-critical, but the result of that is that the company benefits every day from her efforts. In the difficult transition to using the new Underwriters Assoc. Relational Database System, Elma led the way with expertise and unfailing cheerfulness when others were discouraged or negative. The regional programmers indicate that several company-wide adaptations of the system have resulted from the innovative and perceptive understanding Elma has brought to solving our system needs.

Section II: Personal Attributes

	Below	Meets	Exceeds	N/A
Attendance/Punctuality	1	2	<u>3</u>	N/A
Ability to take direction	1	2	<u>3</u>	N/A
Initiative	1	2	<u>3</u>	N/A
Cooperativeness	1	2	<u>3</u>	N/A
Adaptability	1	2	<u>3</u>	N/A
Receptiveness to criticism	1	2	<u>3</u>	N/A
Communication skills	1	2	<u>3</u>	N/A
Interaction with coworkers	1	2	<u>3</u>	N/A

Comments:

Again, I have to admit that it would be hard to imagine a better employee than Elma has been. She is not the most senior member of the programming staff, but her comfortable manner and expertise have made her the odds-on choice for "the person to go to when you think you have made an awful mistake." In all ways she sets a standard for performance we can all emulate.

Section III: Strengths and Weaknesses

Describe employee strengths:

Elma has that sought-after combination of highly tuned skills and comfortable personality that adds up to a tremendous employee. While being a star individual performer, she also manages to be a valuable and comfortable member of the team. We highly value her skills and her impact on the workplace.

Describe employee weaknesses:

If I would have to describe a weakness, it would be the hope that Elma's self-critical attention and unfailing placing of the job and her coworkers ahead of personal needs would not become excessive. While we all might seem to benefit in the short run, in the long run Elma's needs to make sure she is taking care of herself. We don't want her to burn so bright that she burns out.

Describe goals for next performance review:

1. Develop with her supervisor some means of monitoring her personal mental health to avoid possible burnout.

2. Discover and describe some long-term goals she can pursue within the company. She has great value and should explore the possibility that there is an even more rewarding role for her here.

Section IV: Comments

Evaluator:

It is a joy to have Elma as an employee. She has added a lot to this work place both through her expertise and computer innovations and her personal style. I hope we will continue to be able to fulfill her growing job needs and keep her a part of our team.

Employee:

Employee's signature: _____ Date: _____

Evaluator's signature: _____ Date: _____

AV DEPARTMENT: INTERIM REVIEW

Name: Keith Truesdale   Position: Electronic-Equipment Repairer
Date: Jan. 3, 20XX

Performance Rating

On a scale of 1-10, your overall performance rating is a 9. You have demonstrated strong consistency and extensive knowledge of all the audio-visual equipment in your care. You work well independently, and you take responsibility for your work. Usually your work is of a very high quality. You interact well with the other employees and seem to enjoy the oddball requests you often get. It is particularly notable that your turnaround time on repairs is quick, and the "downtime" that results is minimal. Everyone appreciates that.

Strengths

You are very strong in diagnosing and repairing the equipment. You seem to have a sixth sense about where to look for the trouble, which is undoubtedly the result of excellent training and extensive experience.

Weaknesses

The greatest weakness noted to date is your tendency to overcommit. This is a natural extension of your very laudable desire to serve everyone excellently. But when you overpromise, you create a situation in which people plan for the use of equipment they won't have, and disruption and dissatisfaction result. It is also not a good idea to develop expectations of your services that are based on overtime. That expectation will be hard to temper, and that way lies burnout.

Goals and Directions

Continue to enjoy amazing people with quick turnarounds, but modify the way you promise your services. Better to say you <u>may</u> be able to have it for tomorrow and urge them to prepare a backup plan. That way, if you can deliver tomorrow, it is a bonus. But if you cannot, no one is caught short.

In addition, try to encourage the staff to plan ahead enough time so that you have a chance to determine <u>in advance</u> that the equipment they need will be ready so that exaggerated repair turnaround time becomes a luxury, not a necessity.

Forecast

You have begun very well, and I am sure you will continue to be a strong addition to our team. Running a "one-man band" such as your department is always a bit of smoke and mirrors. Be careful not to get caught in overextending to the extent that it impairs your overall performance. We are too glad to have you to have you burn out.

Comments

Employee's signature: _____ Date: _____

Evaluator's signature: _____ Date: _____

PERFORMANCE EVALUATION
Regulatory-Compliance Specialist

Name: Warren Phillips   Date: Mar. 16, 20XX

Performance Rating 1–10

Warren receives a rating of 9.5. He has an encyclopedic knowledge of the tricky OSHA and Environmental Impact Standards and manages to keep us in line with those and other statutory matters without being contentious. This is a crucial matter for the company, and we count on him to keep us operating within the law. This is a highly responsible position, and Warren fills it excellently.

Strongest Work Elements

Earning the respect of the regulatory agencies is a key element in the successful completion of this job. Warren is a recognized expert, and his integrity is without question throughout the regulatory community. This means a great deal in terms of smooth operation and general acceptance of our company's processes and procedures.

Weakest Work Elements

I talked with Warren and asked him what he would like to improve about himself regarding his position with the company. He told me that although he works well independently, he could stand some improvement at being a team player. This has not been an observed weakness, but since this is a goal for Warren we are planning to send him to several training programs that deal with team building and team participation. This can make Warren an even more valued employee.

What We Expect

We expect Warren to continue in his superb work. In the near future, the needs of company compliance will probably exceed what one person can handle. At that time we expect that Warren will play the key role in defining what we need in terms of additional help and in writing a job description, hiring, training, and supervising the additional person or persons.

What Training to Get

As mentioned above, Warren is going to attend several training programs that deal with team building and team participation.

Forecast

I feel Warren has an excellent future with our company. We benefit from the trust and stature he has brought us in the regulatory area. We look forward to enjoying that status for a long time.

Comments

Employee's signature: _____ Date: _____

Evaluator's signature: _____ Date: _____

Sample Reviews for Mid-level Performers

PERFORMANCE EVALUATION

Name: Frank Hartman   Department: Field Engineering
Title: Quality-Assurance Engineer   Supervisor: Fred Haas
Date of hire: 4/15/XX   Review period: From 4/XX to 4/XX

Ratings: Employee is to be rated on a scale of 1 to 3, as described below.

1: Below expectations: Performance is substandard and requires improvement.

2: Meets expectations: Performance fully meets and occasionally exceeds standards.

3: Exceeds expectations: Performance consistently exceeds set standards.

N/A: Not applicable. Lack of sufficient knowledge to evaluate the performance factor.

Section I: Basic Job Skills

	Below	Meets	Exceeds	N/A
Job knowledge	1	2	<u>3</u>	N/A
Quality of work	1	2	<u>3</u>	N/A
Productivity/Timeliness	1	<u>2</u>	3	N/A
Dependability	1	2	<u>3</u>	N/A
Work habits	1	2	<u>3</u>	N/A
Organizational skills	1	<u>2</u>	3	N/A
Resourcefulness	<u>1</u>	2	3	N/A
Problem solving	1	<u>2</u>	3	N/A

Comments:

Frank definitely knows his field and understands what is needed to get the job done under all normal circumstances. On occasion, however, his approach is rather too plodding to achieve needed productivity. Sometimes this results from lack of adequate organization, and sometimes it's because of being too tied to "the letter of the law." In order for Frank to be a top performer, he would need to be willing to apply initiative and imagination to solve situations that are out of the ordinary. His knowledge and skills make him an adequate performer, but his lack of resourcefulness holds him back from top-level performance.

Section II: Personal Attributes

	Below	Meets	Exceeds	N/A
Attendance/Punctuality	1	<u>2</u>	3	N/A
Ability to take direction	1	2	<u>3</u>	N/A
Initiative	<u>1</u>	2	3	N/A
Cooperativeness	1	<u>2</u>	3	N/A
Adaptability	1	<u>2</u>	3	N/A
Receptiveness to criticism	1	<u>2</u>	3	N/A
Communication skills	<u>1</u>	2	3	N/A
Interaction with coworkers	1	<u>2</u>	3	N/A

Comments:

As long as things are going smoothly, Frank is an ideal employee. But when a situation arises that requires flexibility and imagination, Frank has problems. He gets defensive and retreats to reliance on slavish detail rather than on exploring his options. Sometimes this results in incomplete work. If some supervisor will make the decisions, Frank will carry them out marvelously, but he is very reluctant to act on his own. Sometimes this results in friction with other employees and a general breakdown of communication.

Section III: Strengths and Weaknesses

Describe employee strengths:

Frank is a very hard worker. He has top-notch credentials and his attention to detail is way above the norm. He is generally calm and easygoing. He doesn't raise any dust, but he does get the work done and it is almost always of fine quality.

Describe employee weaknesses:

Frank is very reluctant to take any risks. He seems to be afraid that any deviation from established practice will result in criticism of his work. In the cases where established practice applies, he does fine. But in those cases where initiative and problem solving are required, Frank falls apart.

Describe goals for next performance review:

1. Frank should meet with his supervisor to develop strategies to encourage initiative and reassure him that inventive responses to out-of-the-ordinary problems will not draw criticism.

291

2. Frank and his supervisor should explore various means of communicating, conferences, memos, e-mail, etc. A means of keeping Frank reassured that he is acting appropriately when he has to deal with unusual circumstances is much to be desired.

Section IV: Comments

Evaluator:

Frank is a valuable asset to the company, and we want to invest the effort necessary to bring his skills to their highest and best use. To achieve this, both Frank and I need to commit some additional resources of time, effort, and trust to free up Frank to become a top-level achiever.

Employee:

Employee's signature: _____ Date: _____

Evaluator's signature: _____ Date: _____

PERFORMANCE EVALUATION
Management Information Specialist—Mid-level

Name: Sandy Quen
Date: 6/22/XX

Performance Rating 1–10

Sandy's overall performance rating is a 7. She is a dedicated employee. She is reliable and can work independently. Sandy has extensive knowledge of the MIS field and strong people skills that enable her to usually deliver the needed support and training which we require.

Strongest Work Elements

Sandy's strongest attributes are her knowledge and her ability to relate well with people.

Weakest Work Elements

Sandy's weakest attribute has to do with Sandy's uneven performance in a situation where she is expected to work without much supervision. She does very well when she is being supervised but has difficulty maintaining her work levels and completing the task when she has to be self monitoring.

What We Expect

Part of what may help here is better organization, so for a start we are asking her supervisor to help Sandy set up a system for keeping track of her work flow, one that can be monitored from time to time by her supervisor. We expect that over the next three months the need for supervision will dramatically decrease as Sandy is able to see and monitor her own progress.

What Training to Get

As mentioned above, Sandy will receive training in organization and work-flow-management techniques.

Forecast

Sandy is a strong team member. She understands what is needed and wanted and is willing to do it. She can have a strong future with this company if she addresses the issues that are holding back her performance. She communicates well, and she likes her job. In three months, after her retraining program, we will do an interim evaluation.

Comments

Employee's signature: _____ Date: _____

Evaluator's signature: _____ Date: _____

PERFORMANCE EVALUATION

Name: Scott Bogle   Department: Primates Lab
Title: Lab Technician   Supervisor: James Stephenson
Date of hire: 5/15/XX   Review period: From 5/XX to 5/XX

Ratings: Employee is to be rated on a scale of 1 to 3, as described below.

   1: Below expectations: Performance is substandard and requires improvement.
   2: Meets expectations: Performance fully meets and occasionally exceeds standards.
   3: Exceeds expectations: Performance consistently exceeds set standards.
N/A: Not applicable. Lack of sufficient knowledge to evaluate the performance factor.

Section I: Basic Job Skills

	Below	Meets	Exceeds	N/A
Job knowledge	1	2	<u>3</u>	N/A
Quality of work	<u>1</u>	2	3	N/A
Productivity/Timeliness	1	<u>2</u>	3	N/A
Dependability	1	2	<u>3</u>	N/A
Work habits	1	2	<u>3</u>	N/A
Organizational skills	1	<u>2</u>	3	N/A
Resourcefulness	1	2	<u>3</u>	N/A
Problem solving	1	2	<u>3</u>	N/A

Comments:

Scott is certainly a gifted lab technician. He knows and understands his field far beyond the needs of his job. He is also an impressively hard and passionate worker. The difficulty with Scott is that sometimes he gets so involved with some small aspect or some interesting possibility that his productiveness and the usefulness of his work product are impaired. It is an interesting dichotomy that Scott's skills and brilliance as a lab technician get in the way of his job effectiveness.

Section II: Personal Attributes

	Below	Meets	Exceeds	N/A
Attendance/Punctuality	1	2	<u>3</u>	N/A
Ability to take direction	1	<u>2</u>	3	N/A
Initiative	1	2	<u>3</u>	N/A
Cooperativeness	1	2	<u>3</u>	N/A
Adaptability	1	2	<u>3</u>	N/A
Receptiveness to criticism	<u>1</u>	2	3	N/A
Communication skills	1	<u>2</u>	3	N/A
Interaction with coworkers	1	<u>2</u>	3	N/A

Comments:

Scott is an ideal employee in most of the areas that affect his job, as indicated above. He sometimes decides that he "knows better" than the system and departs on his own tangent. When this happens, he is likely to follow his own hunch, despite instruction from his supervisor, and subsequently to react rather poorly to any criticism for his "loose-cannon" behavior. When he is in this mode, he also distresses fellow workers, who are not comfortable with his striking out in an independent direction.

Section III: Strengths and Weaknesses

Describe employee strengths:

Scott is a good, perhaps brilliant, scientist. He is quick, knowledgeable, and intuitive. He has great insight and strong ability to synthesize information and develop a general case from specific details. He is pleasant and attentive and generally has an outstanding work ethic and work habits.

Describe employee weaknesses:

Scott has not developed very good judgment about when to depart from the norm and how far such a departure should go. His interest in learning and expanding our body of knowledge is laudable. But that is not his current responsibility in this job.

Describe goals for next performance review:

1. Bring job performance immediately within the expectations for the current technical position.

2. Explore ways that Scott's gifts can be applied in appropriate channels to benefit the company and encourage and stimulate his growth and creativity.

Section IV: Comments

Evaluator:

I would not want to have a department in which we could not make a place for a man with Scott's gifts. It is a challenge both for Scott and his supervisors to develop ways to maximize his outstanding potential. That said, we need to do that in such a way that we protect the integrity of the work product in the lab and the comfort and confidence of Scott's coworkers. This may be a challenge, but it is one we must work together to meet.

Employee:

Employee's signature: _____ Date: _____

Evaluator's signature: _____ Date: _____

PERFORMANCE EVALUATION
Heating Equipment Technician

Name: Henrietta Dulinskaya   Date: Feb. 1, 20xx

Quality of Work

Henrietta has had a tough row to hoe and many challenges to meet, and overall she has met those challenges with admirable skill and perseverance. However, I would have to rate her currently at about a 7 on a scale of 10. She installs electric and gas systems extremely well, but she still is having a hard time grasping the intricacies of multiple-fuel heating systems and tends to ask for assistance whenever such calls come her way. She has a strong work ethic, maintains a good attendance and punctuality record, and will frequently work overtime to get a job done rather than leave it and come back the next day. On the whole, her work is quite good, but not yet outstanding.

Job Knowledge

Henri has the basic technical know-how to perform routine maintenance and repair in order to keep electric and gas systems operating. For the most part, she is aware of new developments and trends in the home-heating market, although she often loses sight of the newer possibilities in the light of her fascination with the older models of heating systems and the more hands-on approach to servicing them. She is aware that she will have to take some courses to become better acquainted with the more technologically advanced models now coming out on the market.

Strongest Work Elements

Henri works best when she can be part of a team situation, where several people are needed to install a particularly complicated system or to handle a larger job in a corporate or industrial environment. This gives her a sense of security in which she can thrive, and she tends to be more confident and able to work quickly and efficiently. She is also willing and able to work the long hours necessary to servicing our customers. Her dedication to her work is laudable, and her perseverance and diplomacy as a woman technician in a field dominated by men has been exemplary.

Weakest Work Elements

Henri tends to be uncertain of herself, especially when it comes to more complex heating systems that require more time and attention to detail. She often doesn't trust her judgment or expertise well enough to see a job through without having to call in her supervisor or another technician for assistance. Self-doubt makes her too tentative and slows down the completion of a job, which then causes other calls to pile up. She does need further training in installing and repairing more complex and technological models of heating equipment.

Customer Responsiveness

Henri meets expectations in this area. She is unfailingly courteous and patient with customers and has handled the occasional disparaging comments about her sex with aplomb, not to mention plenty of humor. Once she is able to get past a customer's erroneous perception of her abilities, she is able to prove what she is capable of doing and almost always ends up impressing customers with her competent approach to her work. The only complaints might be the amount of time customers are kept waiting while she wraps up a job for another customer.

Dependability

Henri can be considered one of our most dependable employees. She is willing to tackle any call that is assigned to her, even if she finds it daunting, and she can be counted on to show up at each job site in a timely manner and with everything she needs to accomplish the job. She is determined and cheerful and maintains a good attitude about her job. She gets along well with both customers and coworkers.

Forecast/Goals

Being a woman technician in a field that is generally considered to be a man's province has been difficult for Henri from the start, but she has handled it well and is making progress on both a personal and professional level. She has signed up for several courses that will give her more technological proficiency in the more advanced heating systems and enable her to work more independently in the future. She takes refuge in team situations where she has others to bolster and enhance her efforts. But she is needed more often for jobs that she must handle on her own; therefore, she has to become more comfortable with working more autonomously.

Further, Henri needs to assert more confidence in herself and her abilities. I have observed what she is capable of doing, and she clearly has a good instinct for the work she does. If she simply trusts that instinct more and not think so much about the consequences of the decisions she has to make on-site, as opposed to calling for assistance for fear of making a mistake, I believe she would find that she is better than she knows and that her judgment won't let her down.

Employee's Comments

Employee's signature: _____ Date: _____

Evaluator's signature: _____ Date: _____

PERFORMANCE EVALUATION—MID-LEVEL

Name: Graham Clark　　　　　　Department: Marketing
Title: Computer Programmer　　Supervisor: Sharon Corell
Date of hire: 6/15/XX　　　　　Review period: From 6/XX to 6/XX

Ratings: Employee is to be rated on a scale of 1 to 3, as described below.

　　1: Below expectations: Performance is substandard and requires improvement.
　　2: Meets expectations: Performance fully meets and occasionally exceeds standards.
　　3: Exceeds expectations: Performance consistently exceeds set standards.
N/A: Not applicable. Lack of sufficient knowledge to evaluate the performance factor.

Section I: Basic Job Skills

	Below	Meets	Exceeds	N/A
Job knowledge	1	<u>2</u>	3	N/A
Quality of work	1	2	<u>3</u>	N/A
Productivity/Timeliness	1	<u>2</u>	3	N/A
Dependability	1	2	<u>3</u>	N/A
Work habits	1	2	<u>3</u>	N/A
Organizational skills	1	2	<u>3</u>	N/A
Resourcefulness	1	<u>2</u>	3	N/A
Problem solving	1	<u>2</u>	3	N/A

Comments:

　　Graham is a devoted and diligent employee. He is careful to do everything to the letter. He is not very resourceful or self-starting in acquiring new knowledge, and he tends to continue making the same mistake for a long time before he discovers his error and corrects it. He produces an adequate amount of work but does not seem to extend himself beyond meeting the basic requirements of the job. If he were not so meticulous and careful, he would not be an adequate employee. To be a top performer, he must change his complacent willingness to just meet job standards.

Section II: Personal Attributes

	Below	Meets	Exceeds	N/A
Attendance/Punctuality	1	2	<u>3</u>	N/A
Ability to take direction	1	2	<u>3</u>	N/A
Initiative	1	<u>2</u>	3	N/A
Cooperativeness	1	2	<u>3</u>	N/A
Adaptability	1	<u>2</u>	3	N/A
Receptiveness to criticism	1	<u>2</u>	3	N/A
Communication skills	1	<u>2</u>	3	N/A
Interaction with coworkers	1	<u>2</u>	3	N/A

Comments:

Graham is outstanding in his reliability, his cooperativeness, and his following of directions. However, he only meets the basic standards in all other ways. He is very loath to change or adapt and never initiates any ideas or suggestions for improvement or enhancement of the work.

Section III: Strengths and Weaknesses

Describe employee strengths:

Graham is very reliable. He is always on the job and works and produces at a steady if unremarkable pace. Graham excels in the area of computer programming, which requires diligence and repetitive replication of details. He is very accurate and predictable. To the extent that these are desirable traits in a computer programmer, Graham is ideal.

Describe employee weaknesses:

On the other hand, Graham is not creative or inventive nor does he ever seem to have his interest, imagination, or enthusiasm engaged by his work. In order to be a top-level performer, Graham must either develop or disclose enthusiasm, inquisitiveness, and initiative, which are so far not in evidence.

Describe goals for next performance review:

1. Find at least one aspect of the job that incites Graham's imagination and interest and illustrate that there has been demonstrated growth, exploration, and enthusiasm shown in this area.

2. Take advantage of at least one of the company-supported college and technical courses as a means of discovering and developing an area of special expertise and interest related to the job.

Section IV: Comments

Evaluator:

Graham is an enigma. He is clearly bright and talented, but it is frustrating that he does not seem to have any sense of excitement or adventure connected with his job. From my perspective, I am always wishing he would find a way to engage himself in what goes on here at work. I will redouble my efforts to try to find and encourage areas that might foster such development.

Employee:

Employee's signature: _____ Date: _____

Evaluator's signature: _____ Date: _____

RESEARCH TECHNICIAN: INTERIM REVIEW

Name: Mike Curtin   Position: Research Technician
Date: June 27, 20XX

Performance Rating

On a scale of 1–10, your overall performance rating is a 7. You have shown good basic command of the skills of your position and are beginning to get the swing of the job routine. This is a high-energy, high-stress environment and it takes people time to adjust to that reality. You seem to relate well with the others on the staff and are able to cope with the fact that each week, as new tasks and new projects go through the lab, there are somewhat different job requirements. This job requires high "ambiguity tolerance," and you seem to be beginning to pick that up.

Strengths

Your greatest strengths are your basic science and research skills and your pleasant and generally unruffled manner. You are very bright, and you grasp quickly what is the essence of each project. That is impressive.

Weaknesses

Your weaknesses have to do with your difficulty in changing directions in midstream. Often your assignment will change before you have a chance to see one thing through to completion. That is the nature of the kind of service we provide to the scientists we serve. We are the technicians, not the designers of the research, and as such we are called upon to be creative in the way we carry forward the tasks given to us; but then we have to learn to let go, back out, and move on to a new project. You need to work on this adaptability and, frankly, on having the humility of being a technician, not a designer.

Goals and Directions

Continue to share your brilliance on the job, for ultimately this will lead to more and more exciting things for you to do. Listen, listen, listen. There is so much to learn, and although you love to talk—and you do it well and we enjoy listening to you—you can learn more through your ears than your mouth. Concentrate on making this a learning phase of your life.

Be very careful to always do your most accurate and careful work. It is tempting at times to take shortcuts and draw conclusions when your job is really to observe and collect data. Again, practice the humility that your position requires. The discipline you acquire in doing so will serve you well when you advance to greater things—as I know you will!

Forecast

Despite the few rough spots we have talked about, you have begun well. You should expect to make some more gaffs along the road, but be reassured that your ability to learn will help you to improve your "fit" in our laboratory. I firmly believe that you will ultimately become a top performer in this position.

Employee's Comments

Employee's signature: _____ Date: _____

Evaluator's signature: _____ Date: _____

Sample Reviews for Poor Performers

PERFORMANCE EVALUATION
Phone-Service Technician

Name: Danielle Underwood   Date: Sept. 30, 20XX

Quality of Work

Dani's overall work quality has been poor, especially in the past six months. There has been a complete downturn in both her productivity rate and in other aspects of her job performance, such as timeliness, organizational skills, job knowledge, and responsiveness to customers. There have been days when she has been unable to get through her call list, and customers become backed up waiting for her. On several occasions, she failed to call customers to indicate that she would be unable to get to their houses, leaving them waiting at home all day for her arrival, which never came. These customers were understandably upset, since many of them take time off from work to wait for the phone-service technician to come, and it is a waste of their time and money if Dani doesn't come when she's supposed to. This has been impressed on Dani time and again, yet she continues to work at a very slow rate that has imposed on the time of our customers. Additionally, she has made many errors that have caused her to make at least one return visit, and sometimes more, which causes further backups.

Job Knowledge

Dani has been trained well enough and worked long enough that she should have a thorough understanding of all aspects of her job and what is required of her. Unfortunately, she consistently seems to lack that understanding, and time and again has called back to the main office for assistance on problems that she should have been able to handle herself. Additionally, she has failed to keep herself abreast of the latest technology, as well as of company policies and procedures.

Strongest Work Elements

Dani has not demonstrated too many strengths of late. In the past, she was noted for her courtesy toward customers and her willingness to do whatever was asked of her. She is still very polite, but otherwise has allowed herself to fall slipshod in the performance of her work and her attitude toward others.

Weakest Work Elements

The weakest aspects of her work include her disorganization, her failure to keep scheduled appointments with customers, her inability to set priorities well, and her lack of motivation to work on the problems she is currently having. She is also relatively unable to work independently, needing direction and assistance more often than is necessary for somebody of her experience.

Customer Responsiveness

Dani used to have a good relationship with our customers, but it has deteriorated in the last several months. Aside from the problem noted of missing scheduled appointments and keeping people waiting for unnecessarily long periods of time, she has also not demonstrated much respect for our customers' homes. We have received numerous complaints of the mess Dani frequently leaves behind, including bits of wires, and even a tool or two on occasion. She has been reminded numerous times to clean up after herself before she leaves a job site, but has overlooked these instructions on too many occasions.

Dependability

Dani's level of dependability has dropped considerably, for all the reasons enumerated in this evaluation. She cannot be counted on at the present time to be either punctual or productive on a daily basis.

Forecast/Goals

It turns out that Dani has had numerous personal problems that have had a direct effect on both her job performance and her attitude toward her job. When she explained it all to me, I got a clearer understanding of the reasons behind the dramatic slip in the quality of her work over the past six months. However, she should have confided in me a while ago, rather than resisting my attempts to inquire and help previously. The negative reports received about her service, or lack of it, coupled with the accumulation of ways in which she has failed to meet her job criteria had me prepared to give her notice. However, given her years of experience and her good evaluations of years past, she will be given one more chance. Dani is to begin working on all aspects of her job discussed in this evaluation and make tangible improvements within the next three months, especially as regards customer service. She will be evaluated again in three months' time, and if the desired improvement has been made, her probation will be extended for another three months, and additional goals will be set for her.

Employee's Comments

Employee's signature: _____ Date: _____

Evaluator's signature: _____ Date: _____

PERFORMANCE EVALUATION

Name: Virgil Hansen

Title: Lab Technician

Date of hire: 7/15/XX

Department: Oncology

Supervisor: Dana Martin

Review period: From 7/XX to 7/XX

Ratings: Employee is to be rated on a scale of 1 to 3, as described below.

1: Below expectations: Performance is substandard and requires improvement.

2: Meets expectations: Performance fully meets and occasionally exceeds standards.

3: Exceeds expectations: Performance consistently exceeds set standards.

N/A: Not applicable. Lack of sufficient knowledge to evaluate the performance factor.

Section I: Basic Job Skills

	Below	Meets	Exceeds	N/A
Job knowledge	1	<u>2</u>	3	N/A
Quality of work	<u>1</u>	2	3	N/A
Productivity/Timeliness	<u>1</u>	2	3	N/A
Dependability	1	<u>2</u>	3	N/A
Work habits	1	<u>2</u>	3	N/A
Organizational skills	1	<u>2</u>	3	N/A
Resourcefulness	<u>1</u>	2	3	N/A
Problem solving	<u>1</u>	2	3	N/A

Comments:

The nature of an oncology lab is such that reliability is essential, and diligent and resourceful means must be applied to problems that are not readily solved. Questions need to be answered, not left hanging. Virgil leaves an unacceptable number of loose ends and dead ends and his continued employment will be dependent on his ability to rectify those faults.

Section II: Personal Attributes

	Below	Meets	Exceeds	N/A
Attendance/Punctuality	1	<u>2</u>	3	N/A
Ability to take direction	1	<u>2</u>	3	N/A
Initiative	<u>1</u>	2	3	N/A
Cooperativeness	1	<u>2</u>	3	N/A

Adaptability		1	<u>2</u>	3	N/A
Receptiveness to criticism		1	<u>2</u>	3	N/A
Communication skills		1	<u>2</u>	3	N/A
Interaction with coworkers		<u>1</u>	2	3	N/A

Comments:

Virgil is adequate in most ways. But he does not ever rise above adequacy. In several areas, particularly initiative and cooperative interactions with his coworkers as noted above, he is well below acceptable. He must address these lacks and work to find strength in several areas if he is to be an acceptable employee.

Section III: Strengths and Weaknesses

Describe employee strengths:

Virgil is a pleasant and generally cooperative man. He has adequate job knowledge and skills and seems to have plenty "on the ball" in general life skills.

Describe employee weaknesses:

At this point it seems that Virgil is neither interested in nor rewarded by his job. The result is very lackluster and often sloppy job performance. Virgil must find a way to apply himself with energy and accuracy to the job at hand or he will need to find another job that will excite and inspire his careful attention.

Describe goals for next performance review:

1. Develop with the supervisor a list of specific job competency levels to be attained and then document that these levels are being maintained.

2. Chart unacceptable errors in job performance, and demonstrate that through energy and attentiveness this rate has dropped within the acceptable range.

3. Set up a monthly review process for 6 months and then two quarterly reviews to monitor this process and celebrate and support Virgil's success in turning around his job performance.

Section IV: Comments

Evaluator:

I sincerely hope that by charting Virgil's job performance through the next year we can arrive at the next annual review with an entirely different job performance overview: one that is more in line with Virgil's clearly strong abilities. I look forward to celebrating and supporting Virgil's transition to a more effective and productive employee.

Employee:

Employee's signature: _____ Date: _____

Evaluator's signature: _____ Date: _____

9

Model Evaluations for Administrative and Support Workers

This group of workers interpret or apply policy. They often have responsibility for designing and maintaining the systems that they use to do their jobs and have specialized knowledge of the area they administer. Their job titles include:

- Marketing Coordinator
- Administrative Secretary
- Executive Office Assistant
- Accounts Administrator
- Administrative Assistant
- Employee-Benefits Administrator
- Scheduling Coordinator
- Attendance Officer
- Information-Systems Administrator
- Advertising Administrator
- Community and Public-Relations Administrator

Gauging Performance

The overriding concern with these employees is their ability to organize and coordinate all aspects of their job responsibilities in order to accomplish set goals. This frequently means working to get maximum performance from others. There are various combinations of abilities that can accomplish this.

Traits that are admired in these workers include consistency, fairness, the ability to keep priorities straight, and a general evenness of approach and attitude. These workers need to be able to listen, to make decisions, and to handle the buck when it stops with them.

Workers who demonstrate dedication, excellent work habits, strong interpersonal skills, and high output are much admired. One key indicator of these people's strengths is their ability to supervise others while maintaining their own workload. If they get the job done and achieve strong departmental morale while doing so, they have what it takes.

Performance Indicators

The top-level performer

- Has a high level of appropriate knowledge
- Has outstanding supervisory skills
- Has strong communication and interpersonal abilities
- Is highly dependable
- Shows appropriate initiative; can work independently
- Works well in a pressurized environment
- Has excellent organizational abilities
- Is an excellent problem solver
- Is thorough and accurate in accomplishing all tasks
- Is punctual and regular in attendance
- Has a high degree of enthusiasm and commitment towards the job
- Is comfortable and receptive to appropriate criticism

The good performer

- Has a good level of appropriate knowledge
- Can supervise others with little to no difficulty

- Has good communication and interpersonal abilities
- Is dependable and shows initiative without overstepping bounds
- Can generally handle pressure situations well
- Has strong organizational abilities
- Has the ability to spot and solve problems
- Is generally thorough and accurate in accomplishing all tasks
- Is largely punctual and regular in attendance
- Maintains a good, positive attitude
- Can handle appropriate criticism

The poor performer

- Does not possess the appropriate knowledge to do an effective job
- Is a poor supervisor
- Is lacking in communication and interpersonal abilities
- Is not very dependable
- Demonstrates poor judgment in attempts to take initiative
- Is not able to handle pressure situations very well
- Has poor or insufficient organizational abilities
- Is not able to solve problems well
- Is not very thorough or is frequently inaccurate
- Has problems with regular attendance and punctuality
- Is apathetic about the job and demonstrates little interest in improvement
- Has difficulty with criticism

Sample Reviews for Top-level Performers

PERFORMANCE APPRAISAL

Employee Name: Douglas Willison   Interim   Annual ✗
Job Title: Marketing Coordinator (Publishing)
Supervisor: Walter Holmes   Date: 3/1/XX

I: Job Skills

	Sometimes	Usually	Always
			✗

Job Knowledge

Uses/demonstrates the skills and tools necessary to perform job effectively. Can draw upon previous experience to handle new problems or challenges. Makes effort to stay current in field.

Comments:

> Doug effectively utilizes his previous experience in both the editorial and sales fields—and the contacts he made in those positions—to good advantage in his current position. In addition, his strong computer skills enable him to conduct immediate researches and analyses of current trends in the field. He coordinates the efforts of the sales and editorial teams with the goals set by management and does a remarkable job of ensuring a smooth and successful launch to each book for which he is responsible.

	Sometimes	Usually	Always
			✗

Organizational Skills

Can plan, organize and prioritize work effectively. Meets deadlines and completes assignments within specified time frames. Uses time and resources effectively to meet goals.

Comments:

Doug's organizational skills are superb. He is often responsible for the marketing efforts behind several books, many of them published at the same time. Nevertheless, his desk is a model of neatness, and he is always on top of the status of each of his projects. He is extremely attentive to details and is the envy of his coworkers for his ability to find whatever is needed at a moment's notice.

Sometimes	Usually	Always
		X

Teamwork

Works effectively with other employees.
Gives assistance to others when needed.
Shares credit and can balance personal and
team goals.

Comments:

See first comment. Doug is a team player par excellence.

Sometimes	Usually	Always
		X

Communication Skills

Communicates thoughts and ideas clearly
and demonstrates ability to listen and offer
sound feedback. Is concise in both written
and verbal communications. Keeps management and peers well informed.

Comments:

Doug issues regular status reports plotting each book's progress and the status of the marketing plan. He is an active participant in editorial meetings and often provides solid advice on a book's selling points, based on his previous experience in the field and knowledge of the market. He writes well and does not overelaborate when speaking, but sticks well to the point.

Sometimes	Usually	Always
		X

Problem Solving

Can identify and analyze problems and present solutions, using available resources or
creative ideas.

Comments:

> This is one of Doug's strongest credits.

	Sometimes	Usually	Always
Professionalism			X

Accepts responsibility for all aspects of job and is willing to be held accountable for errors. Displays professional attitude and appearance in approach to job.

Comments:

> He can sometimes be too quick to point fingers at others when a crisis occurs, but this doesn't happen very often.

	Sometimes	Usually	Always
Initiative and Motivation			X

Can handle multiple tasks and responsibilities and is willing to take on new challenges. Displays interest in and enthusiasm for the job and completes assignments quickly and efficiently.

Comments:

> As above.

	Sometimes	Usually	Always
Flexibility			X

Adapts to new situations and changing work responsibilities. Is open to suggestions and criticism and able to utilize input from others. Looks for acceptable solutions in conflict situations.

Comments:

> Doug has to cope with the needs and demands of numerous people— authors, editors, sales staff, and marketing staff. He remains flexible at

all times to meet the demands that are put on him and frequently works as a peacemaker when there are disparate points of view regarding the marketing goals of a particular book.

	Sometimes	Usually	Always
			X

Punctuality

Adheres to work hours and is present for work every day. Provides adequate notice of vacation or personal time, and makes arrangements for coverage.

Comments:

He is occasionally tardy and frequently takes several days off without adequate notice. However, he ensures that another coordinator is able to handle whatever questions may arise in his absence.

II: Achievements and Contributions

List the employee's major contributions to company goals, growth, and/or profitability during the appraisal period. Describe what actions the employee took to make these achievements.

Doug coordinated the successful launch of the Atlantis children's series, as well as our two biggest-selling books of the season. He is attentive to all the details of his job and performs extensive market research to back up his recommendations. His enthusiasm and dedication to his work help to inspire his coworkers to bigger achievements. All in all, he has been a positive force for the company.

III: Plans and Goals

List and describe what the employee must achieve for the next performance appraisal period, including skills development, areas of improvement, projects, etc.

Doug will continue to hone his marketing skills and is preparing to embark on a project with the telemarketing department to canvass our customer base to determine whether there is continued interest in our series on the history of the theater. He has expressed an interest in returning to the editorial field, particularly development. He would do well in whatever area he chose.

IV: Appraiser's Summary

Describe employee's overall performance rating.

Excellent! Doug is a real asset to the company and should be supported in his editorial career goals. I recommend a 5 percent pay increase.

V: Employee's Comments

Employee's signature: _____ Date: _____

Evaluator's signature: _____ Date: _____

PERFORMANCE EVALUATION
Administrative

Name: Sean Li   Title: Department Administrator

Date: 10/2/20XX

Job Knowledge

Sean is an able and effective administrator of the marketing department whose experience and abilities have made him uniquely qualified for his position. After nearly two years of bouncing around different departments in varying capacities as a temp, he landed a job in the marketing department as a file clerk and quickly worked his way up to his present position, which he has held for the past year. Along the way, he acquired and retained valuable job knowledge in both office administration and marketing that has served him well. He thus possesses both the skills and the experience to carry out his job.

Quality of Work

Sean's work is superb in every way. He has a number of diverse duties, from general office administration to special assignments given to him by the marketing managers. He coordinates the scheduling of all marketing meetings, serves as reporting secretary, and writes up minutes, in addition to which he follows up in the appropriate areas to ensure that assigned tasks are being carried out properly. He also oversees the secretarial-support staff, hands out assignments, and follows through to make sure that tasks are being completed in a timely and orderly fashion. He orders supplies, takes care of office equipment, and works closely with the head manager on the annual report and other brochures and documents. In essence, he does a lot of all-around work and superbly meets every challenge and opportunity we can throw at him.

Productivity/Timeliness

Sean has almost a mania for effective time management. His ability for scheduling is without peer, and he has been relied upon to put together work-flow charts that enable us to keep track of projects and to know the status of each one and how far along we are. He manages the more mundane aspect of his job with equal efficiency and ensures that all assigned tasks are completed in a timely and presentable manner.

Organizational Skills

His organizational skills are Sean's strongest suit, as should be evident from the remarks above. He manages to effectively balance the needs and demands of his supervisors with the skills and capabilities of those whom he supervises. The overall organization of the department, including files, have improved tenfold since Sean took over and straightened everything out.

Communication Skills

Sean has come a long way since his early days as a temp with our company, and he communicates effectively most of the time. However, he still has some problems with the English language, and if anybody talks to him using long, complicated words with which he is unfamiliar, he runs the risk of misinterpreting an instruction or taking an incorrect action because he is afraid to admit that he doesn't understand something. Sean needs to have the courage to say, "Can you repeat/explain that, please?" and trust that people won't judge him because his English-language skills still need improvement. I should point out that he has little to no problem in writing; it is only the verbal aspect that is still giving him some trouble.

Interpersonal Skills/Leadership

Sean interacts well with everybody, from clerks up to the executive management. He is very popular, well liked, and respected. He inspires the secretarial and clerical staff to excel, and he has proven himself to be invaluable to the managers who use and appreciate his administrative services.

Initiative/Motivation

Sean has plenty of initiative. He is also always motivated to improve both his own performance and the methods by which he administers all departmental functions and services. He is enthusiastic and committed to his job and demonstrates his talent and dedication on a daily basis.

Problem Solving

Sean has terrific problem-solving abilities and is often able to provide sound and well-reasoned solutions to the trickiest of situations. This is a crucial element of his success, in fact.

Goals for Next Review

The only aspect of his performance that Sean needs to work on is his self-confidence. He has the drive, the determination, and the capabilities. He is trusted and relied upon to give his best, and he always delivers. He should work some more on his language skills and trust in himself to know that he is a highly valued and respected member of our team.

Employee's Comments

Employee's signature: _____ Date: _____

Evaluator's signature: _____ Date: _____

PERFORMANCE REVIEW
Executive/Administrative Secretarial Employees

Name: Carol Magnusson

Job Title: Administrative Secretary

Department: Cancer Research

Type of Evaluation:

Interim   Annual X

Date: July 19, 20XX

Evaluation Guide

1 = Excellent (exceptional; exceeds expectations)

2 = Good (consistently meets, and frequently exceeds, usual expectations)

3 = Satisfactory (conforms to standards; meets expectations)

4 = Fair (marginal; only meeting minimum requirements)

5 = Poor (below standard and unacceptable; improvement required or termination will result)

Factors for Review

Job Knowledge   Rating: 1

Degree to which the employee knows and understands his/her job and its functions

Carol continues to expand her job knowledge and excel in every task she undertakes.

Quality of Work   Rating: 1

Accuracy, presentability, neatness, etc.

Her work is top-drawer. Every document she produces is easy to read because it is so well formatted and thoroughly checked for both spelling and grammar as well as neatness. She approaches all other tasks she handles with the same attention to detail and accuracy.

Quantity of Work   Rating: 1

Amount of work consistently produced within requirements of the position

She is fast, accurate, and thorough.

Work Interest   Rating: 1

Employee's attitude toward his/her work, specialized knowledge of the job, receptivity to new work assignments, efforts to acquire new or broader job knowledge

Carol has improved in this area from a rating of 2 up to 1. She has taken numerous computer courses to improve her skills and has sought out others for guidance in understanding the various components of the research center and its scientists. She has also taken on additional responsibilities, such as the processing of visas for foreign scientists.

Resourcefulness   Rating: 1
Adaptability, versatility, dependability, self-reliance, initiative, ease of learning

From the start, she has been motivated to work independently and to find new and creative ways to stimulate her own interest in her work. She learns quickly and is always eager to take on new assignments.

Judgment   Rating: 2
Ability to evaluate situations, draw conclusions, and make sound decisions

An area in which I continue to expect strong growth.

Interpersonal Skills   Rating: 1
Tact, courtesy, self-control, patience, loyalty, and discretion

This is one of her strongest areas. She meets and exceeds all criteria on a daily basis.

Dependability   Rating: 1
Punctuality, regular attendance at meetings, overall reliability

I feel I can rely on Carol.

Work Habits   Rating: 1
Ability to plan and organize work, make efficient use of work time, adhere to established rules and procedures, follow through on work assignments

Excellent organizational skills. She prioritizes her work well and plans each day to achieve maximum effectiveness.

Use of Resources   Rating: 2
Conservation and economization of expendable resources; care of equipment

Another area in which I continue to expect strong growth.

Growth Potential   Rating: 1
Ability to progress to higher level work and assume more responsible duties

Carol has superb potential to advance to a position of greater responsibility.

OVERALL RATING

Since employee's last appraisal, his/her performance has:

_X_ Improved

___ Maintained same level

___ Declined

COMMENTS

Noteworthy performance strengths:

Carol has excellent recall. She is always able to locate important data, records, documents, etc. She maintains a competent, professional manner even during times of stress. She has a superb talent for handling multiple tasks at once. Her ability to follow through on assignments has improved tremendously since her last review. She is frequently left solely in charge of the office and demonstrates good judgment in resolving problems when the director is not available. She responds quickly and efficiently, never complains, and works well with others.

Areas needing improvement:

Carol needs to expand her knowledge of the financial and budgetary concerns of the department and take a more active role in grants management.

Plan of action:

Work with the financial manager to prepare grants, follow up on grant applications, and manage funds.

Employee's signature: _____ Date: _____

Evaluator's signature: _____ Date: _____

EVALUATION FORM

Employee Name: Evelyn Dunn

Employee's Job Title: Executive Office Assistant

Date: June 22, 20XX

Department: Human Resources

Period covered by this evaluation: From 6/XX to 5/XX

Reason for this evaluation: Interim   Annual X   Other _____
                                                                                              (Specify)

Rating levels and definitions

Level 5 = *Performance exceeds job requirements.*

> The employee performs at outstanding level within the criteria and frequently above and beyond expectations.

Level 4 = *Performance meets job requirements.*

> The employee meets the full expectations of the position.

Level 3 = *Performance meets job requirements with room for further development.*

> The employee performs at a satisfactory level within the criteria. However, some further development is necessary.

Level 2 = *Performance needs improvement.*

> The employee does not perform at the required level. Improvement is necessary.

Level 1 = *Unacceptable performance.*

> The employee's performance is clearly unacceptable with the criteria set for the job. Immediate improvement must occur.

PERFORMANCE CRITERIA

A. Job Knowledge   Rating Assigned: 5

Evaluate the extent to which the employee understands the responsibilities of his or her position; is knowledgeable in the latest techniques, skills, and methods pertinent to his or her area of responsibility; and pursues further training or education to improve job know-how and professional capabilities.

Evelyn knows and understands every facet of her job. People within the department, as well as within the company, view her as the primary authority on benefits and tuition reimbursement, as well as an invaluable resource for questions on hiring when a generalist is not available. She provides quality backup to every generalist and goes the extra mile to provide excellent service and accurate information.

B. Quality of Work   Rating Assigned: 5

Evaluate the extent to which the employee's work conforms to established standards and procedures; demonstrates attention to specific directions; is accurate, thorough, and presentable; and is concise and timely.

Evelyn's work is very detail oriented, yet is always clear, concise, and correct. Mistakes are not quantifiable.

C. Accomplishment of Goals and Objectives Rating Assigned: 5

Evaluate the extent to which the employee sets appropriate goals and objectives; demonstrates commitment and enthusiasm in carrying out his or her plan of action; and achieves objectives in a timely and competent manner.

Evelyn is one of the most neatly organized people it has ever been my pleasure to work with. She always keeps her desk cleared of excess paper and knows how to prioritize every task she works on. Her in-basket is almost always empty because of her quick and efficient way of tackling her goals. She does this despite innumerable interruptions on a daily basis.

D. Initiative and Creativity   Rating Assigned: 5

Evaluate the extent to which the employee is aware of what needs to be done and demonstrates the energy and self-motivation to begin and complete work requirements without prompting from others; and approaches his or her work in creative or imaginative ways.

Evelyn played a major role in the redesign of our application forms, making them simpler and easier to read and fill out. She has also suggested innumerable changes in our standard procedures, which she then implemented upon approval. These changes resulted in a cleaner, neater reception area, easy access to all forms needed, and an overall organized feel to the department that was lacking prior to her arrival.

E. Analytic Skills   Rating Assigned: N/A

Evaluate the extent to which the employee can analyze a situation or problem and draw logical and valid conclusions; identifies all critical areas of the issue and can make sound recommendations; and is able to propose several viable alternatives based on recognition of multiple options.

F. Problem Solving   Rating Assigned: 4

Evaluate the extent to which the employee identifies different problems requiring attention; can isolate causes and propose solutions; and is able to foresee the impact decisions made may have on other people or departments and therefore will consult with them.

328

Evelyn reviews all paperwork carefully and is quick to pick out problems or potential problems and bring them to the attention of the appropriate generalist. She often provides an appropriate suggestion for the resolution of the problem.

G. Interpersonal and Communication Skills   Rating Assigned: 5

Evaluate the extent to which the employee demonstrates conciseness, clarity, tact, and cordiality in both written and verbal communications; listens carefully and understands directions; can express an opinion or position while also considering other conflicting points of view; provides accurate and timely information when required; and is considerate and respectful of different levels of personnel as well as people of different types and cultures.

This is probably Evelyn's greatest strength. In addition to her being able to interpret corporate policies and procedures and explaining them clearly and effectively, she also ably assists other personnel with the resolution of any sticky issues, especially those involving benefits and payroll. Many people within the company come to her for advice or counsel of a personal as well as a business nature. It is safe to say that she is in many ways looked upon as an equal-opportunity mother figure, and one in whom enormous trust and confidence can be placed.

H. Teamwork and Cooperation   Rating Assigned: 5

Evaluate the extent to which the employee works effectively and efficiently with others; is willing to offer or accept assistance when necessary; and is flexible and willing to compromise or make concessions in the best interests of the organization.

Evelyn does all of this and more.

I. Consumer Relations/Hospitality   Rating Assigned: 5

Evaluate the extent to which the employee achieves positive relationships with customers, visitors, and all levels of company staff; contributes to a favorable public image of the company; is accessible to users of department services; and has merited the trust and respect of others within and outside the department.

She is responsible for ensuring that the needs and concerns of both salaried personnel and job applicants are met quickly and courteously.

J. Cost Effectiveness   Rating Assigned: 5

Evaluate the extent to which the employee budgets time and remains organized and focused on work assignments; effectively preserves and economizes on expendable supplies and resources; cares for and maintains office equipment; and adheres to departmental cost-containment policies.

Evelyn is very attentive to budgetary concerns and unfailingly meets and exceeds all expectations for fiscal responsibility.

OVERALL PERFORMANCE RATING 5

DEVELOPMENTAL GOALS:

Describe goals for the next 12-month period, along with agreed-upon plan for obtaining goals, the time frame for achieving goals, and the method to be used for measuring achievement.

Evelyn has taken charge of overseeing the conversion of the new computer system containing all personnel records and hiring forms and procedures. She will work with Network Services to complete the transition of all files from the old system to the new and will supervise the efforts of temporary help hired to assist in the entering of all relevant data. She will ensure that the new operations are up and running within the next six months.

Evelyn has the capacity to make an excellent Human Resources Generalist. She is taking courses at a local university with the goal of obtaining the proper academic qualifications for professional advancement.

It seems to be impossible to find anything of a negative or critical nature regarding the quality of Evelyn's work, her professional attitude, or the regard in which she is held by all who come into contact with her. She is a gem!

EMPLOYEE'S COMMENTS

Employee's signature: _____ Date: _____

Evaluator's signature: _____ Date: _____

PERFORMANCE EVALUATION

Name: Maureen O'Herlihy   Title: Administrative Assistant

Date: November 10, 20XX   Interim   Annual X

I. JOB FACTORS:

RATING:

1. Job knowledge   (poor) 1 2 3 4 <u>5</u> (excellent)
2. Quality of work   (poor) 1 2 3 4 <u>5</u> (excellent)
3. Productivity   (poor) 1 2 3 <u>4</u> 5 (excellent)
4. Organizational skills   (poor) 1 2 3 <u>4</u> 5 (excellent)
5. Dependability   (poor) 1 2 3 <u>4</u> 5 (excellent)
6. Interpersonal skills/Teamwork   (poor) 1 2 3 4 <u>5</u> (excellent)
7. Initiative/Motivation   (poor) 1 2 3 4 <u>5</u> (excellent)
8. Communication skills (verbal/written)   (poor) 1 2 3 <u>4</u> 5 (excellent)
9. Analytic skills/Problem solving   (poor) 1 2 3 4 <u>5</u> (excellent)
10. Professionalism   (poor) 1 2 3 4 <u>5</u> (excellent)

Overall Rating   (poor) 1 2 3 4 <u>5</u> (excellent)

(Actual rating = 4.5)

II. SUMMARY/COMMENTS

Maureen is a supremely capable and efficient administrative assistant in the Dean's Office at XYZ University. In addition to her supervision of all secretarial and clerical staff, she is responsible for overseeing and managing the dean's busy calendar, scheduling and organizing numerous ad hoc committee meetings, maintaining an extensive database, and managing an extremely busy and complicated office, along with miscellaneous duties that range from crucial to grunt tasks. She is called upon time and again to be a combination of den mother, big sister, primary bean counter, chief Ms. Fix-It, and supreme organizer—in other words, Wonder Woman. She has duties so numerous and so involved with many different facets of university life that it is impossible to list them all here. Suffice to say that to do what Maureen does requires exceptional organization and administrative abilities, not to mention patience, attention to details, an ability to work well under stress, and resilience. Maureen possesses all of these qualities in spades.

331

She has worked her way up the ranks to her present position, which she has held for the last 5 years. She has been working for the university for the last 15 years and has developed an expertise about both the history and the internal functions of the school that is unparalleled by any other except the oldest staff members. If the answer is unknown, then Maureen is often the court of last resort and the person most likely to provide an accurate answer to whatever the question might be. While she considers herself to be a member of "the old guard," she is highly adaptable to change and is able to adjust to new situations. She is often responsible for the dissemination of information about and enforcement of new policies and procedures as they are handed down by the Board of Trustees and the dean.

Maureen excels at putting out fires. No matter what the situation might be, if there's a crisis that requires the involvement of the dean's office, it will most likely be Maureen who will step in and see the problem through to a successful resolution.

She has full fiscal responsibility for the department, as well as the hiring and training of office-support staff. She has a tendency to be a bit harsh at times, applying rigid standards of behavior on employees that perhaps make them feel imprisoned by their jobs. Maureen should learn not to take everything so seriously and to allow a bit of latitude with her staff. She should trust them to do their jobs and not go overboard with her attention to their professional behavior. This is bound only to cause friction among a staff that should be working closely together.

III. GOALS FOR NEXT REVIEW

It is clear that Maureen is highly dependable and an even more highly valued employee. She keeps every aspect of the Dean's Office running smoothly, with minimal supervision necessary from the dean himself, who trusts her to manage all his administrative affairs and that of his office with the efficiency and capability she has demonstrated so well over the last five years. She has a very admirable work ethic and lives by the principle that idle hands are the devil's playthings. This being the case, it should be noted that she probably pushes both herself and her staff too hard, and it would be good for all concerned if she made some attempt to lighten up a bit and not always be so deadly serious about her work and that of others. This will be an area to work on and will be evaluated based on the number and nature of any comments received about her from others. She should also learn to delegate more work. She has a good-sized, efficient staff, and she should be making better use of them. She has felt in the past that training others to do what just comes naturally to her at this point is more trouble than it's worth, and it's just as easy for her to do it herself. However, aside from overloading herself with responsibilities that can be overwhelming and contribute to a sense of disorganization in her work area, it is a waste of the other resources (clerks and secretaries) who can do the job as easily as she can. Thus, I would like to see her delegate more tasks and authority to others.

IV. EMPLOYEE COMMENTS

Employee's signature: _____ Date: _____

Evaluator's signature: _____ Date: _____

PERFORMANCE EVALUATION

Performance evaluation for: Eleanor Powers   Title: Office Manager
Date: March 1, 20XX

JOB FACTORS:

1. Job knowledge   (weak) 1 2 3 4 <u>5</u> (superior)
   Comments:

   Your years of experience with the company have resulted in an amazing base of knowledge, know-how, and can-do that brings quality result to everything you touch. Also to your credit is that you are always willing to learn new methods and technologies and bring them to bear to your administration of the office if you feel it will benefit the company.

2. Productivity   (weak) 1 2 3 4 <u>5</u> (superior)
   Comments:

   What can I say? You come through every time. The office is run like clock-work thanks to your capable administration and your extraordinary talents.

3. Quality of work   (weak) 1 2 3 4 <u>5</u> (superior)
   Comments:

   You have the golden touch with everything you do. You see to it that all needs are attended to with great skill and attention to detail.

4. Dependability   (weak) 1 2 3 4 <u>5</u> (superior)
   Comments:

   I know of nobody who doesn't rely on you in some way and will come to you when there's a job to be done quickly and efficiently. How you manage to accommodate all the demands on your time is beyond me. I can't praise you enough!

5. Initiative/Motivation   (weak) 1 2 3 4 <u>5</u> (superior)
   Comments:

   You are always thinking of ways to make things better. You have the best interests of the company and its workers firmly in mind as you take it upon yourself to set up offices for new employees, improve operating systems, order equipment and supplies, and so forth.

6. Cooperation/Teamwork   (weak) 1 2 3 4 <u>5</u> (superior)

Comments:

You are not only part of the team, you are a leader. You manage a small staff of just two secretaries, but the fact that they have both stayed for over five years is a clear indication of their regard for you and your leadership.

7. Communication skills   (weak) 1 2 3 4 <u>5</u> (superior)

Comments:

Many managers rely on you to look over their reports and presentations to make sure that they read well and will be effective. Your writing skills are nothing short of superb, as are your verbal interactions with others.

8. Organizational skills   (weak) 1 2 3 4 <u>5</u> (superior)

Comments:

Again there is nothing that can be said. You cannot be equaled in your abilities to organize and prioritize your work.

9. Analytic skills/Problem solving   (weak) 1 2 3 4 <u>5</u> (superior)

Comments:

You are the go-to person when times get tough and fires need to be put out. Your experience and sharp mind always enable you to find a way.

10. Interpersonal skills   (weak) 1 2 3 4 <u>5</u> (superior)

Comments:

I don't know of a single person who doesn't like and admire you and respect your abilities. You have a gift for people. It obviously helps that you love your job, but your interpersonal skills are a great advantage.

OVERALL RATING:

___ Needs improvement in job performance

___ Meets job requirements

<u>X</u> Exceeds job requirements

Comments:

Perhaps next year we can start to discuss the options that will face us and start to plan for how we are going to deal with finding a replacement for you when the time comes—not that you can be replaced. In the meantime, please know how highly your services are valued. We all thank you for doing such an excellent job, which you will continue to do, I am sure.

Employee's Comments

Employee's signature: _____ Date: _____

Evaluator's signature: _____ Date: _____

Sample Reviews for Mid-level Performers

PERFORMANCE APPRAISAL AND DISCUSSION

Employee: Marian Allandale
Department: Information Resources
Prepared by: Robin Littlejohn

Job Title: Administrative Assistant
Time in position: 2 years
Date: 4/1/XX

RATINGS

Select the rating that most accurately reflects the employee's performance:

1 = Outstanding; the employee achieved extraordinary results.

2 = Above average; the employee achieved results that were beyond job requirements.

3 = Average; the employee met job requirements effectively and consistently.

4 = Below average; the employee did not fully meet job requirements. Improvement is encouraged.

5 = Substandard; the employee did not achieve effective results and requires significant improvement.

I. OVERALL PERFORMANCE RATING

Rate and explain employee's overall
performance on all aspects of the job: 1   2   3   4   5

Marian has consistently proven herself to be a conscientious and innovative administrator who continues to improve and excel in her area of responsibility. This year she initiated new Internet search services and also became more proficient in using external and internal resources to answer questions and search inquiries. She assisted in the planning and development of an online database program that will be a valuable resource for the company when it is fully implemented. She is currently assisting in the writing of user documentation for the new program and will be involved in the connection and training of users. Marian has provided numerous useful suggestions to improve and better utilize current search techniques. In addition, she supervises all part-time and temporary help and oversees the satisfactory completion of their work.

II. MAJOR AND OTHER JOB FACTORS

Check the rating that best represents employee's performance in meeting job factors.

Major Job Factors	*Rating*				
Quality: How does the employee's work meet existing criteria (i.e., accuracy, neatness, thoroughness, etc.)?	1	<u>2</u>	3	4	5
Quantity: How does the volume of work the employee produces compare with job requirements?	1	2	<u>3</u>	4	5
Initiative: To what extent is the employee self-motivated in completing assignments and initiating new ideas?	1	<u>2</u>	3	4	5
Dependability: How can the employee be relied upon to complete assignments in a timely manner and acceptable form?	1	2	<u>3</u>	4	5
Cooperation: How does the employee make effective use of all modes of communication and achieve a common understanding with others?	1	<u>2</u>	3	4	5

Other Job Factors	*Rating*				

(List any additional relevant job factors)

Personnel training	1	<u>2</u>	3	4	5

Marian's contributions to training temps and new employees, which included writing job descriptions and training manuals, was crucial to the smooth running of the department.

Problem Solving	<u>1</u>	2	3	4	5

Marian excels in this area.

Customer Response Time	1	<u>2</u>	3	4	5

Marian is attuned to in-house customer needs and is always willing to provide extra effort to make sure that a quick and thorough response is provided to each question received. She is able to draw upon her prior experience to guide and support others within the department to do the same.

Interactive Skills   1   2   3   4   5

   Marian works well with others and is looked upon as a leader within the
   department, as well as a valuable resource to turn to when others are
   stuck with a difficult inquiry or when a problem needs a level-headed
   solution.

III. ACHIEVEMENT OF GOALS AND OBJECTIVES

Review the employee's goals and any special projects assigned at the previous performance appraisal. Indicate whether any goals or projects are still in process or were not
completed and reasons why.

Goal or Project   *Rating*

Improvement of work flow   1   2   3   4   5

   In the past year, Marian was to institute new procedures for improving the
   flow of work within the department. She handled this assignment well,
   first by redefining the job responsibilities of our two part-time secretaries,
   then by redesigning and streamlining the "Request for Information" forms.
   She has also worked closely with various department heads to determine
   their needs and provide guidance in obtaining the appropriate response to
   their inquiries. The result has been an increased confidence in the services our department offers and improved work flow. Good work, Marian!

Increase knowledge of external/
internal resources   1   2   3   4   5

   Marian has done a fine job of meeting this requirement. In addition to her
   implementation of a new Internet search service, she has expanded her
   understanding of various on-line databases and has kept abreast of company product developments to better anticipate questions and search
   inquiries from other departments.

Plan and implement on-line database
program   1   2   3   4   5

   This project is still in process and the effect won't be felt for two or three
   months. However, Marian is taking an active and important role in the
   development of this program.

Increase professional growth   1   2   <u>3</u>   4   5

> Marian has been taking part in business and computer seminars to improve her knowledge of industry standards and resources, as well as her understanding of the Internet.

IV. GOALS AND OBJECTIVES FOR NEXT PERIOD

Describe all goals, projects, and plans of action to be followed by the employee for the next performance-appraisal period. Indicate what is to be done, what the results will be, and what steps will be followed to achieve those results.

Objective: Time Frame:
Implement on-line database program   *6 months*

> When the new database program is ready to be implemented, Marian will be responsible for the training of all company personnel who will be using it, as well as overseeing the continued maintenance of the program.

Reorganize filing system   *6 months*

> As new computer-search techniques are implemented and the overall responsibilities of the department change to accommodate company-wide needs, it has become evident that our filing system has become antiquated and needs to be overhauled. Marian will oversee the hiring and training of temporary help to accomplish this task.

Update all portions of the Information
Resources procedures manual to reflect
changes created by increased
computer use   *3 months*

> Marian will utilize her knowledge of previous and future changes in internal procedures to rewrite the manual used by department employees.

Create guide to online services   *6 months–1 year*

> Marian will write a company guide to assist other employees in online search techniques and services.

Additional Comments:

> Marian has done an outstanding job this year in redesigning and initiating new resources to enhance and improve departmental services. Her interest in automated resources and her desire to explore their potential, as well

340

as to learn about internal business applications, provides a valuable foundation for developing more customer-response services. She enjoys working with others to ascertain and refine their information needs, and she clearly enjoys exploring the variety of resources that can be used to meet these needs. She is an excellent supervisor of temporary and part-time clerical and secretarial staff and motivates others with her enthusiastic attitude toward her job. Overall, she continues to improve her job performance. Her skills and talents are a definite asset.

Overall Performance Rating (from Part I):   1   <u>2</u>   3   4   5

Employee's signature: _____   Date: _____

Evaluator's signature: _____   Date: _____

PERFORMANCE APPRAISAL

Employee Name: Peter Pruitt   Interim   Annual X
Job Title: Office Administrator
Supervisor: Sally Johnston   Date: 12/1/XX

I: Job Skills

	Sometimes	Usually	Always
			X

Job Knowledge

Uses/demonstrates the skills and tools necessary to perform job effectively. Can draw upon previous experience to handle new problems or challenges. Makes effort to stay current in field.

Comments:

Peter has made the classic rise in the ranks, from mail-room clerk to office assistant to administrative assistant and now office administrator. His years of experience and interest in the advertising business have given him a strong background on which to build in his current position. In particular, his knowledge of our varying accounts serves him well in his supervision of client billing. His ability to utilize the specialized job knowledge that he has acquired is his greatest strength.

	Sometimes	Usually	Always
		X	

Organizational Skills

Can plan, organize, and prioritize work effectively. Meets deadlines and completes assignments within specified time frames. Uses time and resources effectively to meet goals.

Comments:

Peter generally does well in this area, although he tends to be flustered when things get very busy and deadlines are looming. He focuses on the

342

"big picture" a little too much, causing him on occasion to overlook important details. I have recommended that he become more list-oriented to ensure that nothing is missed and all details are taken care of, rather than relying solely on his memory so much.

	Sometimes	Usually	Always
			X

Teamwork

Works effectively with other employees.
Gives assistance to others when needed.
Shares credit and can balance personal and
team goals.

Comments:

His job requires him to work with and for personnel at all corporate levels, in addition to supervising the clerical staff. He generally does well, although occasionally he spends more time nurturing connections than he does nurturing his staff. His desire to continue rising in the ranks is quite evident and very laudable, but it should not keep him from remembering that he is part of a team and that the interests of the team should come before his own self-interests.

	Sometimes	Usually	Always
		X	

Communication Skills

Communicates thoughts and ideas clearly
and demonstrates ability to listen and offer
sound feedback. Is concise in both written
and verbal communications. Keeps management and peers well informed.

Comments:

His reports to management are well thought-out and well written, and verbal interactions are satisfactory. Once again, he puts more emphasis on his relationships with his superiors and less with his subordinates. He needs to focus a bit more on ensuring that the clerical staff understand what is expected of them and are fully versed in what they need to know to fulfill their job requirements.

343

	Sometimes	Usually	Always
		X	

Problem Solving

Can identify and analyze problems and present solutions, using available resources or creative ideas.

Comments:

> He does well at solving problems for which he has a historical precedent. He is less adept at handling new situations that he has never before encountered, but has improved in this respect recently as he has matured in his current position. His solutions are not very creative but are always competent.

	Sometimes	Usually	Always
		X	

Professionalism

Accepts responsibility for all aspects of job and is willing to be held accountable for errors. Displays professional attitude and appearance in approach to job.

Comments:

> Peter always dresses and presents himself well. He has experienced some difficulty in accountability and tends to "point fingers" whenever a serious error or problem comes to light rather than dealing with it in a mature, responsible manner. We talked about the fact that when somebody on his staff makes an error, it may be because they had not received adequate instruction from him and therefore he should examine his own role in the cause of such situations and the steps he should take to ensure its not being repeated.

	Sometimes	Usually	Always
		X	

Initiative and Motivation

Can handle multiple tasks and responsibilities and is willing to take on new challenges. Displays interest in and enthusiasm for job and completes assignments quickly and efficiently.

Comments:

Peter is definitely interested in and enthusiastic about his job, and he does well in handling large assignments to which he attaches great importance. He does less well with those tasks that are "rote" and part of his daily routine. As previously stated, he becomes flustered in times of stress, and this is particularly true when he has numerous tasks all requiring immediate completion. It is at these times that he can make better use of his staff by delegating more and assuring that they are adequately informed on what they need to know to provide him with the assistance he needs to effectively juggle all the demands on his time.

	Sometimes	Usually	Always
			X

Flexibility

Adapts to new situations and changing work responsibilities. Is open to suggestions and criticism and able to utilize input from others. Looks for acceptable solutions in conflict situations.

Comments:

He generally does well, especially in adapting himself to increasing or changing work duties. He has a small problem with criticism, particularly that which comes from me. He denies having any problem working with a woman supervisor, although I suspect that may be the reason why he gets defensive when I speak to him about errors and areas for improvement. He does not tend to get into conflict situations with his peers. Lately he has improved in his efforts to mediate disputes among his clerks, and at my suggestion he has begun a weekly staff meeting to provide a forum for their concerns and complaints.

	Sometimes	Usually	Always
			X

Leadership

Effectively trains and supervises staff to accomplish goals and objectives. Coaches and counsels others. Is sought out by peers and supervisors for ideas and opinions in a variety of situations.

345

Comments:

> As indicated in other comments, Peter has had some difficulty in keeping his staff fully trained and adequately utilized. He needs to follow up with them more and be available to them to resolve problems and make decisions that may be beyond their capacity. His interactions with higher managers are much more positive, and he is frequently included in key meetings to provide the benefit of his ideas.

II: Achievements and Contributions

List the employee's major contributions to company goals, growth, and/or profitability during the appraisal period. Describe what actions the employee took to make these achievements.

> Peter instituted a new system for ordering office supplies, utilizing a new vendor, that has resulted in a reduction of expenditures on consumables by approximately 20 percent. He also revamped the client-billing procedures to make invoices and their terms easier to understand and installed a follow-up procedure to improve the collections process.

III: Plans and Goals

List and describe what the employee must achieve for the next performance-appraisal period, including skills development, areas of improvement, projects, etc.

> Peter is to improve his organizational skills and that of his staff. He should institute a system of periodic reviews with the clerks and examine whether any revision of their job descriptions will help to improve efficiency in overall operations. He should also delegate more responsible work to those whose efforts merit it. I would like to see improvement in accountability for his job, including accepting the responsibility and correction of those errors made by his subordinates.

IV: Appraiser's Summary

Describe employee's overall performance rating.

> Overall, Peter's performance has been good. He is ambitious, and that ambition has perhaps caused him to focus more than he should on nurturing his business contacts and doing the "glamour" jobs that will put him in the spotlight. However, he has demonstrated a desire to improve his supervisory skills and has already acted upon some of my suggestions in this area.

I believe Peter's strengths far outweigh his weaknesses and that he will work hard to improve his rating in every job-skills area. I fully expect that by his next review, he will be in line for a promotion.

V: Employee's Comments

Employee's signature: _____ Date: _____

Evaluator's signature: _____ Date: _____

PERFORMANCE EVALUATION
Administrative

Name: Burt Simpson   Title: Computer Administrator
Date: Nov. 6, 20xx

Job Knowledge

Burt possesses all the necessary skills and knowledge to do an effective job as Computer Administrator. His extensive experience working with all types of computer systems has enabled him to set up an office-wide network of computers that will greatly enhance efficiency company-wide. He is currently at work on a database program that will provide crucial product and customer information at the touch of a finger for all employees. He brings a real sense of competency and assurance to his work.

Quality of Work

On the whole, Burt's job performance is quite good. Although there have been some issues of the time it has taken him to complete assigned projects and his management of staff, as described below, the end result of his efforts is always top-notch. He sets high standards for himself and his staff when it comes to programming, installations, and response to service calls.

Productivity/Timeliness

There have been complaints received about the amount of time it takes for Burt to return calls and respond to inquiries and requests for service. On the larger projects, he has yet to meet a promised deadline, frequently completing a job a month or more later than expected. It is to be expected that there would be problems in this area, since Burt's position and the whole computer network are new to this company, and there is a lot to get used to yet. However, it is to be hoped that Burt can find ways to manage his time and his responsiveness to calls more effectively, in order to handle his large workload and the heavy volume of demands on his time and attention.

Organizational Skills

Organization both in terms of how he manages his resources and how he schedules and uses his time provides a point of concern in terms of han-

348

dling the overall problem of timeliness and productivity. Burt has noted that he does feel overwhelmed and falls behind so much because he has a hard time juggling multiple tasks. I am working with him now on ways in which he can delegate more authority and can structure his schedule so that he may use his time more effectively and efficiently and not always be so overwhelmed.

Communication Skills

Burt has solid communication skills. He is always clear and concise in his speech and has a way of explaining computers and programs to our novices that makes this whole transition easier for many who have been frightened by the new technology.

Interpersonal Skills/Leadership

Burt's supervision of his staff could use some work. He is well liked and respected, which is a strong start. Now he needs to make better use of their talents and willingness to assist in this massive new operation. Burt tends toward a hands-on approach, needing to be involved in every aspect of every job, which puts too much pressure and demand on him. I have suggested a more structured system that allows him to delegate certain responsibilities to a few key people and free up his time for more administrative matters.

Initiative/Motivation

Burt has initiative and motivation in spades. He designed the new computer network after extensive research into what was needed for our company. He is also in the process of designing the new database. He is highly committed to his job and is unquestionably hard working and highly motivated.

Problem Solving

His genius for problem solving has become legendary. He is so familiar with every aspect of the computer system that he is often able to pinpoint and take care of problems even before they occur. This is unquestionably one of his strongest points and what makes him so valuable to us.

Comments/Goals for Next Review

Burt has many strengths, and he has been invaluable to the company from the first date of his employment. Without him, we would not have the superb new computer network now making life easier for so many of our employees. The issues that keep this from being an outstanding review overall can be easily solved. Specifically, Burt can improve productivity within his department and reduce the number of complaints received by making better use of the resources provided by his able staff. Rather than delegating assignments and issuing instructions, he should take a risk and start designating real responsibility and decision-making power to those technicians he trusts most. By splitting up the work more and relieving himself of some of the stress of having to make both simple and complex decisions, it will undoubtedly promote higher efficiency. It may require a small investment of time for training purposes, but it would be worth it in the long run. I am working with him now on ways he can implement the new structure and will review his progress periodically. He is to feel free to come to me for advice at any time.

Employee's Comments

Employee's signature: _____ Date: _____

Evaluator's signature: _____ Date: _____

PERFORMANCE EVALUATION

Name: Karen Dalloway   Title: Administrative Secretary
Date: April 30, 20XX   Interim ____   Annual X

I. JOB FACTORS: *RATING:*

1. Job knowledge   (poor) 1 2 <u>3</u> 4 5 (excellent)
2. Quality of work   (poor) 1 2 <u>3</u> 4 5 (excellent)
3. Productivity   (poor) 1 2 <u>3</u> 4 5 (excellent)
4. Organizational skills   (poor) 1 2 <u>3</u> 4 5 (excellent)
5. Dependability   (poor) 1 2 <u>3</u> 4 5 (excellent)
6. Interpersonal skills/Teamwork   (poor) 1 2 <u>3</u> 4 5 (excellent)
7. Initiative/Motivation   (poor) 1 2 <u>3</u> 4 5 (excellent)
8. Communication skills (verbal/written) (poor) 1 2 <u>3</u> 4 5 (excellent)
9. Analytic skills/Problem solving   (poor) 1 <u>2</u> 3 4 5 (excellent)
10. Professionalism   (poor) 1 2 <u>3</u> 4 5 (excellent)
Overall Rating   (poor) 1 2 <u>3</u> 4 5 (excellent)

II. SUMMARY/COMMENTS

Karen has been a good, steady employee who does all that is expected of her exactly according to the standards that have been set for her. While she cannot be said to excel in any sort of extraordinary fashion, she does do a consistently good job and gets things done within established time frames and procedures. She keeps all the operations of our home office running smoothly, maintaining schedules and charts of the responsibilities and whereabouts of all our sales reps and coordinating meetings and all interactions between Sales and Marketing. She also acts as a liaison for the sales reps, fielding phone calls, typing up reports, and handling general administrative work for them. She is relied upon to keep them well informed and well supplied with promotional brochures and other materials essential to their work, as well as to ensure that they submit weekly activity reports in a timely fashion. She is responsible for putting together, editing, and issuing monthly status reports, as well as the company newsletter reporting staff news and corporate happenings. In addition to all this, she oversees all office administrative matters and supervises our two clerks plus any temporary secretarial help that we get.

Clearly Karen has many responsibilities, and she manages them all with competency. She seems to especially enjoy her editing responsibilities and spends a lot of time on that aspect of her job. All the same, she cannot be said to be a spectacular worker. She does only what is expected of her, and no more. She has made no move to change anything in the way of office procedures since she took over the job and seems content to run things exactly the way they've always been run. Her analytical and problem-solving skills are weak, and unless she has faced the situation previously, she generally can't handle problems on her own and must ask for assistance.

III. GOALS FOR NEXT REVIEW

It is important for Karen to remember that the old ways of doing things don't necessarily work when circumstances change. We are now faced with the imminent expansion of our product line due to our acquisition of ABC Company's line of computer software, which will require additional sales reps and expansion of our office staff. Karen will need to assume greater responsibilities and change the office structure. To be up to the task, she has to be willing to take some risks and be more daring in her approach to her job. Thus, she is to work on issues of initiative and motivation and concentrate more on her administerial duties. I will be helping her during this transition period. I am certain that with her talents Karen is capable of achieving much more proficiency in her job than she is currently demonstrating.

IV. EMPLOYEE COMMENTS

Employee's signature: _____ Date: _____

Evaluator's signature: _____ Date: _____

PERFORMANCE EVALUATION
Administrative

Name: Julian Merkel   Title: Department Administrator

Date: 6/8/XX

Job Knowledge

Julian possesses strong job knowledge skills that he puts to good use in his administrative functions. He has worked in several different departments throughout his ten years with the company and so has acquired a broad understanding of the corporate structure and the products and services we sell. His computer expertise is invaluable as he has assisted in the planning and development of a new database system. His overall administrative skills are excellent, although there have been a few problems in terms of the detail work.

Quality of Work

Julian has a strong work ethic and maintains high standards in his approach to his job. In fact, he probably sets his standards a little too high, concentrating too much on the forest and not enough on the trees. He enjoys working on high-interest, high-profile assignments and tends to avoid the more rote aspects of his job, or at the very least tends to put them off until the last minute. As a result, activity reports are sometimes submitted late, and filing piles up. If he delegated more of this work to his subordinates, he would probably be better off.

Productivity/Timeliness

As noted, he does fine on projects that have a greater interest for him on both a personal and professional level, but shows a poorer productivity rate on those tasks that are routine and of less interest to him. His overall productivity rate is not so high as it could or should be, given his skills.

Organizational Skills

He has strong organizational abilities, and in fact when he sets up systems for filing and managing the traffic of paper, he creates a smoother-

353

working environment for all. However, he needs to stay on top of the systems that he sets up, making sure that they are being used to their full effectiveness. Once again, his preference is for tasks that will challenge him and give him a greater opportunity to show what he can do, but he must remember that the machinery needs to be kept oiled or it will break down.

Communication Skills

He has strong skills in both oral and written communications.

Interpersonal Skills/Leadership

Julian gets along very well with his peers and supervisors and is at his best when working on complex, challenging projects that have him interacting closely with others on an administrative or managerial level. He has issues to work on regarding his leadership of others. He does not delegate or train very well and tends to get impatient with clerical staff when they don't understand his instructions or make errors. He creates more work for himself as a result, because he takes an attitude of "they're useless, I might as well do it myself." But then he can't manage the extra pressure this puts on him, not to mention that the lesser, more clerical chores do not attract him. He has definitely created a conundrum for himself.

Initiative/Motivation

Julian is highly motivated to work on special projects and high-interest assignments. He is not so motivated when it comes to the basic day-to-day chores. His initiative is put into play when it suits him.

Problem Solving

He has solid problem-solving skills and likes nothing better than to have a tricky dilemma to work out. This is one of his strongest suits.

Goals for Next Review

It should be clear from this evaluation that Julian possesses many strengths, but one major weakness, and that is his failure to deal with clerical matters in an effective manner. He is an immensely bright and talented individual who leans toward the creative side of his work more than toward any other area; he has concentrated his efforts more on major projects than on the effective management of routine office matters. This is a major point of concern. To be a true member of a team, one must interact with all the other members of the team, not just selected individuals. Julian is ambitious and wants to move on to larger, more creative responsibilities. This is fine, but he has to prove himself in his current position first and demonstrate that he is capable of delegating tasks and authority and working effectively just as well with subordinates as he does with superiors and peers. To that end, his next evaluation will concentrate on this aspect of his job. Considerable improvement must be demonstrated in his ability to be an administrator in <u>all</u> areas, not just selected ones, if he is to be considered for future promotion.

Comments

Employee's signature: _____ Date: _____

Evaluator's signature: _____ Date: _____

INTERIM PERFORMANCE EVALUATION

Performance evaluation for: Howard Balsam
Title: Executive Office Assistant
Date: July 1, 20XX

JOB FACTORS: *RATING*

1. Job knowledge   (weak) 1 2 <u>3</u> 4 5 (superior)
   Comments:

   You have adequate skills, but seem to lack the incentive to improve the
   base of your knowledge and to learn more about the company and its
   operations and employees. You content yourself with learning only what is
   told or given to you, and you rarely attempt to stretch your own horizons.
   Make more of an effort to mingle with others and learn something in the
   process.

2. Productivity   (weak) 1 2 3 <u>4</u> 5 (superior)
   Comments:

   You do very well, in the sense that you ensure that your assigned tasks
   are completed in a timely manner and to the general satisfaction of
   those who have given you the assignment. In fact, you seem to bury yourself in your work and become preoccupied by it at times.

3. Quality of work   (weak) 1 2 <u>3</u> 4 5 (superior)
   Comments:

   You ensure that daily routine tasks are attended to. On special projects,
   you tend to do things strictly according to instructions and rarely take
   the initiative to make something more of it—for example, apply a little creativity, change the formatting of a document or presentation, etc.

4. Dependability   (weak) 1 2 <u>3</u> 4 5 (superior)
   Comments:

   You can be counted on to get the job done, but not necessarily to go the
   extra mile and push beyond the limits of your instructions.

5. Initiative/Motivation   (weak) 1 2 <u>3</u> 4 5 (superior)
   Comments:

   See #4.

6. Cooperation/Teamwork   (weak) 1 2 <u>3</u> 4 5 (superior)
    Comments:

    Although you are responsible for the supervision of two other people, and the nature of your job requires you to interact with others, you generally prefer to keep to yourself and work on tasks in solitude. When you have to work with others, you do so without complaint, but you seldom volunteer for team assignments and have stuck with a solitary attitude.

7. Communication skills   (weak) 1 2 <u>3</u> 4 5 (superior)
    Comments:

    Written skills are strong, but you have difficulty expressing yourself in person, and you occasionally mumble. It is clear that you are shy, and this gives an impression of standoffishness. I think you should work on this by attempting to interact more with others. You can start by making more of a contribution in staff meetings. It's taking a risk, but it's a start.

8. Organizational skills   (weak) 1 2 3 <u>4</u> 5 (superior)
    Comments:

    Your organizational skills are quite strong. You have dedicated yourself to the assigned task of a complete overhaul of the office filing system and are making admirable progress. You should try to get others to help you, however, and not feel you have to tackle it all alone.

9. Analytic skills/Problem solving   (weak) 1 2 <u>3</u> 4 5 (superior)
    Comments:

    You can and do analyze situations and solve problems when you have to, but your preference clearly is to pass off the responsibility to somebody else whenever you can. You need to be more assertive about this and take the risk of making a mistake every now and then. This falls into the area of initiative, as well.

10. Interpersonal skills   (weak) 1 <u>2</u> 3 4 5 (superior)
    Comments:

    As already indicated, your interpersonal skills are very weak.

OVERALL RATING:

___ Needs improvement in job performance

_X_ Meets job requirements

___ Exceeds job requirements

357

Comments:

You do a good, steady job for the most part and meet all the requirements of your position. However, there are several areas you need to work on. First and foremost is your relationship with others. Your shyness inhibits you and gives the wrong impression to others. In our office situation, it is essential that you be part of the team. You cannot operate as a solitary unit, however effectively you do your job. This is all the more important because you must oversee the work of two others, and they rely on you for direction and guidance. I feel certain that if you address yourself to this issue, the other improvements will follow in short course. Please feel free to come to me for advice at any time.

Employee's Comments:

Employee's signature: _____ Date: _____

Evaluator's signature: _____ Date: _____

Sample Reviews for Poor Performers

PERFORMANCE EVALUATION

Employee Name: Monica Simmons   Date: June 22, 20XX

Employee's Job Title: Computer Administrator   Department: Library Services

Period covered by this evaluation: From 6/XX to 5/XX

Ratings: Employee is to be rated on a scale of 1 to 3, as described below.

   1: Below expectations: Performance is substandard and requires improvement.

   2: Meets expectations: Performance fully meets and occasionally exceeds standards.

   3: Exceeds expectations: Performance consistently exceeds set standards.

N/A: Not applicable. Lack of sufficient knowledge to evaluate the performance factor.

Section I: Basic Job Skills

	Below	Meets	Exceeds	N/A
Job knowledge	1	<u>2</u>	3	N/A
Quality of work	1	<u>2</u>	3	N/A
Productivity/Timeliness	1	<u>2</u>	3	N/A
Dependability	<u>1</u>	2	3	N/A
Work habits	1	<u>2</u>	3	N/A
Organizational skills	<u>1</u>	2	3	N/A
Resourcefulness	1	2	<u>3</u>	N/A
Problem solving	1	<u>2</u>	3	N/A
Care of office equipment	1	2	<u>3</u>	N/A

Section II: Personal Attributes

	Below	Meets	Exceeds	N/A
Attendance/Punctuality	1	<u>2</u>	3	N/A
Ability to take direction	<u>1</u>	2	3	N/A
Initiative	1	2	<u>3</u>	N/A
Cooperativeness	<u>1</u>	2	3	N/A
Adaptability	<u>1</u>	2	3	N/A
Receptiveness to criticism	<u>1</u>	2	3	N/A
Communication skills	1	<u>2</u>	3	N/A
Interaction with coworkers	<u>1</u>	2	3	N/A
Courtesy/Hospitality	<u>1</u>	2	3	N/A

Section III: Strengths and Weaknesses

Describe employee strengths:

Monica's greatest strength is the initiative she takes in examining the department's resources, processes, and organization and in proposing methods for improvement and enhancement. She concentrates with an almost fierce dedication on attaining the goals that have been set and takes personal ownership of her responsibilities. She has been especially active in creating and enhancing the company's presence on the Internet, helping to set up our company's Web site and providing increased customer responsiveness through the use of Internet mailing lists. She also continues to educate herself about the company's business directions in order to select the most useful sources of information for her electronic catalog.

Describe areas for improvement:

Monica often does not respond well to direction. She is aware that she needs to be more of a team player in terms of receiving and implementing ideas and suggestions that are not her own and has made attempts to improve her combative attitude. She is justifiably proud of her abilities, but can be impatient with others who are not so quick or computer-literate as she is. She must therefore make more of an attempt to monitor herself and contain the occasional impulsive and sarcastic comments she is prone to making.

Section IV: Goals Assessment/Comments

Describe goals previously established for employee, how well they were met, and objectives for next performance appraisal:

In addition to her almost single-handed creation of our Web site, Monica assisted me in the planning and development of new, Internet-based electronic catalog to provide access to the Library Services materials and resources from desktop PCs. She also assisted in the writing of user documentation for the program, as well as the connection and training of in-house users. She conducted a survey of the pilot group to collect suggestions for additions and improvements in our electronic collections, then helped to plan and implement many of the improvements. She continues to connect new users to the system and provides troubleshooting assistance, when needed.

There are signs of strong potential here on some projects. Monica was charged with creating a tracking system to evaluate messages and requests coming in via our Web site. In a typical three-day period, 41 inquiries from 9 different countries were received. I have received messages from many of our external customers stating that Monica's activity on the Internet mailing lists provides great value to them and enhances the company's positive public image. Given this good response, she will continue to develop updates and enhancements to our World Wide Web site.

Monica will continue to expand the electronic catalog and investigate further opportunities for its application by both internal and external users. Unfortunately she is unable to oversee the training of new personnel in the uses of the system, because of her attitude toward co-workers.

I would like to see some attempt made at developing self-control and curbing the tendency to respond in a short-tempered or sarcastic manner whenever her patience is tested. I would like to see her improve in her relationships with co-workers, so she will be able to oversee the computer training program.

Section V: Employee Comments

Employee's signature: _____ Date: _____

Evaluator's signature: _____ Date: _____

PERFORMANCE EVALUATION

Name: Barbara Medway   Title: Office Manager
Date: January 10, 20XX   Interim   Annual X

I. JOB FACTORS: *RATING:*

1. Job knowledge   (poor) 1 <u>2</u> 3 4 5 (excellent)
   Comments:

   Barbara does not seem to be motivated toward expanding the scope of
   her job responsibilities or instituting new systems to improve or enhance
   overall office efficiency. She relies too much on old methods and technology that were in place before she took over the job.

2. Quality of work   (poor) <u>1</u> 2 3 4 5 (excellent)
   Comments:

   The quality of Barbara's work has declined considerably in the last few
   months. She does only the barest minimum of what she needs to do to
   keep the office running and has fallen behind on her bookkeeping chores
   and other general administrative duties.

3. Productivity   (poor) <u>1</u> 2 3 4 5 (excellent)
   Comments:

   Filing is backlogged and subordinates are confused about what is expected of them because Barbara has not taken an active enough role in their
   training and the monitoring of their work. She hands out work assignments
   without providing adequate instruction and often fails to follow up on
   assigned work. Office efficiency has dropped considerably as a result,
   and there have been numerous complaints lodged about Barbara's failure
   to respond to special requests more immediately.

4. Initiative   (poor) 1 <u>2</u> 3 4 5 (excellent)
   Comments:

   She has demonstrated little to no initiative in either enhancing current
   office systems or offering new ideas.

5. Dependability   (poor) 1 <u>2</u> 3 4 5 (excellent)
   Comments:

   She has become less dependable in recent months.

362

6. Interpersonal skills/Teamwork   (poor) 1 <u>2</u> 3 4 5 (excellent)
   Comments:

   Barbara has good people skills and gets along fine with her peers. However, she has gone through phases where she ignores her staff, and she has generally failed to build a good team spirit among her subordinates.

7. Decision-making abilities   (poor) 1 <u>2</u> 3 4 5 (excellent)
   Comments:

   She does not think through some of her decisions very carefully and sometimes reacts impulsively rather than in a considered manner. Her quick purchase of a color copier machine from vendor X without carefully considering all other options resulted in numerous complaints and the loss of hundreds if not thousands of dollars due to her purchase of a less than superior model machine that was subject to frequent breakdowns.

8. Problem-solving abilities   (poor) 1 <u>2</u> 3 4 5 (excellent)
   Comments:

   Barbara has the ability to solve problems, but not the interest. Her reaction to subordinates who come to her with a question or dilemma is more often than not, "Figure it out for yourself."

9. Organizational skills   (poor) 1 <u>2</u> 3 4 5 (excellent)
   Comments:

   Barbara has certainly not led her staff by example. Her desk is always a mess and she seems to always be losing or misplacing important documents. Her inefficiencies and lack of attention to detail have sometimes had an adverse effect on personnel who have trusted her with important responsibilities and been let down by her failure to complete those assignments in a timely manner or with any real accuracy.

10. Communication skills   (poor) 1 2 <u>3</u> 4 5 (excellent)
    Comments:

    If she has a strong suit, this is it. She has good verbal and written skills and expresses herself fairly well.

11. Analytic skills   (poor) 1 <u>2</u> 3 4 5 (excellent)
    Comments:

    She should be able to analyze systems and situations better in order to exercise good judgment and reasonable follow-through.

12. Receptiveness to criticism (poor) 1 2 <u>3</u> 4 5 (excellent)
    Comments:

    She handles criticism of her work well and concedes that she has been having problems of late that have been affecting office efficiency.

13. Management of resources (poor) 1 <u>2</u> 3 4 5 (excellent)
    Comments:

    Her failure to make arrangements with new vendors, to find ways to cut costs, and to monitor expenditures have caused her to go over budget in three successive quarters.

14. Professionalism (poor) 1 <u>2</u> 3 4 5 (excellent)
    Comments:

    She does not display a high degree of professionalism in either appearance or attitude.

15. Punctuality (poor) 1 <u>2</u> 3 4 5 (excellent)
    Comments:

    Frequently late, she also spends too much time on the telephone and far too much time away from her desk—for instance, taking lunch breaks that often last an hour and a half.

Overall Rating (poor) 1 <u>2</u> 3 4 5 (excellent)

II. SUMMARY/COMMENTS

Barbara seems to have lost complete interest in her job in the past few months. She has been slow in completing chores, has delegated a large portion of her work to subordinates, and spends a great deal of time either on the phone or away from her desk, visiting people in other offices.

III. GOALS FOR NEXT REVIEW

Overall improvement must be made in professional deportment, attention to details, and more timely accomplishment of general goals and objectives. In addition, I want Barbara to make recommendations for improving office efficiency, including upgrading computer applications and enhancing current office procedures, then to demonstrate initiative and thoughtful attention to detail in implementing those recommendations. Failure to comply with expectations for sustained improvement will result in dismissal. Barbara has been given three months to demonstrate significant changes.

IV. EMPLOYEE COMMENTS

Employee's signature: _____ Date: _____

Evaluator's signature: _____ Date: _____

10

Model Evaluations for Managers

These workers direct the efforts of other individual workers or groups of workers. They have the responsibility of being fully informed about what their workers do, how they do it, and their individual strengths, weaknesses, and idiosyncrasies. They usually have prior experience in doing the tasks being accomplished by those they manage. They derive much of their credibility and effectiveness from their ability to apply both their experience and strong interactive skills to increase the effectiveness and job satisfaction of those they manage. Their job titles include:

- Customer Service Manager
- Sales Manager
- Manager of Development
- Department Manager
- Convention-Services Manager
- Group-Sales Manager
- Financial Manager
- Fiscal-Systems Manager
- Information Systems Manager

- Advertising Sales Manager
- Construction Project Manager
- Project Manager
- Building Maintenance Manager

Gauging Performance

The overriding concern of these workers is their ability to inspire top performance from others. These are the folks who can make it all happen and achieve corporate goals through their management skills. There are various combinations of abilities that can accomplish this.

Traits that are admired in these workers are fairness, consistency, ability to keep priorities straight, and a general evenness of approach and attitude. Whether these workers lead through counseling models or through more authoritative approaches, these people need to be able to listen, to make decisions, and to handle the buck when it stops with them.

Employees who demonstrate excellent work habits, strong interpersonal skills, and high output are much admired. But ultimately the strongest test of these people is the quantity and quality of the work being done by those whom they lead. If they get the job done and maintain strong morale while doing so, they have what it takes.

Performance Indicators

The top-level performer

- Has outstanding leadership abilities
- Has a good rapport with employees; can inspire and motivate
- Is fully informed about the job responsibilities for every employee
- Has a high degree of appropriate skills and knowledge
- Has superior communication and interpersonal skills
- Is highly productive and elicits the highest productivity from employees
- Has outstanding problem-solving skills
- Is well organized and adapts well to changing situations and demands
- Is an active and involved participant in the formation of company policy and procedure

- Has outstanding fiscal-management skills
- Displays thoroughness and accuracy in all work areas
- Demonstrates a high level of sensitivity to cultural diversity in the workplace
- Is sensitive to individual special needs of employees
- Works extremely well in pressure situations
- Works with energy and a cheerful, inspirational attitude
- Is comfortable and receptive to appropriate criticism

The good performer

- Has good leadership abilities
- Has a good rapport with employees
- Is generally informed about the job responsibilities for every employee
- Has the appropriate skills and knowledge to do a good job
- Has sufficient communication and interpersonal skills
- Can generally motivate employees to perform at expected levels
- Usually has no problem-solving difficulties
- Is well organized and able to adapt to changing situations and demands for the most part
- Takes part in company meetings and submits ideas toward the formation of company policy and procedure
- Has adequate fiscal-management skills
- Is largely thorough and accurate
- Generally demonstrates an adequate level of sensitivity to cultural diversity in the workplace
- Is generally sensitive to individual special needs of employees
- Can handle most pressure situations
- Approaches work energetically and maintains a positive attitude
- Is generally comfortable and receptive to appropriate criticism

The poor performer

- Has problems taking charge and leading employees
- Has a poor rapport with workers and has difficulty inspiring or motivating them

- Is unaware or not fully informed of job responsibilities in certain positions
- Lacks appropriate skills and knowledge to do an effective job
- Has poor communication and interpersonal skills
- Experiences difficulties in producing work in a timely and efficient manner
- Has less than adequate problem-solving skills
- Is poorly organized
- Has difficulty adapting to changing situations and demands
- Is not an active participant in company meetings and overall management
- Is not able to handle budgets or other fiscal responsibilities
- Produces incomplete or inaccurate work
- Is not sensitive to cultural diversity in the workplace or to individual special needs of employees
- Does not handle pressure situations well; is easily flustered
- Has a bad attitude or is apathetic toward the job
- Has difficulty with criticism

Sample Reviews for Top-level Performers

PERFORMANCE EVALUATION

Name: Melissa Kane
Date: March 30, 20XX

Title: Customer Service Manager
Interim   Annual X

I. JOB FACTORS:

RATING:

1. Job knowledge   (poor) 1 2 3 4 <u>5</u> (excellent)
   Comments:

   Melissa remains completely on top of our book list at all times. She inter-acts with the Marketing and Editorial departments to stay aware of the status of projects and projected publication dates. She also works closely with Order Processing to ensure that her department is always aware when books are out of stock. She maintains easy-to-use reference lists for her staff that summarize the status of all books, including those that are out of print or not yet published.

2. Quality of work   (poor) 1 2 3 4 <u>5</u> (excellent)
   Comments:

   Melissa is justifiably proud of the quality of her work, which is enhanced by the excellence of her well-chosen staff.

3. Productivity   (poor) 1 2 3 4 <u>5</u> (excellent)
   Comments:

   Excellent turnaround time on handling customer calls and correspondence. Because files are neatly organized and established procedures are fol-lowed, it is rare that any member of Melissa's staff takes any longer than one day to resolve a particular issue.

4. Responsiveness to customers   (poor) 1 2 3 4 <u>5</u> (excellent)
   Comments:

   Melissa keeps her staff well trained in how to respond to particular types of customers, issues of telephone courtesy, proper ways to write letters, and so forth. As a result, customers have confidence that their problem will be handled quickly and courteously.

5. Dependability   (poor) 1 2 3 4 <u>5</u> (excellent)

Comments:

Melissa is a dedicated and hard-working employee—possibly our most dependable one.

6. Interpersonal skills/Teamwork   (poor) 1 2 3 4 <u>5</u> (excellent)

Comments:

She employs excellent interpersonal skills as she not only supervises her staff but interacts with other departments to ensure not only that she is fully informed on projects and decisions affecting her department, but that they are fully informed on customer response to new products or to company policies that may affect their relationship with the customer.

7. Adaptability   (poor) 1 2 3 4 <u>5</u> (excellent)

Comments:

Melissa is able to handle any challenge that is thrown her way.

8. Organizational skills   (poor) 1 2 3 4 <u>5</u> (excellent)

Comments:

She devised the current office system and setup of files that is responsible for the organizational efficiency of her department.

9. Communication skills (verbal/written) (poor) 1 2 3 4 <u>5</u> (excellent)

Comments:

She is very keenly attuned to language and how it is used in interactions with customers (as well as with other staff). She makes communication skills an important part of the training of any new employee.

10. Computer skills   (poor) 1 2 <u>3</u> 4 5 (excellent)

Comments:

This is probably her only weakness. Melissa has concentrated her efforts on reorganizing office systems and proper training of staff in context with the current computer system. She knows only what she absolutely needs to know to use the computer to research customer inquiries. This will be an area for development.

11. Professionalism   (poor) 1 2 3 4 <u>5</u> (excellent)

Comments:

Melissa is a consummate professional.

12. Punctuality   (poor) 1 2 3 <u>4</u> 5 (excellent)

Comments:

Although she is generally punctual, she sometimes takes longer lunch hours than is allowed by company policy.

Overall Rating   (poor) 1 2 3 4 <u>5</u> (excellent)

II. SUMMARY/COMMENTS

The overall efficiency of Melissa's department, along with their courteous and timely responsiveness to customers, has developed a reputation for our company of quality, efficient service that is always attentive to customer needs and desires. This has contributed to the increase in sales over the past year, as college bookstores have chosen to place new orders with our company rather than go through the used-book market. She is an excellent supervisor who has put together a dedicated staff. In fact, the turnover rate in her department has dropped dramatically since Melissa took over as manager. All in all, she has proven herself to be a valuable asset for our company.

III. GOALS FOR NEXT REVIEW

Melissa is to enhance her computer skills to become more proficient and better versed in new applications that may improve the service of her department in the future. She has attended seminars and workshops on customer service and supervisory skills, and that should continue to add to her professional growth. Meanwhile, we expect that she will continue her excellent management of her department, which has contributed greatly to company profitability.

IV. EMPLOYEE COMMENTS

Employee's signature: _____ Date: _____

Evaluator's signature: _____ Date: _____

PERFORMANCE EVALUATION
Managerial

Name: Elizabeth Loehr   Title: Archives Manager

Date: 12/4/XX

Job Knowledge

Elizabeth is a superb manager of our corporate archives. Her knowledge of both the company and her field is beyond the pale. Prior to joining the XYZ Company, she had eight years of archival experience, working her way up from a clerical position to a managerial post at the prestigious ABC Corporation. We recruited her to head our archives program a year ago and have not regretted the choice. In addition to her impressive credentials in archives acquisitions and management, she has been actively involved in both national and regional archives associations and has led numerous workshops on the collection and preservation of appropriate materials for archives. She is one of the most knowledgeable experts on document preservation in the field.

Organization and Administrative Skills

As our corporate archives had been sadly neglected before she got here, Elizabeth was faced with the task of taking mountains of unorganized documents, photos, film clips, and product samples and creating a well-organized resource for researchers, employees, and any member of the public who wishes information on the history of our company. She created a filing-and-retrieval system that allows for near-immediate responses to inquiries and requests for specific materials or information. To do this monumental job has taken both skill and patience, which Elizabeth possesses in abundance. It has also taken superb administrative skills; she must manage a staff of five people, check their work, assign special projects, and ensure that they are submitting daily reports on requests received, which she then edits into a monthly status report to management. Since the archives has swung into full operation and its value has become better known, the number of requests received has risen monthly. Recently over 125 requests were received and processed in a single month. That these requests were handled and processed in a timely fashion by her dedicated and hard-working staff is a tribute to Elizabeth's outstanding organizational and administrative skills.

Productivity/Timeliness

The overall productivity rate is tremendous. As noted above, requests made to the archives are processed quickly and efficiently. In addition, there are many other tasks to be seen to, including the ongoing sifting of material not yet entered into the archives, determining what is to be catalogued and arranging for the appropriate preservation of these materials, creating a descriptive inventory of all records and files, and entering all information into a comprehensive database. All these tasks are skillfully accomplished by Elizabeth's staff under her direction. The output from her department is nothing short of amazing, and she and her staff deserve our highest praise for all the work they've accomplished in just one year.

Quality of Work

Other comments in this review should make clear that the overall quality of Elizabeth's work is nothing short of outstanding.

Leadership/Interpersonal Skills

Elizabeth manages her staff exceptionally well. She provides clear, concise directions to each member of her team and has instilled a real sense of teamwork by providing for linking and overlapping of jobs, requiring everybody to interact with and support each other, and making it possible for another person to fill in as needed when somebody is absent. She keeps an "open-door" policy; her employees are comfortable about going to her with questions, concerns, and problems. She has a good relationship not only with her staff, but also with her supervisors and her peers in the company. When a problem arises, she always handles it with diplomatic skill.

Communication Skills

Elizabeth has a wonderful command of language and expresses herself well, both verbally and in writing. Her monthly Activity Report is a model of concise reporting. She also works on newsletters and assists employees with presentations for which historical materials are needed. In addition, she provides for an education outreach program that informs and teaches about the resources in the archives and how both employees and the interested public can take advantage of the materials and services the archives has to offer.

Adaptability/Dependability

She is highly dependable, and also very adaptable. Recently she was asked to assist with a major research project that has taken precious hours away from her regular duties, not only for the amount of grunt work it has entailed, but also for an extensive amount of traveling. To adjust to the new (but temporary) demands on her time, she delegated certain tasks to members of her staff and hired a freelance editor to edit and prepare her monthly Activity Report, thus saving her many hours of work and enabling her to devote her time to this crucial, time-sensitive project. When put to the test, Elizabeth always finds a way.

Fiscal Management

The only possible flaw I can find in her work is a minor one. She tends to go slightly over budget in ordering preservation materials, as well as for other expenses, such as travel. A lot of this has been due to what has been necessary to get the archives organized and up and running. However, there are certain financial constraints that she must observe, and we have discussed this at length. She has submitted a new budget requesting additional funds that allows for the continued expansion of the archives and its valuable services and has assured me that with the approval of this budget, any overexpenditures will be kept in check.

Comments/Goals for Next Review

It should be clear that I think highly of Elizabeth and can't praise her enough for all she has done since coming to XYZ and taking charge of what had been a woefully deficient archives until she got hold of it. Her contributions have been invaluable. Several members of management had expressed doubts at the beginning regarding the value of an archives pro-

376

gram, but Elizabeth has completely won them over with her efficient management of the department and the quickness and ease with which she turned it into an indispensable resource and provider of historical research services to employees and public alike.

We want Elizabeth to continue developing the department. She will be challenged by the rapid increase in requests for materials, data, and other services, but I have no doubt that she will be up to whatever comes her way. Elizabeth will represent XYZ at archival conferences and workshops, in addition to taking on special assignments for company management. She will have the budget under control within the next three months.

Her supervisors join me in thanking Elizabeth for a job superbly done!

Employee's Comments

Employee's signature: _____ Date: _____

Evaluator's signature: _____ Date: _____

PERFORMANCE REVIEW
Managerial/Supervisory Employees

Name: Ben Maxwell

Job Title: Financial Manager

Date: 8/14/XX

Type of Evaluation:

Interim   Annual X

Evaluation Guide

1 = Excellent (exceptional; exceeds expectations)

2 = Good (consistently meets, and frequently exceeds, usual expectations)

3 = Satisfactory (conforms to standards; meets expectations)

4 = Fair (marginal; meeting only minimum requirements)

5 = Poor (below standard and unacceptable; improvement required or termination will result)

Factors for Review

Job Knowledge   Rating: 1

Degree to which the employee knows and understands his/her job and its functions

Organization and Administrative Skills   Rating: 1

Ability to establish goals/objectives, prioritize, anticipate problems, implement plans, etc.

Delegation of Authority   Rating: 1

Ability to assign appropriate duties to subordinates

Written Communication   Rating: 1

Ability to organize thoughts and present them clearly and concisely in writing; effectiveness of prepared reports, correspondence, etc.

Oral Communication   Rating: 1

Ability to present information and ideas to others in an articulate and effective manner, as well as to listen effectively, comprehend, and respond to the ideas of others

Judgment   Rating: 1

Ability to reason through problems, review alternative solutions, reach sound conclusions, and modify decisions when necessary

Cooperation and Interpersonal Skills   Rating: 2

Tact, courtesy, self-control, patience, loyalty, and discretion; ability to work harmoniously with others, both subordinate and superior

Adaptability   Rating: 1

Ability to learn new skills, concepts, and processes; resourcefulness; flexibility in thinking

378

Work Quality   Rating: 1
Accuracy, presentability, neatness, thoroughness; and reliability of finished product.

Persuasiveness   Rating: 2
Ability to negotiate, argue persuasively, get things done by influencing others

Initiative   Rating: 1
Ability to act independently without specific instructions

Imagination and Originality   Rating: 1
Ability to visualize and anticipate new problems and to conceive new ideas or techniques

Supervisory Skills   Rating: 2
Ability to accept responsibility and to guide or lead other employees to successful work performance

Stability under Pressure   Rating: 2
Mental and emotional balance under stress due to pressure of work

Dependability   Rating: 1
Attendance and conscientiousness

Fiscal Management   Rating: 1
Ability to develop a fiscally sound operating budget and to manage effectively within established fiscal constraints, as well as to recognize, develop, and implement cost-effective operating changes

OVERALL RATING: 1

EVALUATOR'S COMMENTS

Summarize your overall evaluation of the employee's performance, noting any strengths and weaknesses. Provide goals and plan for further development and current estimate of the employee's capacity and ambition for future growth.

Ben continues to perform at a superb level. He meets and almost always exceeds all expectations placed on him. His strengths include his organizational abilities and effectiveness in communication, both written and verbal. He did the primary work on putting together the company's five-year plan and justified anticipated expenses so well that the budget was passed by the board with only a minimum of discussion. He has an effective way of transmitting information in an organized and lucid manner.

379

The quality of Ben's work is always neat, presentable, thorough, and accurate. He has a remarkable ability to plan and control all aspects of his job and is able to follow through on a logical and effective course of action for major projects that ensures the achievement of project objectives. This has been very helpful to me, especially during the crunch times when cool, level-headed thinking is crucial.

The company's recent growth has added a great deal to Ben's workload, yet he continues to meet all challenges presented to him willingly and efficiently. His sound and effective management of the company's finances has contributed significantly to a 15 percent increase in profits over the last year. He saved the company approximately $300,000 by challenging or pursuing errors in accounting procedures.

Ben's only weakness may be an aggressive manner that occasionally clashes with other employees, particularly subordinates. This is no doubt due to his striving for perfection and his desire for others to live up to his standards. He is a strong and effective leader, but he resorts to sarcasm to make his point a little too often and has offended other employees with his comments. We have discussed this problem, and he has agreed to monitor himself to be more tactful in the future.

PLAN FOR ACTION

As the company continues to grow, Ben will be responsible for overseeing the expansion of individual departments and what they will need in terms of new employees, equipment, supplies, and increased budgets. He is currently working on projections for sales and future growth that will be presented at the Board of Directors meeting in September, and will be a key element in the development of the next five-year plan. To meet increasing demands on his time and energy, he will hire and train an executive assistant to take over some of his areas of responsibility.

EMPLOYEE'S COMMENTS

Employee's signature: _____ Date: _____

Evaluator's signature: _____ Date: _____

PERFORMANCE EVALUATION
Managerial

Name: Helen Griffin   Title: Operations Manager

Date: July 1, 20xx

Job Knowledge

This position has required extensive knowledge of computer-programming, order-processing, and customer-service functions, as well as company products and services. Helen meets all these qualifications with flying colors, having had many years of experience in all those areas and a capacity for learning new methods and technologies that has served her well time and again. Her knowledge and experience has enabled her to adjust to the ever-changing nature of our business, and she has a talent for adapting previous experience and methods to new situations.

Organization and Administrative Skills

Helen has been overseeing the updating and expansion of our mainframe-computer system to accommodate the increase in business resulting from ABC's acquisition of the XYZ line of computer software. This massive project has really preoccupied her and made it necessary for her to delegate many tasks to her staff. She nevertheless has kept tabs on all that has been happening within the department and has seen to it that systems are running smoothly and according to correct policy and procedure. She holds weekly staff meetings to review production levels, discuss problems, and work out solutions, as needed. She juggles multiple tasks with great ease.

Productivity/Timeliness

Under Helen's supervision, her staff manages a terrific productivity rate, with all orders processed within 24 hours of receipt and all customer service calls resolved within 24–48 hours. In addition, reports are unfailingly submitted to management in a timely manner. She works exceedingly well under pressure and is never daunted by deadlines. She will do whatever it takes to get a job done.

Quality of Work

As evidenced by these remarks, Helen's productivity and the quality of her work is remarkable, given all that she has to do. She manages all aspects of her job with skill, competency, and attention to detail.

Leadership/Interpersonal Skills

Mention has already been made of Helen's ability to delegate and to maintain contact with her staff despite the demands on her time. If she has a flaw, it may be that she becomes impatient with those employees who are not working up to the same high standards that she sets for herself and puts excessive pressure on them to produce at an even greater rate than they are currently managing. She should be trying to encourage them more than drive them; this is an area to be worked on in the future. Otherwise, she maintains a good working relationship with both management and peers and works closely and effectively with the managers of other departments as she solicits their input on the development of the new computer system.

Communication Skills

Helen is deeply involved in her work and can sometimes be so distracted by what she is doing that she forgets to pass on a vital piece of information or to issue appropriate instructions to her staff. However, these moments are rare. By and large, she has above-average communication skills. Her reports at the monthly management meetings are always clear, concise, and well presented.

Adaptability/Dependability

We count on Helen highly, especially given the recent expansion of the company. With all the new products we have acquired from XYZ and the new headaches that have come with the acquisition, she has been the one who has coordinated a smooth transition and integrated vital information into our computer database, making it possible for employees to have quick and easy access to important data.

Fiscal Management

Helen manages her budget very well, keeping a close eye on costs and ensuring that expenditures are tightly controlled.

Comments/Goals for Next Review

Helen is a strong and valuable asset to our business. In a crucial position, she is clearly knowledgeable and reliable. She should continue with the superb job she has been doing, especially as it relates to the installation of new computer systems and the upgrading of our programs. Some attention needs to be paid to issues of flexibility and patience where her staff is concerned. I will fully expect that she will continue on this course of excellence.

Employee's Comments

Employee's signature: _____ Date: _____

Evaluator's signature: _____ Date: _____

PERFORMANCE APPRAISAL

Employee Name: John Keriotas   Interim   Annual X

Job Title: Construction Project Manager

Date: 10/1/XX

I: Job Skills

	Sometimes	Usually	Always
			X

Job knowledge

Uses/demonstrates the skills and tools necessary to perform job effectively. Can draw upon previous experience to handle new problems or challenges. Makes effort to stay current in field.

Comments:

John always keeps abreast of the latest technologies and construction techniques. In addition, he has taken numerous postgraduate courses to keep himself informed on the latest in construction management. He makes a concerted effort to understand his field and the products he is using, as well as the resources available to him to retain control of every phase of a construction project. He knows building codes inside and out, which is a crucial ability to have.

	Sometimes	Usually	Always
			X

Organizational skills

Can plan, organize, and prioritize work effectively. Meets deadlines and completes assignments within specified time frames. Uses time and resources effectively to meet goals.

Comments:

John is superbly confident in his abilities, and that confidence is demonstrated by the way he approaches each project he tackles. He takes meticulous notes and effectively implements all blueprints and instructions from the home office into a superbly run operation in the field that results in a quality finished product.

	Sometimes	Usually	Always
			X

Teamwork

Works effectively with other employees.
Gives assistance to others when needed.
Shares credit and can balance personal and
team goals.

Comments:

If John has a flaw, it is that he doesn't make more of an effort to know
and develop a rapport with employees such as the secretaries and office
assistants who play a key role in project development and customer relations. He can also be a little too harsh with his workers in the field.
However, he strives for perfection and expects the same high standards
from others. He is very much a part of the team, given that his responsibilities involve effecting translation of customer and home-office desires and
instructions into a strong working unit that will bring the project to satisfactory completion.

	Sometimes	Usually	Always
			X

Communication skills

Communicates thoughts and ideas clearly
and demonstrates ability to listen and offer
sound feedback. Is concise in both written
and verbal communications. Keeps management and peers well informed.

Comments:

He exceeds all the requirements of the job. Although he has occasionally
been tough on his workers, his own experience in the field gives him an
understanding of where they are coming from, and he communicates on
their level. He also communicates well with company executives and is
unfailingly gracious with customers. He has a remarkable ability to help
them understand the ins and outs of a project, and he will spend considerable time and effort with a customer in explaining and justifying expenses.

	Sometimes	Usually	Always
			X

Problem solving

Can identify and analyze problems and present solutions, using available resources or creative ideas.

Comments:

> John has frequently demonstrated a great ability to analyze and solve a problem even before it occurs. His meticulous examination of the blueprints and his detailed work with customers and architects ensure that he understands every phase of the construction project and can anticipate problems before the blueprints reach the construction site. He is then well prepared when problems do arise and is able to handle them quickly and efficiently.

	Sometimes	Usually	Always
			X

Professionalism/Accountability

Accepts responsibility for all aspects of job and is willing to be held accountable for errors. Displays professional attitude and represents the company well.

Comments:

> He always accepts full responsibility whenever something goes wrong—which is rare.

	Sometimes	Usually	Always
			X

Flexibility

Adapts to new situations and changing work responsibilities. Is open to suggestions and criticism and is able to utilize input from others. Looks for acceptable solutions in conflict situations.

Comments:

> This goes hand-in-hand with his problem-solving abilities. Each job is different and comes with its own unique set of difficulties. In addition, there

are the continuing changes and advancements in the field, and John must always be prepared to adapt to those changes. He does superbly in this regard.

	Sometimes	Usually	Always
			X

Leadership abilities

Effectively trains and supervises staff to accomplish goals and objectives. Coaches and counsels others. Is sought out by peers and supervisors for ideas and opinions in a variety of situations.

Comments:

Although, as previously noted, John can drive his workers too hard and occasionally antagonize them, he is nonetheless an effective leader who always achieves the best results because he hires the best workers and monitors every phase of their work.

II: Achievements and Contributions

List the employee's major contributions to company goals, growth, and/or profitability during the appraisal period. Describe what actions the employee took to make these achievements.

John has overseen the timely completion of five major construction projects in the last year. Thanks in large part to his hard efforts, the company enjoyed a growth rate of 30 percent in 20XX. Customer satisfaction is at an all-time high. More important, John takes total responsibility for controlling the cost of every phase of a project. He understands the importance of keeping costs within the budget estimates, which always come within a 3–5 percent accuracy upon project completion. He follows up every phase of construction, including work that is farmed out to subcontractors, whom he also monitors to ensure compliance with estimates.

John is supremely confident in his abilities, and that confidence translates into quality results. His honesty and attention to detail, as well as his perfectionism in keeping costs under control, has brought about tremendous customer satisfaction, which in itself has brought about increased business due to word-of-mouth advertising.

III: Plans and Goals

List and describe what the employee must achieve for the next performance appraisal period, including skills development, areas of improvement, projects, etc.

John's impressive skills and accomplishments have put him on track for promotion. He must work to improve his interpersonal skills with employees at all levels of the company.

He should also continue taking courses or seminars to stay current with new standards and technologies.

IV: Appraiser's Summary

Describe employee's overall performance rating.

Excellent. John's work does credit to both the company and himself.

V: Employee's Comments

Employee's signature: _____ Date: _____

Evaluator's signature: _____ Date: _____

Sample Reviews for Mid-level Performers

PERFORMANCE REVIEW—MANAGERIAL

Name: Steve Stanley

Job Title: Construction Project Manager

Date: April 4, 20XX

Type of Evaluation:

Interim   Annual X

EVALUATION GUIDE

1 = Excellent (exceptional; exceeds expectations)

2 = Good (consistently meets, and frequently exceeds, usual expectations)

3 = Satisfactory (conforms to standards; meets expectations)

4 = Fair (marginal; meeting only minimum requirements)

5 = Poor (below standard and unacceptable; improvement required or termination will result)

FACTORS FOR REVIEW

Job Knowledge	Rating: 2
Work Quality	Rating: 3
Organization and Administrative Skills	Rating: 3
Staff Management/Supervisory Skills	Rating: 2
Persuasiveness	Rating: 2
Communication Skills	Rating: 2
Judgment	Rating: 3
Interpersonal Skills	Rating: 2
Adaptability/Dependability	Rating: 3
Initiative	Rating: 2
Stability under Pressure	Rating: 2
Fiscal Management	Rating: 4

OVERALL RATING: 3

EVALUATOR'S COMMENTS

Summarize your overall evaluation of the employee's performance, noting any strengths and weaknesses. Provide goals and plan for further development and current estimate of the employee's capacity and ambition for future growth.

Steve is a very popular project manager and is particularly outstanding for his handling of his crew. Like his crew, he is young and has more enthusiasm and energy than experience. He has boundless energy, works at a terrific pace, and is very much "on task" all the time. In this way he sets an excellent standard for his crew to follow.

Steve has had difficulty estimating how long each part of the project will take. The result has been either delays caused by materials or personnel arriving later than needed or overlap from having workers waiting for the next step when materials arrive before they can be used. This has a bad effect on worker morale and serious negative financial implications.

GOALS/ACTION TO BE TAKEN

Steve must get this scheduling issue under control. We suggest that he go over his job plans with another, more experienced manager and factor that manager's time/work-flow estimates into his job schedule. He should also begin to keep a notebook of actual job-performance schedules to assist him in future estimating. Although this problem of schedule management is a serious one and keeps Steve from receiving a top-level evaluation at this time, it should be able to be rectified. When this has been done Steve should become one of the firm's best construction managers. Keep up the good work!

EMPLOYEE'S COMMENTS

Employee's signature: _____ Date: _____

Evaluator's signature: _____ Date: _____

PERFORMANCE REVIEW
Managerial

Name: Bill Perkins

Job Title: Customer Service Manager

Date: 4/6/XX

Type of Evaluation:

Interim   Annual X

EVALUATION GUIDE

1 = Excellent (exceptional; exceeds expectations)

2 = Good (consistently meets, and frequently exceeds, usual expectations)

3 = Satisfactory (conforms to standards; meets expectations)

4 = Fair (marginal; meeting only minimum requirements)

5 = Poor (below standard and unacceptable; improvement required or termination will result)

FACTORS FOR REVIEW

Job Knowledge	Rating: 1
Work Quality	Rating: 2
Organization and Administrative Skills	Rating: 1
Staff Management/Supervisory Skills	Rating: 3
Persuasiveness	Rating: 3
Communication Skills	Rating: 3
Judgment	Rating: 3
Interpersonal Skills	Rating: 3
Adaptability/Dependability	Rating: 1
Initiative	Rating: 2
Stability under Pressure	Rating: 3
Fiscal Management	Rating: 2

OVERALL RATING: 3

EVALUATOR'S COMMENTS

Summarize your overall evaluation of the employee's performance, noting any strengths and weaknesses. Provide goals and plan for further development and current estimate of the employee's capacity and ambition for future growth.

Bill has been with the foundation for a long time and knows and understands all of the things that go on here. He is well known and well liked by all the staff, both those in his department and those from other departments. He is very experienced and skilled in performing the customer ser-

391

vice functions of his department and provides excellent leadership based on that knowledge and experience.

There have been several times when Bill has reacted inappropriately to questions, concerns, or actions from members of his staff. In some cases he has overreacted, and what should have been a small matter blew up into a major concern. In other cases he reacted very little or not at all, and a situation that could have been headed off at the pass was allowed to develop into a significant problem.

Bill seems to be having trouble in the transition from staff member to manager. He is very comfortable and skilled at doing what the staff is called upon to do. He is not yet taking hold in his management role of making it possible for his staff to do those things.

GOALS/ACTION TO BE TAKEN

Probably these matters will be resolved with time. We need to take steps to assure that this is happening and to hasten the time when these issues will not keep reoccurring. As Bill is in a new position, there is no one in the foundation to whom Bill can go who has done his precise job. I have asked Barbara Galley, of Personnel, to meet with Bill on a weekly basis and to provide some ongoing guidance to help Bill identify these problem issues and handle them more effectively. Barbara manages a similar staff and has done so effectively for several years.

We will do an interim review in three months to monitor Bill's progress.

EMPLOYEE'S COMMENTS

Employee's signature: _____ Date: _____

Evaluator's signature: _____ Date: _____

392

INTERIM PERFORMANCE EVALUATION
(Middle-management employee)

Performance evaluation for: Jack Daniels

Date: September 1, 20XX

JOB FACTORS

1. Job knowledge   (weak) 1 2 3 <u>4</u> 5 (superior)

   Comments:

   You are an excellent manager and have earned the loyalty of your staff. You know how to use their skills and abilities to your advantage. Now keep honing your own skills through management courses and seminars.

2. Productivity   (weak) 1 2 3 <u>4</u> 5 (superior)

   Comments:

   You're doing well in meeting deadlines and you work very effectively under pressure—very good!

3. Quality of results   (weak) 1 2 3 <u>4</u> 5 (superior)

   Comments:

   Your presentations to management have never failed to impress. You make excellent use of graphics and charts to demonstrate your department's sales performance and future trends. Only complaint: You concentrate a little too much on only your department's accomplishments and not enough on overall company goals.

4. Initiative   (weak) 1 2 <u>3</u> 4 5 (superior)

   Comments:

   You are excellent in carrying through on projects assigned to you, but hesitate too much in proposing ideas of your own. Try to take more risks and trust your creative instincts.

5. Teamwork   (weak) 1 2 <u>3</u> 4 5 (superior)

   Comments:

   You are remarkably patient with your staff, but less so with some of your fellow managers. In particular, your testiness when you are interrupted tends to antagonize others. Try to control this.

6. Decision making   (weak) 1 2 <u>3</u> 4 5 (superior)
   Comments:

   You make good decisions in matters of office procedure and organizational details. However, you have been weak when called upon to make
   weightier decisions that require more abstract thinking. You should get
   away from nitty-gritty details and more into tough decision making.

7. Problem solving   (weak) 1 2 3 <u>4</u> 5 (superior)
   Comments:

   You have a keen ability to identify and analyze problem areas in your
   department's day-to-day operations. Don't be afraid of applying more creative solutions to resolving weaknesses.

8. Organization   (weak) 1 2 3 4 <u>5</u> (superior)
   Comments:

   Your organizational abilities are your strongest suit. Department efficiency
   has improved greatly since you reorganized your staff reporting structure
   and filing system. Congratulations!

9. Communication   (weak) 1 2 <u>3</u> 4 5 (superior)
   Comments:

   As already indicated, you interact with your staff well. You are clearly
   able to convey your instructions and handle problem situations with those
   who work under you. You need to apply these skills to your interactions with
   your peers and managers. Be less reticent and more assertive, and make
   an effort to play a bigger role in company-wide team operations and decision making.

10. Receptiveness to criticism   (weak) 1 2 <u>3</u> 4 5 (superior)
    Comments:

    You seem to handle criticism well on the whole, but occasionally you misin-
    terpret it as an attack on your ability to do the job. Don't let negative
    remarks get you down.

OVERALL RATING:

___ Needs improvement in job performance

<u>X</u> Meets job requirements

___ Exceeds job requirements

1. *Work over the past three months:*

   Overall, your work has been exemplary. You handle your staff well and have both improved morale and reduced turnover by your implementation of incentives and Employee Recognition Day. Your department's performance has also improved considerably due to your reorganization efforts. Your timely and top-notch completion of the five-year plan for your department was passed with flying colors by the Chief Operating Officer. You are quick to act on any assignments given to you, but slow to propose ideas of your own.

2. *Goals for the coming three months:*

   As we talked about, you should take a couple of courses in marketing techniques to help you come up with more creative approaches to your department's sales goals, rather than relying on the "tried-and-true" way of doing things. Also work on developing a more patient working relationship with other managers. Your department is performing well, but shouldn't be an isolated unit within the company.

3. *Additional comments:*

   You have made some valuable contributions to the company's profitability and are deservedly proud of your department's performance in this quarter. Please don't let it go to your head; try to control your "tunnel vision" where your department is concerned and remember you and your staff are part of a very large team.

   I would like to schedule a follow-up review for 30 days from today.

Employee's Comments

Employee's signature: _____ Date: _____

Evaluator's signature: _____ Date: _____

PERFORMANCE EVALUATION
Managerial

Name: Mary Ann McGuire   Title: Convention Services Manager
Date: 12/30/XX

Job Knowledge

Mary Ann has experience both in food services and operations and brings a wide and extensive knowledge to her position. She is particularly adept at blending various available features from each department into unique, attractive, and memorable conventions and conferences.

Organization and Administrative Skills

Mary Ann has demonstrated a weakness in keeping control of all the complicated schedules and activities that make up a convention event. There have been several occasions when her planning did not allow for cleanup and setup times in the transition from one activity to another.

Productivity/Timeliness

Mary Ann has booked more convention business than we have been accustomed to having, and we are very appreciative of that increase. She must work on her coordinating skills to be sure that this added pressure on the system does not result in breakdowns.

Quality of Work

Other than the scheduling/planning issues referred to, which are serious, Mary Ann has done fine quality work and raised the quantity and quality of our convention services dramatically.

Leadership/Interpersonal Skills

Mary Ann is well liked by the entire staff, and even her blunders have been responded to with good will in all quarters. She is respected by the staff and is popular with the customers. She must get on top of some of her operational difficulties or she will lose staff patience.

Communication Skills

Mary Ann has failed several times to post her room use far enough in advance to assure that others, particularly in Operations or Sales, do not double-book a space. Convention business must not be allowed to displace normal hotel functions, and careful space management is the key to this. Mary Ann must be sure that she schedules her use of space carefully and allows for cleanup/setup times in the plans.

Adaptability/Dependability

Mary Ann is very hard working and dependable and generally handles the "pressure cooker" of the convention office with ease and grace. She must not, however, think that her ability to "shoot from the hip" will make up for good planning and communication.

Fiscal Management

Except for the negative impact of the scheduling and communications difficulties listed elsewhere, Mary Ann has an excellent fiscal record and is a high revenue producer.

Goals for Next Review

If Mary Ann will focus on doing away with the scheduling and communications difficulties, she will become one of our top-producing employees. We look forward to that.

Employee's Comments

Employee's signature: _____ Date: _____

Evaluator's signature: _____ Date: _____

PERFORMANCE REVIEW
Managerial

Name: Ruth Lambert

Job Title: Store Manager

Date: May 18, 20xx

Type of Evaluation:

Interim   Annual X

EVALUATION GUIDE

1 = Excellent (exceptional; exceeds expectations)

2 = Good (consistently meets, and frequently exceeds, usual expectations)

3 = Satisfactory (conforms to standards; meets expectations)

4 = Fair (marginal; meeting only minimum requirements)

5 = Poor (below standard and unacceptable; improvement required or termination will result)

FACTORS FOR REVIEW

Job Knowledge	Rating: 1
Work Quality	Rating: 2
Organization and Administrative Skills	Rating: 2
Staff Management/Supervisory Skills	Rating: 3
Persuasiveness	Rating: 2
Communication Skills	Rating: 3
Judgment	Rating: 3
Interpersonal Skills	Rating: 3
Dependability	Rating: 1
Initiative	Rating: 3
Stability under Pressure	Rating: 2
Fiscal Management	Rating: 2

OVERALL RATING: 3

EVALUATOR'S COMMENTS

Summarize your overall evaluation of the employee's performance, noting any strengths and weaknesses. Provide goals and plan for further development and current estimate of the employee's capacity and ambition for future growth.

Ruth has been running a generally successful store operation for the past year. Her sales are high, and the store has high traffic and is clean, cheerful, and generally well run. One of the challenges for any 24-hour convenience store is the high turnover of staff and the difficulty in finding and training good staff members.

To be a top-performing manager, Ruth needs to develop better skills for recruiting, training, managing, and retaining staff. The staff-turnover rate for this store is the highest in the district, even though the store's location should offer a better-than-average labor pool from which to select staff.

GOALS/ACTION TO BE TAKEN

It is suggested that Ruth study the manuals and videos in the training room that outline the franchise-wide program for recruiting, training, and retaining staff. One of the strong suggestions is that every potential staff member be sent through the entire prehiring cycle and every new hire be sent through the entire training program, observing the suggested minimum time requirements. The program is very repetitive, and it does drive away some potential employees, but it is more cost effective to wash out persons who are not a "good fit" during training rather than after a brief time on the job. The jobs are repetitive, and dealing with that repetition consistently and cheerfully is what makes for a good employee.

If additional management support would be helpful in addressing this staffing issue, Ruth should feel encouraged to seek help from the District Manager. Help is available. We want to see you solve this problem. We are willing to have you solve it in the way that works best for you.

EMPLOYEE'S COMMENTS

Employee's signature: _____ Date: _____

Evaluator's signature: _____ Date: _____

Sample Reviews for Poor Performers

PERFORMANCE REVIEW
Managerial/Supervisory Employees

Name: Jose Salazar

Job Title: Restaurant Manager

Date: Feb. 28, 20xx

Type of Evaluation:

Interim   Annual X

Evaluation Guide

1 = Excellent (exceptional; exceeds expectations)

2 = Good (consistently meets, and frequently exceeds, usual expectations)

3 = Satisfactory (conforms to standards; meets expectations)

4 = Fair (marginal; meeting only minimum requirements)

5 = Poor (below standard and unacceptable; improvement required or termination will result)

FACTORS FOR REVIEW

Job Knowledge	Rating: 3
Work Quality	Rating: 4
Organization and Administrative Skills	Rating: 4
Staff Management/Supervisory Skills	Rating: 5
Communication Skills	Rating: 4
Judgment	Rating: 4
Interpersonal Skills	Rating: 4
Adaptability	Rating: 3
Initiative	Rating: 4
Imagination and Originality	Rating: 4
Stability under Pressure	Rating: 4
Dependability	Rating: 3
Fiscal Management	Rating: 3

OVERALL RATING: 4

EVALUATOR'S COMMENTS

Summarize your overall evaluation of the employee's performance, noting any strengths and weaknesses. Provide goals and plan for further development and current estimate of the employee's capacity and ambition for future growth.

Jose manages one of our key locations in the heart of the city. Because of where it is situated, the restaurant should be attracting plenty of business clientele during both the lunch and dinner hours and operating at full or near-full capacity most of the time. In addition, there are numerous opportunities for special functions that would add to the restaurant's profitability. Despite this, bookings for functions have dropped by 50 percent, and overall business is down. Jose has not met expectations, and investigation into the causes has revealed a number of problems. Primarily, he has not succeeded in developing a good working relationship with his staff, who seem to take advantage of his easygoing attitude. In unofficial inspections, I have observed a rampant disregard for and violation of corporate policies and procedures as well as a laxness on the part of the wait staff that has directly affected the quality of the service provided to customers. The time it has taken for an order to be delivered to a table has sometimes exceeded 40 minutes. When the primary customer is a business executive who needs to return to the office in a timely fashion, such a delay is unacceptable and can be directly related to the decline in business. In addition to this, Jose has an abnormally high absentee rate and frequently finds himself understaffed, which only adds to delays and to mounting customer frustration.

The problems with the wait staff have also led to problems with the chefs and other kitchen staff. Turnover in the kitchen is 20 percent higher than at other locations, and this has affected the quality of the food served. Customer complaints have been on the rise, and our reputation has suffered to the extent that our salespeople are experiencing increasing difficulty in booking special business functions at this location.

All in all, Jose has unfortunately been unable to effectively manage either his staff or the varying demands on his time and efforts. He is frequently overwhelmed and has experienced emotional distress due to the pressures of mounting problems. He has agreed that matters cannot continue as they now stand, but would still like the chance to prove his potential adeptness as a restaurant manager. It is probably true that this high-stress location was assigned to Jose before he was ready to take it on. Therefore, he will be given another opportunity, as outlined below.

GOALS/ACTION TO BE TAKEN

The key location of this particular restaurant, along with Jose's inability to effectively manage his staff, does not allow for corrective action to be taken on-site. Jose will be transferred to the home office and will be reentered into the management-training program. He will then be assigned to another location that will provide less stress and more opportunity for professional and personal growth. Should he fail again to meet expectations in his new assignment, he will be terminated from the corporation.

EMPLOYEE'S COMMENTS

Employee's signature: _____ Date: _____

Evaluator's signature: _____ Date: _____

PERFORMANCE EVALUATION

Name: Matthew Loebman   Title: Store Manager Trainee

Date: September 15, 20XX   Interim X   Annual

I. JOB FACTORS: RATING:

1. Job knowledge   (poor) 1 <u>2</u> 3 4 5 (excellent)

   Comments:

   Matt has not yet acquired sufficient job skills to merit confidence in his abilities to take over a responsible position. His primary weakness appears to be difficulty in familiarizing himself thoroughly with all or most of the merchandise in our specialty stores (although his knowledge of specific products can be excellent). In addition, he is still struggling with the computer system and needs to overcome his fear of it.

2. Quality of work   (poor) 1 <u>2</u> 3 4 5 (excellent)

   Comments:

   Matt allows himself to be distracted a little too easily and seems to have a hard time juggling his differing responsibilities. Thus, while he has proven himself to be capable in certain areas (such as stock ordering and responsiveness to customer needs), the overall quality of his work suffers due to his difficulties with the computer and his lack of human-resource skills (see #5).

3. Productivity   (poor) 1 <u>2</u> 3 4 5 (excellent)

   Comments:

   Matt is not so productive as he is capable of being. He needs to learn some basic, effective time-management skills.

4. Organizational/Administrative skills   (poor) 1 <u>2</u> 3 4 5 (excellent)

   Comments:

   He has a lot to learn about how to organize his time and manage his resources. This is one of his weakest areas.

5. Supervisory skills   (poor) 1 <u>2</u> 3 4 5 (excellent)

   Comments:

   Matt seems to work best with people who are self-motivated and do not require any concentrated supervision from him to ensure the competent completion of their duties. He is rather diffident and clearly doesn't like being put in the position of having to discipline or criticize an employee. This

403

could be the biggest factor that prevents him from finishing the training program, as he must learn how to manage people effectively if he is to succeed in his chosen career path.

6. Interpersonal skills　　　　　　　(poor) 1 2̲ 3 4 5 (excellent)
   Comments:
   As above.

7. Adaptability　　　　　　　　　　(poor) 1 2 3̲ 4 5 (excellent)
   Comments:
   Matt has demonstrated that he has the ability to adapt to any location.

8. Initiative　　　　　　　　　　　　(poor) 1 2 3̲ 4 5 (excellent)
   Comments:
   He made this a personal goal and generally has succeeded in introducing and implementing some creative new ideas for merchandising in certain stores, based on store location and clientele. This is where he has shown his potential.

9. Communication skills　　　　　　　(poor) 1 2 3̲ 4 5 (excellent)
   Comments:
   He manages to get his ideas across, and he interacts well with customers. There is a certain lack of skill in dealing with employees (see #5).

10. Analytic skills/Problem solving　　(poor) 1 2̲ 3 4 5 (excellent)
    Comments:
    Although he has proven he can analyze customer needs and put together a working merchandising plan, Matt has difficulty in handling other aspects of the job that require him to troubleshoot, particularly if it involves employee relations.

11. Professionalism　　　　　　　　　(poor) 1 2 3 4̲ 5 (excellent)
    Comments:
    Matt tries his best to present a professional demeanor. He is always neatly dressed in a suit and tie and maintains a courteous, interested manner in his dealings with customers.

12. Fiscal management　　　　　　　　(poor) 1 2̲ 3 4 5 (excellent)
    Comments:
    This is not a strong suit for Matt, and he will have to work to strengthen his skills in this area.

Overall Rating　　　　　　　　　　(poor) 1 2̲ 3 4 5 (excellent)

II. SUMMARY/COMMENTS

Matt is almost a mid-level performer at this point, but he has several areas he needs to work on if he wants to advance out of the training program and into a management position. The weakest areas are summarized above; he particularly needs to work on his supervisory skills. His strengths lie in his ability to visualize customer desires and to make suggestions for merchandising in various store locations. In this regard, it should be pointed out that he stays on top of current trends and is frequently able to provide valuable information to upper management on the potential success or failure of new products. It is my belief that Matt's skills are better suited to a marketing position than to direct sales. However, he feels he would be happier in a retail setting than in an office environment and wishes to continue along the present lines. He is aware that he has a way to go and seems determined to apply himself to meeting the goals that have been set for him.

III. PLAN OF ACTION

First and foremost, Matt needs to get over his fear of the computer and needs to learn to use it to his advantage, particularly as regards familiarity with merchandise. Second, he must strengthen his human-resource skills and become more assertive with employees. Finally, I want him to take at least one course in accounting and budgeting to learn how to better manage his fiscal responsibilities. He will remain in the training program for at least another three months to determine whether there is any merit in further professional development and the possibility of graduating to a responsible managerial position.

IV. EMPLOYEE COMMENTS

Employee's signature: _____ Date: _____

Evaluator's signature: _____ Date: _____

PERFORMANCE REVIEW
Managerial

Name: Christine Sandberg

Job Title: Customer Service Manager

Date: August 15, 20XX

Type of Evaluation:

Interim   Annual X

EVALUATION GUIDE

1 = Excellent (exceptional; exceeds expectations)

2 = Good (consistently meets, and frequently exceeds, usual expectations)

3 = Satisfactory (conforms to standards; meets expectations)

4 = Fair (marginal; meeting only minimum requirements)

5 = Poor (below standard and unacceptable; improvement required or termination will result)

FACTORS FOR REVIEW

Job Knowledge	Rating: 1
Work Quality	Rating: 3
Organization and Administrative Skills	Rating: 4
Staff Management/Supervisory Skills	Rating: 5
Persuasiveness	Rating: 4
Communication Skills	Rating: 4
Judgment	Rating: 5
Interpersonal Skills	Rating: 4
Adaptability/Dependability	Rating: 2
Initiative	Rating: 5
Stability under Pressure	Rating: 4
Fiscal Management	Rating: 4

OVERALL RATING: 4

EVALUATOR'S COMMENTS

Summarize your overall evaluation of the employee's performance, noting any strengths and weaknesses. Provide goals and plan for further development and current estimate of the employee's capacity and ambition for future growth.

Christine has had the experience and currently has the knowledge needed to manage her department. At this time, however, she is not demonstrating the management skills necessary for the position. Her most significant problems can be summarized as inappropriate response to the individ-

406

ual needs of her staff. She has alienated many on her staff, and serious problems are already manifesting themselves in terms of poor attendance, lowered morale, and loss of several key experienced staff members.

Christine often reacts in anger when the effective response would be listening and quiet support. Christine is defensive or hostile when approached with legitimate concerns or routine types of questions. These situations seem to be perceived as threats or challenges when they are not meant as such. Probably Christine may be uncomfortable and may feel inadequate in her new position. She must find ways to change these behaviors and reverse the tide of staff distress if she is to remain in this position.

GOALS/ACTION TO BE TAKEN

Arrangements have been made to have Christine attend several three-day management-training seminars within the next few weeks. Cathy Weeks, the consultant who helps shape the form of this new Customer Service department that Christine heads, will be brought in to substitute for Christine during those seminars and will remain in the department for the next month to assist Christine in identifying the things that lead to these difficult situations and will develop effective strategies to handle such things.

At the end of the month, we will reevaluate the situation. If progress is being made, Cathy will be retained in an on-call, advisory mode for another one or two months to assist Christine in the transition to handling the staff effectively on her own. At the end of three months, it is hoped that there will be a clear indication that Christine will be able to rise to the challenge of her position.

EMPLOYEE'S COMMENTS

Employee's signature: _____ Date: _____

Evaluator's signature: _____ Date: _____

PERFORMANCE REVIEW
Managerial/Supervisory Employees

Name: Edmund Olzewski
Job Title: Operations Manager
Date: 4/6/XX

Type of Evaluation:
Interim   Annual X

Evaluation Guide

1 = Excellent (exceptional; exceeds expectations)
2 = Good (consistently meets, and frequently exceeds, usual expectations)
3 = Satisfactory (conforms to standards; meets expectations)
4 = Fair (marginal; meeting only minimum requirements)
5 = Poor (below standard and unacceptable; improvement required or termination will result)

Factors for Review

Job Knowledge   Rating: 3
Degree to which the employee knows and understands his/her job and its functions

Organization and Administrative Skills   Rating: 3
Ability to establish goals/objectives, prioritize, anticipate problems, implement plans, etc.

Delegation of Authority   Rating: 4
Ability to assign appropriate duties to subordinates

Written Communication   Rating: 4
Ability to organize thoughts and present them clearly and concisely in writing; effectiveness of prepared reports, correspondence, etc.

Oral Communication   Rating: 4
Ability to present information and ideas to others in an articulate and effective manner, as well as to listen effectively, comprehend, and respond to the ideas of others

Judgment   Rating: 3
Ability to reason through problems, review alternative solutions, reach sound conclusions, and modify decisions when necessary

Cooperation and Interpersonal Skills   Rating: 4
Tact, courtesy, self-control, patience, loyalty, and discretion; ability to work harmoniously with others, both subordinate and superior

Adaptability   Rating: 3

Ability to learn new skills, concepts, and processes; resourcefulness; flexibility in thinking

Work Quality   Rating: 4

Accuracy, presentability, neatness, thoroughness, and reliability of finished product

Persuasiveness   Rating: 4

Ability to negotiate, argue persuasively, get things done by influencing others

Imagination and Originality   Rating: 3

Ability to visualize and anticipate new problems and to conceive new ideas or techniques

Supervisory Skills   Rating: 4

Ability to accept responsibility and to guide or lead other employees to successful work performance

Stability under Pressure   Rating: 4

Mental and emotional balance under stress due to pressure of work

Dependability   Rating: 3

Attendance and conscientiousness

Fiscal Management   Rating: 4

Ability to develop a fiscally sound operating budget and to manage effectively within established fiscal constraints, as well as to recognize, develop, and implement cost-effective operating changes

OVERALL RATING: 4

EVALUATOR'S COMMENTS

Ed has suffered some setbacks since his return from sick leave five months ago. In the three months that he was gone from the office, a major portion of his responsibilities was taken over by the Customer Service and Order Processing managers (Joe and Katherine), under my supervision. Operations ran smoothly during his absence, and when he first returned, he seemed content to allow the situation to continue on the same course, with minimal interference from him. Two months ago he began implementing new policies and procedures that reclaimed his personal authority in the department and superseded decisions and procedures that had been instituted by Joe and Katherine. Unfortunately, this resulted in a clash between him and his staff, who had become used to the way things were run during his absence and resented his stripping control of certain functions from Joe and Katherine. A series of meetings were held to resolve the crisis, during which time Joe left the company and Katherine transferred to another department. Ed then instituted a new organizational and reporting structure and at the present time is backlogged but catching up quickly.

I have discussed this crisis at length with Ed. He felt that his authority as head of the department had been usurped by Joe and Katherine, who had gone on a "power trip," in his opinion. He rightly felt that, while he appreciated their efforts in his absence, they should have respected his position upon his return and conceded to him the authority they had assumed while he was away. While I agreed with this wholeheartedly, I pointed out that he had erred in not reestablishing his authority immediately upon his return from sick leave and that by allowing the situation to continue for several months before he took action, he had inadvertently led staff to assume that they would retain their current modus operandi. In addition, because of his aloofness from them, the support staff were not given any reason to believe that the situation would change, therefore they continued to go to Joe and Katherine when decisions had to be made. In other words, corrective action was not taken soon enough, and therefore Ed was also responsible for the crisis that ensued after he decided to take back control of the department.

The situation brought to light other problems that Ed has in supervising his staff. He is too often remote and does not interest himself too strongly in the questions and concerns that arise in the course of a normal day, which gives him little understanding of what his order-processing and customer staffs are doing and the problems they are encountering. He issues directives without discussing them first with the supervisors who must implement them and does not hold regular meetings to review what has been happening in his department or to solicit any input. As a result, he has not established a good rapport with his staff, and this also contributed to the recent crisis.

Prior to his illness, Ed was in the process of designing a new computer system to improve order-processing and customer-service efficiency. This system was to have been in place by now, but work on it was suspended during

Ed's illness because of his crucial role. I believe both the aftereffects of his illness and the pressure that is now on him to get the new system up and running as quickly as possible have been major factors in his managerial problems. With the restructuring of his department, he should be delegating more authority to his staff to allow him the time to concentrate on the computer system, while at the same time monitoring the situation in his department by holding regular staff meetings.

ACTION TO BE TAKEN

Ed is to work more closely with Order Processing and Customer managers to delegate decision-making authority and solicit reasonable input on systems and procedures, rather than issuing peremptorial directives. He is also to consider organizational and administrative issues that will arise when he has completed setting up the new computer system and has worked out all the bugs. In addition, the company's recent acquisition of My Books, Inc., and the transfer of their operations to our corporate headquarters will increase the workload of Ed's department twofold, an event for which he must begin preparing now.

Ed is to submit a new budget for his department, taking into account the hiring of new staff, expansion of office space, and the need for additional equipment and supplies as the company and his department grow.

EMPLOYEE'S COMMENTS

Employee's signature: _____ Date: _____

Evaluator's signature: _____ Date: _____

PERFORMANCE EVALUATION
Managerial

Name: Nancy Greene   Title: Convention Services Manager
Date: May 30, 20XX

Job Knowledge

Nancy came to us with a record of sales and food-service experience, and we invested considerable time in bringing her up to speed on the operations end of the convention business. Nancy should be equipped to handle the challenges of her position, but that does not seem to be happening. Particular difficulties seem to occur in the operations area, although there has also been evidence of lack of understanding of some of the food-service issues involved in convention planning.

Organization and Administrative Skills

Nancy fails to prepare a coherent plan for each event. The result is many operations and food-service problems, with the resulting confusions and ill will.

Productivity/Timeliness

Nancy has made a good sales record matching previous records but she has not been able to bring off the events successfully, and this has already resulted in some loss of repeat and contract business.

Quality of Work

The surface appearance of Nancy's convention plans is very attractive and she brings flair, imagination, and ingenuity to each project. This has resulted in a good sales volume. Her lack of skills and planning in carrying out the plans has resulted in disappointed customers and angry and frustrated staff.

Leadership/Interpersonal Skills

Nancy has significant issues with the staff that will need to be carefully tended and mended if Nancy is to continue as Convention Services Manager. We have a gifted and dedicated staff, many of whom are highly skilled artists in one or another facet of the hospitality business. Nancy has created situations in which many of these people have either been unable to do their job, or in which their work has not been able to be presented in a manner that reflected the artistry, quality, and care that they bring to their work. Nancy must see that this does not happen anymore and must make significant overtures of apology to many of these fine artisans.

Communication Skills

Nancy is capable of communicating effectively, but at present she is not in control of her projects well enough to use those skills to advantage.

Adaptability/Dependability

Nancy is very dependable, but she has thus far not adapted well to the demands of her position.

Fiscal Management

The significant problems with the conventions this spring have not only been frustrating and embarrassing, they have also had a serious negative financial impact that will likely have negative impact on future business even if we turn things around immediately. If we do not immediately reverse the current situation, the financial impact on the hotel will be unimaginably bad.

Goals for Next Review

We will schedule weekly supervision beginning immediately. In one month we will monitor the situation and expect significant change. If things are going well in one month, we will continue weekly supervision and monthly reviews until a completely satisfactory situation is solidly established. It is expected that Nancy will prepare and execute comprehensive plans for each event, which will accommodate all needed activities and services and allow appropriate time, space, staff, and materials for success.

Employee's Comments

Employee's signature: _____   Date: _____

Evaluator's signature: _____   Date: _____

PERFORMANCE REVIEW
Managerial

Name: Margaret Travis
Job Title: Store Manager
Date: August 8, 20XX

Type of Evaluation:

Interim   Annual X

EVALUATION GUIDE

1 = Excellent (exceptional; exceeds expectations)

2 = Good (consistently meets, and frequently exceeds, usual expectations)

3 = Satisfactory (conforms to standards; meets expectations)

4 = Fair (marginal; meeting only minimum requirements)

5 = Poor (below standard and unacceptable; improvement required or termination will result)

FACTORS FOR REVIEW

Job Knowledge	Rating: 3
Work Quality	Rating: 3
Organization and Administrative Skills	Rating: 5
Staff Management/Supervisory Skills	Rating: 4
Persuasiveness	Rating: 3
Communication Skills	Rating: 3
Judgment	Rating: 4
Interpersonal Skills	Rating: 4
Dependability	Rating: 2
Initiative	Rating: 3
Stability under Pressure	Rating: 4
Fiscal Management	Rating: 4

OVERALL RATING: 4

EVALUATOR'S COMMENTS

Summarize your overall evaluation of the employee's performance, noting any strengths and weaknesses. Provide goals and plan for further development and current estimate of the employee's capacity and ambition for future growth.

Margaret came to us with experience and what seemed to be the knowledge needed for this position. Perhaps some of the special demands of running a 24-hour convenience store are beyond her expertise. If so, there are training manuals and videos, management-training seminars (one of which

414

Margaret has attended), and a detailed set of practices and procedures written up for use in the store.

One of the challenges for a store with a round-the-clock operation is consistency of practice and level of service with varied and often rapidly changing staff, and a high-volume and sometimes difficult clientele. Margaret has not been clear about the practices and procedures she expects and has not demanded consistent compliance with those practices and procedures by all personnel.

There have been close-downs of the store when staff has failed to report. There has been a dramatic increase in shelf loss and "shrink." There have been reports of staff rudeness and inattention and lack of store cleanliness. There have even been reports of tobacco and liquor sales to minors and charging prices for goods that are different from the ones marked or advertised.

GOALS/ACTION TO BE TAKEN

Within one week of receiving this review, Margaret must arrange to meet with the District Manager to review the issues raised herein. It is expected that Margaret, working with the District Manager, will be able to chart a plan that will accomplish immediate reversal of these difficulties if she is to remain as store manager.

EMPLOYEE'S COMMENTS

Employee's signature: _____ Date: _____

Evaluator's signature: _____ Date: _____

PERFORMANCE REVIEW
Managerial

Name: Martin Maxson

Job Title: Construction Project Manager

Date: December 2, 20XX

Type of Evaluation:

Interim   Annual X

EVALUATION GUIDE

1 = Excellent (exceptional; exceeds expectations)

2 = Good (consistently meets, and frequently exceeds, usual expectations)

3 = Satisfactory (conforms to standards; meets expectations)

4 = Fair (marginal; meeting only minimum requirements)

5 = Poor (below standard and unacceptable; improvement required or termination will result)

FACTORS FOR REVIEW

Job Knowledge	Rating: 2
Work Quality	Rating: 4
Organization and Administrative Skills	Rating: 5
Staff Management/Supervisory Skills	Rating: 5
Persuasiveness	Rating: 3
Communication Skills	Rating: 3
Judgment	Rating: 4
Interpersonal Skills	Rating: 3
Adaptability/Dependability	Rating: 5
Initiative	Rating: 5
Stability under Pressure	Rating: 4
Fiscal Management	Rating: 5

OVERALL RATING: 4

EVALUATOR'S COMMENTS

Summarize your overall evaluation of the employee's performance, noting any strengths and weaknesses. Provide goals and plan for further development and current estimate of the employee's capacity and ambition for future growth.

Marty is a capable project manager. He has the knowledge and skills needed to do the project and guide other workers in their tasks. He has, however, been late or missing from the work site several times each week. When these attendance problems occur, the office staff has tried to reach him at his home and has been unable to reach anyone. When he arrives late, he seems to have a chip on his shoulder, perhaps in embarrassment at being late. When he misses an entire day, he arrives the next day bright and eager as if nothing had happened.

This behavior has left the crew leaderless on many occasions. Several workers have stepped in to try to keep things going, but this is not really their responsibility, and they often don't have the information needed to really manage the situation.

Worse, when he arrives late and surly, the crew is plunged from leaderlessness into the awkward and uncomfortable role of fall guys for Marty's bad temper. We have lost several subcontractors due to this behavior.

GOALS/ACTION TO BE TAKEN

Everyone has issues and problems to deal with in life. A good manager must find ways to keep these things from having a negative impact on his or her job performance. Whatever is causing this erratic behavior on Marty's part, the behavior must be eradicated or Marty will no longer be able to hold this position.

It is expected that from this point onward there will be no more instances of lateness or absence without prior notice to the construction office. If the office is informed in time, another staff member can be sent to the job site to fill in. Furthermore, the frequency of attendance issues, even with notification, must be reduced to a more normal level.

If there are extenuating circumstances that require special accommodations, the company will make every effort to accommodate them. It is Marty's responsibility to make these needs known to the company and arrange to get whatever help is required to become a reliable and productive employee.

EMPLOYEE'S COMMENTS

Employee's signature: _____ Date: _____

Evaluator's signature: _____ Date: _____

11

Handling Salary Reviews Successfully

Ask any manager to name the least enjoyable aspects of overseeing the work of others. Odds are that among the answers you get there will be some reference to the mind-numbing chore of composing and delivering individual salary reviews for staff members.

Unlike firings and layoffs (two other items likely to show up on the manager's list of Things Not to Look Forward To), salary reviews are a predictable, scheduled part of professional life. Managers can never completely cross them off their to-do list; they are unavoidable, like death and taxes.

It's easy to see why so many managers put off this chore until the last minute. Salary reviews are time-consuming, fraught with potential legal perils, and, all too often, the source of unpleasant face-to-face conflicts with disgruntled employees.

Although performance evaluations can be scheduled several times a year, salary reviews are generally scheduled only once a year. Salary increases usually reflect employees' performance appraisals. Employees who have been given an outstanding rating have reason to expect a larger increase in salary than those who have achieved mid-level ratings. However, depending on your company's salary program and corporate practice, this may not always be the case. For this reason, the salary review may well be the setting for the vast majority of tense, openly antagonistic exchanges between employees and their managers.

Defusing High Emotions During the Face-to-Face Meeting

Emotions are usually highest during the face-to-face meeting, which is the customary way in which salary-review matters are handled. In most cases, the employee is bound to feel his or her worth is being judged, and that is an uncomfortable feeling for everyone involved. Even when the news is good and a substantial increase in salary is being recommended, there may be elements of the review itself that will pinch like a cheap pair of shoes.

As the manager, you are the person in the power position. Therefore, you can afford to assume some slack on your side of the table. Be prepared for the possibility of difficult, emotionally charged feelings to come out in the meeting, and think about how you will or will not react to those feelings. Your best option is to refrain from reacting as much as possible and to attempt to move the meeting on to other, less emotionally charged activities as quickly as possible. Don't allow an employee's shock or momentary flare-up to become an extra burden in your own emotional baggage. Chances are good that it won't be long before the employee calms down and a good working relationship can be reestablished; so there is no need for you to be unduly upset by an employee's reaction.

Successful Interpersonal Strategies

Since high emotions are bound to be a reality during salary reviews, here are several strategies that can help to reduce levels of anxiety:

- Don't play "cat and mouse." This is a poor time to demonstrate power. It is already implicit, so get to the point.
- Avoid personalizing further what is already too personalized a process by saying what needs to be said calmly and clearly, in a quiet voice and with a neutral manner.
- Be specific, but don't belabor the matter.
- Be positive as much as possible, but without being saccharine.
- Provide the employee with a copy of the review. Many people don't hear clearly when they are anxious, which can result in misunderstandings. Having it in writing helps to clarify the discussion for both parties.

Sample Salary Reviews

Here are two sample reviews—one showing the style you should use; the other showing the style you should not use.

The Writing Style to Use

SALARY REVIEW
MIS Data Entry

Name: Myra Westbridge   Date: February 15, 20XX

Overall Evaluation: Failure to follow through on assignments, Poor communication skills, Poor work pace

In the past year, Myra continued to demonstrate a sincere concern and commitment to her job. Her emphasis on the integrity of the database is commendable. She also makes a consistent effort to understand and carry out the guiding philosophies of the MIS department. Unfortunately, she is often overly committed to a goal of absolute perfection in entry, which can have a counterproductive effect on her overall performance. I want to recommend three steps Myra can take to contribute to the smooth and efficient operation of the department.

1. PRODUCTIVITY

An operations study done in October of the past year shows that Myra's processing times fall well behind those of her fellow workers. Specifically, Myra's average time for data entry of a 25-item batch of source documents was 59 minutes. This is approximately 50 percent above the office average of 40 minutes per batch and approximately 100 percent above the average of 29 minutes by the other staffers doing data entry. This is a matter of particular concern, as the department has been given a high-priority goal of 24-hour total processing time for all new entry items, and a high standard of productivity is needed from everyone if this goal is to be met. Myra should continue to emphasize accuracy, but she should also exercise more faith in the system and concentrate on quicker processing. I suggest a target of 40 minutes for manual batches, and I will work with Myra to help make this happen.

2. COMMUNICATION

Myra's powers of observation are keen, and she can often spot serious system problems. When she is able to focus herself and communicate this information in a nonthreatening way, she makes key contributions. Occasionally, however, her tone of voice can be intimidating to others in the MIS department. I encourage Myra to share the information she uncovers in a positive way; I suggest that we meet on Monday afternoons at a mutually agreeable time so that we can discuss the best ways to do this and that we focus particularly on developing written communication skills that will allow Myra's observations to reach the people who can assess and react appropriately to them.

3. COOPERATION AND FLEXIBILITY

This is an area where commitment to improvement is very important. Myra needs to work on developing greater workplace flexibility; there have been a number of situations in which Myra has felt something not to be within her area of responsibility and has simply not completed important assignments in such areas as developing written summaries of work, responding to specific customer requests, and following up with status reports on key issues. I am concerned about this approach, and I want to work to help Myra to adopt a more open-ended attitude toward tasks that she feels are not part of her formal job description. (It's worth noting her job description, like those of everyone else in the department, includes duties described as "other unforeseen tasks related to the attainment of key goals in the department.") I want to be very clear: Change in this area is essential. Failure to improve on Myra's part may well result in disciplinary action.

SUMMARY

Myra has a real gift for spotting technical problems, and this can and should be pointed in a constructive direction that will benefit the company and her own career here. At the same time, she needs to focus with greater energy on her work pace, on appropriate communication patterns, and on carrying out instructions from supervisors.

Given Myra's performance over the past year, I am afraid I cannot authorize a pay increase at this time, but I want to schedule a meeting now for the first of March 20XX to discuss her progress toward the goals outlined here. If the current trend changes, and I have every reason to believe that it can, it may be appropriate to institute a salary increase at that time.

EMPLOYEE'S COMMENTS

Employee's signature: _____ Date: _____

Evaluator's signature: _____ Date: _____

SALARY REVIEW
MIS Data Entry

Name: Myra Westbridge   Date: February 15, 20XX

Overall Evaluation: Failure to follow through on assignments, Poor communication skills, Poor work pace

Even though Myra talks a good game about her interest in the company and her job, we never get to see much profit from what she says. We need her to "put her money where her mouth is." She is a nut about the database, and while we all agree that having an accurate database is important she goes way overboard and acts like a crazy woman about even tiny mistakes. The result is that Myra just doesn't get her work done. She is so hung up on her perfectionist stuff that she doesn't get much done. So, I have to make three demands of her for the next year if she is to keep her job.

1. PRODUCTIVITY

We spent a lot of money to prove what we already knew: Myra is a really slow worker. It took her almost an hour to do what the average good worker could do in about two-thirds that time. And it took her twice as long as the people whom we pay to do her specific job. We're never going to meet the departmental goal of overnight data processing if people like Myra don't pull their weight. Myra has to be careful not to get sloppy with her work, but she has to get a lot faster, and right away!

2. COMMUNICATION

Myra has a wicked tongue on her when she gets going. She is always wasting time watching for other guys to make mistakes and pounces on them with a vengeance. This is such a big problem that I am going to have to take part of my Monday afternoon to meet with her each week to work on fixing this mess. She has to learn to put things in writing and go through the proper channels if she wants to make suggestions.

3. COOPERATION AND FLEXIBILITY

Now we come to the really big problem. Myra has taken a "it's not my job, man" attitude and just lets a lot of stuff fall through the cracks. She has to learn that it's her job to do written summaries of work, respond to specific customer requests, and following up with status reports on key issues. Who does she think she is that she doesn't have to do these things, which everybody else does just fine? (Her job description, just like them all, has "other unforeseen tasks related to the attainment of key goals in the department" to take care of stuff like this.) Get this straight: You have to fix this now! If you don't fix this I'll have to write you up for disciplinary action.

SUMMARY

Myra has to work faster, keep her thoughts to herself, and pitch in on projects around the office that don't necessarily appeal to her.

Obviously, Myra isn't getting any raise. In fact, if she doesn't improve, and fast, she may not even have a job. I'm going to check up on her in a bit and see what's happening.

EMPLOYEE'S COMMENTS

Employee's signature: _____ Date: _____

Evaluator's signature: _____ Date: _____

Sample Memo for Salary Increase

Here is a sample of a memo requesting a raise for a manager who has implemented significant increases in efficiency.

TO: Salary Review Committee   Date: May 15, 20XX
CC: Mary Rockwell
FR: Ellen Hungerford
RE: Ramon Ybarra

I'd like to request a 10 percent salary increase for Supervisor of Cash Management Ramon Ybarra this year, from $34,912 to $38,403, effective with his June 29 anniversary date.

Ramon has continued to be one of the most effective managers in the department. This year he has outdone himself with efforts that have paid off dramatically for the organization.

Ramon has a great deal of valuable technical expertise. This year he applied it in setting up a sophisticated new charge-card payment-processing system that uses direct modem communications with our bank-processing center. This has saved us at least $75,000 per year in credit-card fees. It has also cut in half the staff time needed for processing credit cards. The greatly reduced turnaround time has benefited cash flow, interest earnings, and customer service.

Ramon has a real talent for improving efficiencies within a department. This year he continued to tighten up processing procedures and security measures, resulting in faster delivery, fewer wasted mailings, and fewer customer service calls and letters, with a correspondingly positive effect on expense budgets.

On top of all this, Ramon has a great deal of dedication to his staff of seven employees, five of whom are minorities. He has done wonders in cross training, and the improvement in morale in his department has been significant. He has also very ably and sensitively handled several difficult personnel situations this year, again with an overall net benefit to the morale and productivity of the department.

Ramon is an extremely valuable employee and deserves to be recognized and encouraged accordingly.

12

Preparing a Paper Trail for a Worker You Wish to Terminate

Clark Kerr, after he had left the University of California at Berkeley and acquired a position with the Carnegie Foundation, used to say with great glee, "I left Berkeley the same way I arrived: Fired with enthusiasm." Not everyone reacts with such equanimity to a firing. But then, not everyone moves on to the Carnegie Foundation. The people you need to fire will probably not be so cheerful.

When It Is Time to Part Company

Sometimes the hire was a mistake from the beginning, and sometimes what was once fine is now no longer acceptable. But usually there will come a time when a worker needs to be terminated. Sometimes both parties realize the hour is at hand. Other times, however, while it is evident to you, the worker doesn't have a clue. What do you do then?

First of all, talk with the firm's legal-support staff. Whether it's an entire department or just a friendly lawyer down the hall, this is one time when you can't risk "going it alone." The legal minefields in current practice are very real and very costly for the unwise, the rash, or the uninformed.

427

Why You (Often) Can't Just Fire the Person

In many companies, there may be union or corporate termination policies in place. Even if that is not the case, if an employee wishes to take the matter to court, it will be expected that you have followed a procedure similar to the one outlined here, which is often the most typical case involving an employee termination.

1. There have been several regular unsatisfactory performance reviews.
2. Given this, you have set up a series of goals to be met in order to address the problems.
3. You have allowed an ample timetable to address the problems. (Usually this is anywhere from 6 to 18 months.)
4. You have provided significant support and training to help the employee meet the desired expectations.
5. Having taken those steps, the employee still does not meet minimum standards.

If you terminate the worker, you will be responsible for unemployment compensation and will be required to keep the former employee informed of his or her COBRA rights and other legal matters.

What You Must Establish on Paper

Whatever the chain of events leading up to the termination, you will be expected to be able to illustrate with concrete, verifiable documentation that the employee was not meeting the expectations clearly outlined in the job description. You will also need to be able to carefully document all the steps you have taken to avoid having to terminate this employee and will need to provide copies of all the documents with which you kept him or her informed every step of the way.

Sample Documentation

- The job requirement includes making 100 customer calls every quarter. This is clearly stated in the job description.
- The employee has been unable to meet this requirement for the last three quarters.
- The number of calls made was: Quarter 1: fifty; Quarter 2: fifty-two; Quarter 3: thirty.
- I suggested the following steps to improve performance: (1) attending the Sales Seminar offered by the Corporation; (2) working closely with the team manager to improve calling skills; (3) preparing Calling Notes to help streamline the call process.
- The employee chose not to attend the Sales Seminar.
- The team manager reported that the employee appeared to resent offers of suggestions or assistance.
- I met with the employee on a monthly basis to monitor progress and review performance.
- Despite our best efforts, the results did not improve.
- I offered the employee another position that does not require making customer calls—a position as assistant clerk.
- The employee declined to accept this offer.
- We have concluded that it is necessary to terminate employment at this time.

What May Not Go into the Evaluation

Nothing that cannot be verified objectively and demonstrated with concrete examples can play a role in this process.

If you have an employee with a bad attitude, it is not enough for you to say so; in fact, you must avoid saying so, at all costs. If you wish to make this point, you must have copious, recurrent specific instances where several people can verify that misbehavior occurred. You must also be able to illustrate, chapter and verse, what steps you have taken to remedy the situation, and you must be able to document with similar clarity that the problem continued unabated through the entire course of the termination process.

Face-to-Face Meetings with the Worker

While creating a paper trail is the most important part of the termination process, each piece of paper will generally need to be presented, explained, and discussed in a face-to-face meeting. When such meetings take place, you must prepare carefully for them so that no matter how much you are provoked, you will never respond personally or unprofessionally. It is often helpful to have a third party, usually selected by the employee, in attendance at each meeting to ensure that your appropriate behavior has been witnessed and is verifiable.

The Waiting Game

As outlined here, there is a lot of time built into the usual termination process. You must document the problem over a protracted period, often a year or more, and then you must document the failed attempts at a solution over a similar period. Nothing happens quickly. The game is so protracted and the impact on the company often so negative that many firms remove an individual only when the entire position can be eliminated and no equivalent position exists.

When Is It Time to Schedule the Termination Meeting?

The answer probably is, when the lawyers tell you it's okay. Certainly you won't schedule such a meeting without extensive preparation and careful planning. If you are not sure that you can fire the worker and make it stick, it's best not to bring it up at all.

Termination Strategies

As mentioned earlier, attrition, the elimination of a position, can be a termination strategy. But don't even think of removing a position this month to get rid of a problem employee and then putting the position back next month.

There are whole books of legal barriers that will rise up before you if you attempt anything like that.

The best strategy is simply to prepare for the termination with effective, verifiable documentation and to keep the employee aware that her or his job is in jeopardy so that an adequate chance for improvement is provided. If you fire a worker without any prior warning, you are leaving yourself open to a lawsuit.

Sometimes it is a good plan to enthusiastically help the worker to find a job elsewhere, one in which there is a better chance for success and happiness. Whatever your plan may be, your best resource throughout the ordeal is the legal advice of your firm.